The
Economist
PUBLICATIONS

Pocket Negotiator

Related titles in this series:

The Pocket Economist
Rupert Pennant-Rea and Bill Emmott

The Economist Pocket Accountant
Christopher Nobes

The Economist Pocket Banker
Tim Hindle

The Economist Pocket Entrepreneur
Colin Barrow

The Economist Pocket Guide to Defence
Michael Sheehan and James Wyllie

The Economist Pocket Lawyer
Stanley Berwin

The Economist Pocket Guide to Business Numeracy
David Targett

The
Economist

PUBLICATIONS

Pocket Negotiator

Gavin Kennedy

Basil Blackwell

and

The Economist Publications

Copyright © Gavin Kennedy 1987

Jointly published 1987 by
Basil Blackwell Ltd
108 Cowley Road, Oxford, OX4 1JF, UK
and
The Economist Publications Ltd
40 Duke Street, London, W1A 1DW

Basil Blackwell Inc.
432 Park Avenue South, Suite 1503
New York, NY 10016, USA

All the information in this book is verified to the best of the author's and publisher's ability, but they do not accept responsibility for loss arising from decisions based upon the information presented. Where opinion is expressed it is that of the author, which does not necessarily coincide with the editorial views of The Economist Newspaper

British Library Cataloguing in Publication Data

Kennedy, Gavin
The Economist pocket negotiator.
1. Negotiation in business
I. Title
658.4'5   HD58.6

ISBN 0-631-15451-5

Library of Congress Cataloguing in Publication Data

Kennedy, Gavin.
Pocket negotiator.

1. Negotiation in business.   2. Negotiation.
I. Title.
HD58.6.K47 1987   658   87–6302
ISBN 0-631-15451-5

Typeset in 10 on 12 pt Bembo
by Alan Sutton Publishing Ltd, Gloucester
Printed in Great Britain by
Billing and Sons Ltd, Worcester

For Florence

Contents

Preface

We often find ourselves in conflict with others, such as customers and clients who want it yesterday, rivals who can supply it today, suppliers who won't deliver to our deadlines and certainly not to when they promised, clients who claim they never received what we posted a week ago, colleagues who can't see us when we need them, and can't see what we know to be in their best interests, employees who want more (and time off), spouses who spend it before we earn it, children who think we are a bottomless pit, and bosses who think they know whose fault it is.

To find acceptable solutions to these and other problems, we negotiate. We start with two solutions (ours and theirs) to the same problem, be it two prices, two shares, two delivery dates, two wage rates, two quality standards, two appointment times, two budgets, two amounts of pocket money, two views on who was to blame, and so on. Negotiation is about searching for a single solution mutually acceptable to both negotiators.

Everybody has some negotiating experience. We reach adulthood through long apprenticeships as negotiators – from the quantity of cabbage we must eat before we get some ice cream (guess who usually wins?), through to the reward for a tidy room, to the 'price' for borrowing the family car. What is teenage courtship but a series of negotiations (not all of them successful)? What is our early employment experience but an induction into how resources are allocated between colleagues at work?

Mostly, our negotiating experience is taken for granted; it is an unthought about, almost unconscious, activity. Yet, if we tap the rich seam of our own experience, apply ourselves to some obvious, but oft forgotten, techniques, and begin to think about what we normally do without thought, we can improve our negotiating performance quite dramatically.

This book helps you to understand the process of negotiation. It highlights appropriate skills. It does not promote devious 'Machiavellian' bluffs and double bluffs, which usually are counter-productive. Instead, it concentrates on what actually happens when people negotiate. It looks at actual moves, tactics and ploys, and suggests what your best move might be when you recognize them (though the author disclaims all liability for taking his advice!). You are warned of the traps that lurk within otherwise attractive proposals, for *Pocket Negotiator* aims to be a practical as well as an informative guide to negotiating.

Pocket Negotiator makes reference to negotiating practice around the world. Mainly the context is competitive business, but, where appropriate, examples have been taken from other contexts, such as diplomatic, industrial and domestic negotiation. Some entries are relevant to others and these are indicated by the use of small capitals.

Currencies have not been specified. This saves readers having to convert a chosen currency into their own. A price of '1,000' can be taken to refer to any currency, according to your convenience.

Space precludes coverage of every aspect of negotiation, and every important contributor to the literature and practice of negotiating. Among the many authors and negotiators around the world whom I have listened to, read, or consulted over the years, I acknowledge with respect and gratitude: Robert Allen, Gerald Atkinson, John Benson, Edward de Bono, Hank Calero, John Carlise, Herb Cohen, Daniel Druckman, John Fayerweather, Roger Fisher, Patrick Hearn, Tom Hopkins, Ashok Kapoor, Chester Karass, Albert Lowry, Robert McKersie, John McMillan, P.D.V Marsh, Tony Martin, John Nash, Howard Raiffa, Anatol Rapoport, Masura Sakuma, Thomas Schelling, Glenn Snyder, William Ury, John Winkler, Oran Young, William Zartman, and the thousands of negotiators who have contributed to my clinics and workshops since 1972 in Europe, North America and Australasia.

Special thanks are offered to my colleagues at Heriot–Watt University, Edinburgh, in particular to Professor John Small for permitting me time-out to complete the manuscript, and to our dedicated secretariat, Diann MacDonald, Kath Birkenfield and Margaret Tait, who cheerfully printed the manuscript through more than one resource crisis.

Readers with views on what is included, or missed out of the *Pocket Negotitator* are invited to send them to me. Those interested in reading my other books, or seeing my videos, or attending a clinic can write to me direct at: Negotiate Limited, 10 Forth Street, Edinburgh, Scotland, UK (phone 031 557 4633; telex 72165, fax031 553 1739). In Australia call Rose & Heriot on 054 261 808; in North America call Washington Speakers Bureau on 703 684 0555; in Scandinavia call Kris Helgerson on (Oslo) 472 288661.

Gavin Kennedy

Acknowledgements

We are grateful for kind permission to reproduce cartoons from the following: *Punch*, pp. 35, 116, 159, 183, 244 and 251; *Private Eye*, pp. 18, 72 and 222; Marc, p. 3; *Scottish Business Insider*, p. 152; and Barry Fantoni, p. 24.

A

Add-on. A tactic to increase the quoted terms for a transaction. The add-on is a plausible *extra* such as for delivery, or fitting, or for some necessary component (batteries, wires, plugs, etc.), added to the main item.

Car sellers use the add-on to boost the gross sales value of the transaction. You assume that the price on the windscreen is the gross price for the car. If you agree to buy the car, the seller may add extra charges:

'That'll be 9,725, sir.'
'But the sticker says 8,800.'
'Yes, but the on-the-road price costs 300 for delivery, 400 for the aluminium wheels and performance tyres, 250 for the in-car entertainment centre, and 25 for fuel.'

Counter: Find out what you get for your money *before* you give a buying signal.

Sometimes it is necessary to add-on when your first offer is accepted:

'My normal price is 1,000 per twenty windows.'

You expect them to negotiate you downwards. Instead they reply:

'Fine. Send me the invoice.'

Now spring the add-on:

'There'll also be charge of 500 for delivery, installation, and fitting the anti-theft switches you require.'
'OK.'
'Plus 50 a window for the premium glass.'

Your add-ons take the gross price from 1,000 to 2,500 (should you be selling to a price-blind buyer).

Even a small add-on across all your sales increases gross selling value. This is why restaurants charge for the main meal plus for starters and coffees. Some restaurants charge for the main dish and then add-on for the vegetables. Quote *basic* prices only – they look smaller – and then try the add-on for ancillaries. Divide your product or service into component parts, and set prices for the main component and add-on prices for the others.

See BROOKLYN OPTICIANS and TAKE-OFF.

Adjournments. Negotiator's equivalent of a time-out. You agree to terminate the current negotiating session, and adjourn for a while – minutes in the corridor, hours in another room, days back at your own site, etc. You need a break to think about what has been said, to reconsider your position, to regroup your team, to consult with your advisers or more senior decision-makers, or simply to rest and recuperate.

Some negotiations are spread over several weeks, or months (major international projects take several years). Adjourn if only to rest, but take advantage of the break to prepare for the next session. Adjournments are risky. While absent, circumstances change – your rivals make irresistible proposals, the war swings against you, your product becomes redundant, they find another solution to their problem. The negotiator calling for an adjournment creates expectations that he may be unable to fulfil on his return. The other side believe you adjourned to consider an improvement in your previous proposals or acceptance of theirs. If you do no more than re-state your pre-adjournment position, you risk creating hostility.

The benefits of adjourning are often worth the risks. To avoid false expectations, make clear why you are adjourning. If it is to rest and recuperate, say so, choosing, if possible, a 'natural break': lunch time, end of the working day, midnight, late on Friday (Wednesday in the Middle East), or when it is mutually clear that both negotiators could benefit from a break. If you want to adjourn to think over what has been put to you, say so.

Either negotiator can call for an adjournment. It is best to agree to one. Also, avoid 'valedictory' exhortations and speeches once an adjournment is called. They only waste time, and always risk further argument.

Advance. Payment of part (a deposit) or all of the charge for services yet to be performed. Advance payments are common in publishing, household repairs, furniture stores, small boat building and bespoke products of all kinds.

If asked to make an advance payment, ask yourself: 'Will the service be performed after I have paid for it?' Avoid advance payments to household plumbers, painters, roof repairers and people you don't know. If they are short of cash. they are unreliable. They might turn up and start the job, but then they

'All right. If you behave for the rest of the journey, mummy promises not to go topless when we get there'

might not. Also, it is notoriously difficult to find them again, let alone get your money back. If, plausibly, they need money for materials, buy them yourself, and deliver them to your premises, not theirs. Tell them they get the next tranche of money as a PROGRESS PAYMENT when they perform, and not before.

If a reputable business wants an advance payment (get a signed and dated receipt), require a discount on the price at least equivalent to the interest you lose while they have your money. Banks don't lend money for nothing, so why should you?

If asked to perform a service before payment and without an

advance, ask yourself: 'Will they pay for it afterwards?' You risk not getting paid when payment is due, or not getting paid at all, or not getting paid the full amount. Remember: it's easier to avoid debts than to collect them.

They get the benefits of your services, which cost you for materials and your time. You are dependent on their goodwill (see HOOKER'S PRINCIPLE). Once you have performed the service what SANCTIONS do you have against their quibbling over payment? Get them to agree on a price before you perform the service, and put your charges in writing. You must get a signature from the client on a signed order, or an instruction to proceed on their notepaper.

Send a letter outlining your terms for performing the service, stating that 'unless we hear to the contrary, we will proceed on this agreed basis'. Their silence is evidence of a contract.

There is another problem with advances. A well-known author took an incredibly large advance against ROYALTIES for a 'bodice-ripping' blockbuster novel. It flopped, and he owed the publisher $800,000 in unearned royalties. They could have asked for it back, but he had already spent it. Instead, they required him to produce other formula-written 'blockbusters' until their earnings cleared the advance. It will take the author years of compulsory writing to clear the (then) 'biggest ever advance in publishing'.

Agenda. An order of business. It sets out the sequence of the issues to be negotiated; it is a helpful organizer of what would otherwise be a wandering debate. It can have important implications for the negotiators, causing them to debate what is negotiable and what is non-negotiable.

For example, Britain is willing to negotiate anything with Argentina, except the issue of the sovereignty of the Falkland/Malvinas Islands; Argentina resists negotiating with Britain until the sovereignty of the islands is included on the agenda. Until they agree to a common agenda, they are unable to negotiate.

Negotiators can agree on the composition of an agenda but disagree on the order in which items will be discussed. For example, employees prefer to negotiate wage rises before they discuss productivity or manning changes; the company prefers to quantify the productivity changes before committing itself to a wage rise. One solution: first, negotiate for a (small) basic wage rise, then for productivity changes, and finally negotiate for an increase in wages for the agreed changes. Alternatively, agree to negotiate the items in any order on the basis that 'nothing is agreed until everything is agreed'.

Extremely hostile relationships between negotiators preclude detailed agendas. Much coaxing is required just to get the negotiators to agree to an agenda. But agreement to consider an agenda is a step forward, and the less specific the headings on the agenda, the more likely the parties are to agree to meet.

Agent. Somebody who represents a PRINCIPAL to third parties. Used in REAL ESTATE transactions for the buying and selling of goods and services.

In Britain the law treats commercial agents at arm's length, whereas on the Continent, and in some Third World countries, specific laws protect agents, making it difficult to terminate an agency – at least cheaply – if circumstances suggest you should do so. Many countries require foreigners to operate exclusively through nationals who act as commercial agents (GO-BETWEENS), but some specifically prohibit the use of local agents (because of bribery scandals), and it is essential to know about local practices to avoid unplanned jail sentences.

In negotiating an agency CONTRACT check on the legal complications of doing so for the country where the contract is to operate. You are liable to a third party for your agent's actions, promises and negligence. Avoiding a formal contract may not protect you if the local courts judge that there is an implicit agency relationship between you. Strictly defining your agent's authority, and the limits to your liability, might help.

If the agent requires an exclusive agency, strictly define the territory, reserve the right to terminate the agency if sales and profit targets are not met, if payments are not made on time, if the agent is taken over by another party, if he is discovered to be in breach of trust (e.g. fiddling the books), or if he fails to maintain declared standards of quality. (Consider other reasons for revoking the contract using the 'WHAT IF?' technique.) Also, include a dated TERMINATION clause that enables you to reassign the agency to another party, redefine the extent of the territory, or take over direct distribution of your own product.

An agency agreement seeks to enable both parties to make PROFITS. Either, the GROSS Income from agency sales goes direct to the principal, who returns the agent's COMMISSION, or the gross goes to the agent, who retains his commission, passing on the NET income to the principal. The former is more secure for the principal, and the agent's INCENTIVE is assured if the commission is paid promptly; the latter is riskier, but may be administratively convenient. Consider invoicing stock on despatch to the agent. This motivates the agent to recover his outlays, and reduces your risks.

Agreement. Preferred name for a CONTRACT. Agreements are on the angel's side of the trust boundary; contracts lie just over it. Negotiating an agreement sounds more trusting than negotiating a contract. Later, if agreed obligations are not met, call your agreement a contract. The legal connotations of a 'contract' carry a message without being unduly threatening.

Record what was agreed during the negotiation, not after you have dispersed. If you can't agree what was agreed while you are together, it is unlikely that you will do so later. So if you can't agree, carry on negotiating until you can.

Beware of stretching the truth when writing up an agreement. You might get away with it, but you might also jeopardize trust and sour the relationship. The world's courts are full of disputes about what was actually agreed between the parties, and charges of malpractice are the most bitter (and often the most expensive). Record the agreement in any mutually acceptable form: a formal contract, an exchange of minutes, a letter of agreement, a telex, a verbal undertaking (supported by an early letter summarizing your understanding of the undertakings you and they have agreed to).

All agreements should outline the action to be taken by each party to implement the agreement.

Any relevant qualifications, or limitations, to obligations, explanations of specific clauses and what each negotiator understands by them, or reference documents necessary to follow what the negotiators intended, should be included as appendices to the formal contract and confirmed in writing. Such references, if not included in the wording of the agreement, should be unambiguous and relate to the formal contract.

Alternatives. If the negotiated possibilities are inferior to the available alternatives, it is better to abandon an attempt to negotiate the differences. (Cf. BEST ALTERNATIVE TO A NEGOTIATED AGREEMENT, BATNA.)

For example, in March – June 1982 any negotiated settlement of the Falklands crisis was less attractive to Britain than to Argentina. MEDIATION inevitably meant Argentina acquired some form of sovereignty in exchange for withdrawing its military forces from the islands. Regaining the islands by force was a more attractive option to Britain than negotiating under duress. Military defeat for Argentina reinforced British claims to the islands, removed the occupation forces and restored unambiguous sovereignty to Britain.

Negotiators overstate the attractiveness of their alternatives. Sellers deny that failure to agree to their terms is a disaster for them because another buyer will meet their terms, and soon; buyers deny that failure to agree to their terms is a disaster for them because another seller is about to settle with them. Tactically, each negotiator attempts to persuade the other that they have real alternatives to doing business on the offered terms. Buyers mention sellers waiting to see them; sellers mention buyers queuing in the waiting room clutching fistfuls of offers.

Ambiguity. May be intentional or unintentional. Intentional ambiguities arise when there is a need for a face-saving formula to break a DEADLOCK: 'You interpret it your way and we will interpret it our way.'

The UK's employer–union procedure agreements that operated from the 1920s to the 1960s were classic examples of ambiguity. They stated that : 'The employers have the right to manage their enterprises and the unions have the right to exercise their functions'. Clearly, these rights overlapped, and depending on the circumstances and the economic climate, one side's interpretation could (and often did) trespass on the other's.

Ask 'WHAT IF?' questions during the drafting of the agreement to avoid, or reduce, unintentional ambiguities. Ask 'What if this happens?', 'What if that happens?', 'Does this mean that?', and so on. Decide whether you should take action while drafting, or whether, having spotted a potential ambiguity, it is best left as it is (intentionally), perhaps to avoid rubbing salt in the other negotiator's wounds, or your own, or to avoid exposing you to additional liabilities.

Apples and pears. Principle that things may be substitutes but they need not be the same.

Negotiators compare one proposal with another. With several proposals they have difficulty in making accurate comparisons because the proposals differ in more than one respect. In fact, they may not be comparable at all. Each proposal varies in a different respect to the other; with one it might be a different specification, another might involve differences in delivery and installation, others have different features, some tackle the problem one way, others another, some look good on price, but not so hot on finance and credit, others offer training with support, or training without support, some offer 'hot lines' for emergency advice, others charge for the advice, but not for the training and updating. They are similar in that they are fruit, but one is an apple and the other is a pear.

When a negotiator tells you it is all down to price, he is saying that you and your competitors have all put in bids that are apples. This is most unlikely, and if it is true, then it is time to reconsider what you are doing in this particular market, because if you are supplying homogeneous goods, and it is down to price, its time you got into another line of work – there is never a low price that can't be beaten by somebody else of a Kamikaze disposition.

Arbitration. Use of a private tribunal or person to adjudicate a dispute between parties instead of recourse to litigation.

In most countries there are legal implications in the use of arbitrators, particularly where provision for arbitration is written into an agreement. In many cases, the decision of a commercial arbitrator is legally binding on the parties. Industrial relations law can require a binding arbitration on the parties (Australia and the United States). It can also be a voluntary arrangement (even non-binding) when it arises out of a conciliation process, such as the UK government's Advisory, Conciliation and Arbitration Service (ACAS).

Arbitrators exercise arbitrary power. They make an award, and the negotiators (normally) accept their decision. Hence take care when selecting an arbitrator (avoid using in-laws to arbitrate domestic disputes). Negotiators unable to resolve a dispute refer the issue to a mutually acceptable third party who, for a fee, receives submissions from each side (written or oral), exercises judgement and then pronounces a verdict.

Arbitrators are selected from numerous sources. The Pope arbitrated between Argentina and Chile over the islands of the Beagle Channel; the Secretary-General of the United Nations arbitrated between New Zealand and France over the *Rainbow Warrior* affair.

Many contracts nominate either named persons or the officials of named institutions to arbitrate if a dispute arises. It is common for the president of a chartered professional association (accountancy, surveyors, architects etc.) to be nominated to choose an arbitrator. Alternatively, each party nominates one person each, and the two nominees choose a third to form a panel.

The International Chamber of Commerce provides an arbitration service for commercial contracts (for details contact ICC Court of Arbitration, 38, Cours Albert 1er, 75008 Paris).

Once a dispute goes to arbitration the negotiators cease to influence the outcome. Their case stands or falls on its merits in the eyes of the supposedly independent arbitrator. The arbitrator, examining a dispute over a price or wage rate, may choose some compromise between the parties' final proposals. In PENDULUM ARBITRATION, the award must be one or the other party's FINAL OFFER.

In disputes over facts – was the grain shipment of the claimed quantity? did the carrier give due and proper notice of a delay? were the specifications changed by an authorized officer of the company? – arbitration is more useful than in disputes over interpretation of the law. While, in general, arbitration is better than litigation (it should cost less and be quicker), negotiation is better than both while avoiding disputes is best of all.

Argument. Eighty per cent of a successful negotiation is spent arguing (an unsuccessful negotiation is 100 per cent argument). All behaviour that involves statements of position, criticism of the other negotiator's positions, SUMMARIZING what has been said, or QUESTIONS and answers, constitutes argument. Argument can be either constructive or destructive.

Some negotiations never get beyond argument. The negotiators feel strongly about the issues, they know they are in conflict over means or ends (and often both), they feel that their interests are at stake (as well they might be), they have an urge to state their principles, prejudices, beliefs, suspicions and grievances. Differences in their value systems raise the temperature of the argument, if only because they excite THREAT perceptions.

Only PROPOSALS can be negotiated. Destructive argument through the use of emotive language, point scoring, blaming, swearing and cursing, attacking the other negotiator's integrity, questioning their authority, interrupting, shouting down, mocking and generally being obstructive, prevents proposals being formulated, or if formulated, prevents their being considered constructively. Constructive use of argument involves LISTENING to the other negotiator; refraining from indulging in, or responding to, destructive argument; questioning views and assumptions (and listening to the answers); summarizing the issues in dispute and how each side sees the problem; and SEEKING CLARIFICATON of the views and positions of each side. The objective is to discover, or confirm, the INTERESTS and INHIBITIONS of the other negotiator, and to search for SIGNALS that indicate potential for movement.

Aspiration. The world is full of unfulfilled ambitions. Being tough is not enough; merely aspiring high in a negotiation need not produce the result that was sought. Some research shows that high aspirations produce better results than low aspirations. Other research shows high aspirations produce higher risks of DEADLOCK. Negotiators balance the prize of high aspirations with the price of unfulfilled ambition.

When a party with high aspirations meets a party of low aspirations, the outcome depends on how the parties perceive each other. The less ambitious party sometimes reacts to the higher demands of the more ambitious and gives way: ambition becomes self-fulfilling. Alternatively, the over-ambitious negotiator irritates or antagonizes the less ambitious. Worms turn; they fight back; sometimes they even intimidate the INTIMIDATOR into making major concessions ('I was only kidding . . .'). (See INTIMIDATION.) More often, bruised egos retire without agreement.

It should not be concluded from this that you should necessarily aim low. NEGOTIATING WITH YOURSELF by lowering your aspirations is as self-defeating as trying to coerce a stronger opponent into submission (See REALISTIC OFFER).

Assumption. In business and *affaires de coeur*, assumptions are inevitable. Some of our assumptions, particularly about the other negotiator's intentions, are often totally false; 'I'll never get the business unless I cut my prices'; 'They only buy from multinationals'; 'He's only interested in social partners under 25'; 'My intentions are good, therefore I make everybody happy'.

Acting on our assumptions, we price cut when it is not necessary, miss out on profitable business with the Fortune 500, feel passed over at 26 and unintentionally make everybody else miserable. Validate your assumptions before acting upon them. Ask QUESTIONS. For example, if we assume that the other party is more interested in price than in delivery, we react to the assumed price problem by shaving our prices. LISTENING to what they tell us about their attitude to price, delivery and so on, and questioning them carefully about their attitudes, we test our assumptions. Finding out what is important to the other side is not difficult: they often tell you, loudly. Ask them: 'What aspects of my proposals do you find attractive and what aspects are unattractive?' What you assumed to be true, maybe false. For instance, you assumed that your prices were higher than your rivals', but that your service was so good you were in front of the competition. They tell you that your price is competitive but your service is below standard.

Assumptive close. Used by sellers. The seller asks a question which assumes that the prospective buyer has decided to purchase. If the buyer answers the question, he commits himself to buy.
- 'Will you collect or shall we deliver?'
- 'Is it cash or charge?'
- 'Do you want them in batches of 50, or 100?'

If you're buying, seek additional movement from the seller before you give a BUYING SIGNAL. Tell the seller:

'I am not in a position to answer that question until I have decided whether to do business with you. First you must tell me what you propose in respect of the following.'

This blocks the assumptive close, tells the seller he has more work to do and passes the initiative to you.

Auction. System of selling that puts maximum pressure on buyers. (Maximum pressure is put on sellers by the BID system.)

In the regular auction buyers call out their bids in an ascending order to the auctioneer. The *last* bidder wins. In a DUTCH AUCTION the auctioneer asks for bids in a descending order. The *first* bidder to call out wins. In a 'Vickery sealed-bid auction', the highest bidder wins at the second highest bidder's price.

Bids can be public, usually with the buyers in the same room. Each knows the value of the last bid. A good auctioneer creates sufficient excitement about the bidding that buyers bid more than they intended to. This raises the price of the item and the auctioneer's commission. Auctions can also be private, as with property sales in Scotland. Each prospective buyer submits a sealed bid by a specific time and the highest bidder (normally) wins.

Authority. Negotiating with people without authority to settle is similar to being at an AUCTION, except that you are often only bidding against yourself. The other party forces you to change your offer because it is not yet good enough for acceptance by the higher authority. Negotiators without authority leave you vulnerable if the higher authority seeks concessions from you in exchange for agreement.

Union representatives often claim to have insufficient authority to sign an agreement: 'It must be referred to the membership first.' This reflects the power balance inside the union: the members do not trust their representatives to make decisions on their behalf, hence, they demand a vote. Company offers are thus vulnerable to what happens at the members' meeting. The risk is reduced if the representatives recommend the offer to the meeting. A lukewarm presentation of what has been agreed damns its prospects with feint support. Hence, willingness to recommend an offer should be secured:

'On condition that you recommend what we have agreed, the company will make a final offer that incorporates some of your requirements regarding overtime working.'

Managers also state that anything they agree to is 'subject to board approval'. Many companies sensibly require board endorsement of expenditures above a certain limit. There is also the owner/entrepreneur who insists that 'I didn't get where I am today by letting my managers spend a cent without my approval'.

Normally, managers lack authority because their role is to filter out totally unacceptable proposals. Sometimes, board approval of what has been agreed is a formality. But if somebody upstairs wants to change something (seldom other than to his own advantage), they come back for more concessions. They assume that the offer was padded in anticipation of further concessions and hence they ask for them. To avoid the embarrassment, therefore, PAD your offers.

Being ambushed with the 'no authority here' tactic, after you have moved as far as remains profitable for you, is disconcerting, and expensive. Avoid this by asking the negotiators whether they have the full authority to settle. Don't necessarily believe the answer you get. People don't like admitting to being the 'monkey' and not the 'organ grinder'. Hold back something in the proposal for that final traded concession to get agreement.

When asked if you have authority when you haven't, and you don't wish to disclose the fact, say 'yes'. When it's time to refer the proposal upstairs for approval, take an ADJOURNMENT to 'consider the proposal' and refer it upstairs. If the decision-makers upstairs want further concessions, claim that the required changes resulted from your consideration of the total package. Don't try this more than once with the same person in the same negotiation. Scepticism is not correlated with intelligence.

Authority levels are often obvious from the company structure. Government officials seldom have total authority, except on low budget items. Spending proposals often involve managers from finance besides the user departments. Junior managers normally need to refer to their bosses.

Most decisions take time and therefore your proposal is unlikely to be decided at a single meeting. To assess authority levels, ask:
- 'What are your procedures for making decisions of this nature?'
- 'Who in your company participates in these decisions?'
- 'How long do decisions of this nature normally take?'
- 'Does the company have a purchasing policy and can I see a copy?'

Avoidance–avoidance model. Application of an insight from psychology to the economics of negotiation.

Briefly, people faced with two relatively unattractive choices try to avoid both. The closer they are to an unattractive choice, the more they try to avoid making it. The model was first applied to a negotiation between a union and a company by C.M. Stevens in 1958, from the earlier work of John Dollard and Neal E. Miller (1950). It has affinities with the economic models of John Hicks (1930).

The company's choices are to settle on the union's terms, and thus reduce its profitability, or to stick to its current position (the status quo) of a lower wage offer than the union is seeking, and thus suffer the costs of a strike. The company wishes to avoid both choices. It seeks a compromise: a wage rise smaller than the union's demands, but better than its own opening offer.

The union adopts tactics from one or both of the following classes of objectives:

• Those that increase the company's tendency to avoid sticking to its opening offer.

• Those that reduce the company's tendency to avoid meeting the union's demands.

Among the former tactics, the union asserts that the costs of a strike are higher than the company's own estimates (SECONDARY BOYCOTTS). Among the latter tactics, the union claims that the company's competitors are raising their wage costs, thus reducing concern of a competitive disadvantage emerging if the company meets the union's demands.

B

Bagatelle. As in 'mere bagatelle'. A tactic to overcome resistance to major changes perceived to be onerous or unacceptable to the other party. Sometimes called 'salami' tactics because it comes in thin slices.

Instead of demanding, for instance, that everybody in employment receives a pay rise, the union demands that an additional payment be made to all employees with ten years' service. The company might accept (or by circumstances be forced to accept) the principle of long service payments, but respond by narrowing the criteria – 'everybody with 25 years' service', etc. They only consider the cost of implementing the policy for a few cases, which is a fairly small sum initially – it's a mere bagatelle – and not what it will cost over the years as the number of people qualifying increases.

Faced with a bagatelle demand, increase the complexity of the qualifications: 'Everybody with 25 years' service, with unblemished discipline records, who are ex-service men and women, who have families with more than one child, whose children are in college, who do community service, who . . .'. The more credible the qualifications, the more negotiating room to resist future attempts to extend the bagatelle's applicability.

The bagatelle is a favourite ploy of sellers of anything relatively expensive. The bagatelle widens the market for their products. The most common bagatelles are used in selling repayment schemes to make the cost appear trivial: 'Drive this new Ford away today for only 49 a week' (its true cost is 20,000, before interest on the loan); 'Everything you have wanted in home entertainment for less than a can of beer a day' (it costs the equivalent of five years' beer drinking).

To protect yourself from the illusion of the bagatelle, always gross up to the full cost (price per slice times the number of slices). Find out what you pay.

To use the bagatelle, break down the total cost of your product into small slices, using a per minimum unit price or some imaginative comparative price. For instance, sell photocopying paper by the sheet; annual fees for hospital insurance by the cost per day; cable TV entertainment by the cost per hour; overseas calls by the cost per three minutes ('Call Timbuktoo for only 3.52'). Timeshare companies use a brilliant bagatelle: 'A week in Acapulco for ever, for the cost of a week in Acapulco.'

Balloon. Ballon loans stave off the pain of repayment. Instead of paying off a loan in regular instalments (monthly, quarterly), like an ordinary mortgage, the entire loan, plus the accumulated interest, is paid off in one ('balloon') payment on a specified date.

If you are presently, and hopefully only temporarily, strapped for cash to pay for something you want (need desperately), a balloon may be the answer (if you find somebody willing to lend money on those terms). You might offer to take a balloon, for example, if you were expecting a legacy in five or seven years' time. Meanwhile, enjoy the benefits of the loan without the hassle of paying for it. When the windfall arrives, pay it off. As the day of reckoning approaches, however, the burden of the balloon looms ever larger. If you do not arrange your affairs appropriately – and foolishly (unavoidably?) spend your cash on something else – and cannot pay off the loan when due, the security for the loan (a house?) is forfeit. If this security is worth less than the loan plus interest, you still owe the difference.

Faced with a looming balloon, you desperately sell the security for the loan. Desperate sellers sell cheap; buyers get good bargains from balloon borrowers in trouble.

Should you agree to lend on balloon terms? Yes, if the borrower has appropriate security and can pledge it against the loan and the accumulated interest (insist on holding the title and having a signed acknowledgment of your interest in the security to prevent the borrower disposing of it without your knowledge). You do not get any income from your loan until it is due in full. Only lend what you can wait a long time for. You are vulnerable if the pledged security does not maintain its value (reserve your right of regular inspection and survey). Consider these risks. You could, for a price, offer a balloon loan if you wish a large lump sum (the loan plus interest) at some date in the future, without having the hassle of making regular savings yourself, say, when you retire, or face school fees, or want to make a large purchase, or because of tax advantages.

Banks. Banks lend money that does not belong to them. If they don't lend, they go bust. The art of successful banking is to lend any amount of money at a profit to anybody who can pay back what they borrow, and to avoid lending anything at all to anybody who can't.

Successful negotiating with banks depends on how you feel about debt. If the bank's loan is a salvation for pressing financial problems, you are almost certainly a supplicant psychologically. You are grateful for any favours the bank manager imposes, such as onerous interest and security terms. Debtors in trouble tend not to be choosy.

If debt is an opportunity to enhance your NET WORTH, you negotiate on the basis of equality: the bank sells access to money, you sell access to a profitable relationship.

Negotiating a loan to finance your lifestyle is a disaster area. You'll end up broke, as interest payments gobble up your income (if you have any). Unless you are a prodigal child, there is no future in such borrowing.

To get rich using other people's money, never borrow to finance income. Only borrow to finance net worth (broadly, what you own minus what you owe).

Banks lend money to make a profit. The profit on a loan is negotiable. You don't have to accept a fixed borrowing charge if you can give the bank a credible reason why you should be charged less. Banks have their loan charges printed so that all their managers are informed of the most profitable lending rates, but they are not written in stone. Avoid INTIMIDATION by a printed interest list.

Your negotiation for better terms depends on your LEND-ABILITY FACTOR. A high lendability factor gives you access to larger amounts of money, with less hassle and at lower cost than a low lendability factor. But whatever offer the bank makes, remember it is only their FIRST OFFER, not their only offer.

Bargaining. Getting something you value highly for something you value less.

Trade is based on the exchange of things that the parties concerned value differently. When you are hungry you buy food in exchange for cash. At the moment when you buy the food you value the food more than you do the cash, otherwise you would keep your cash and stay hungry. What happens after you have consumed the food is irrelevant, even if you wish you had kept your money. The person selling the food values the cash more than the food, otherwise that person would keep the food and do without the cash. At the moment of the trade you each get a

'Or for a little extra you can have the "Gucci" heart.'

bargain. The same is true of all transactions in an open market. If, however, you are coerced into buying or selling something, the extent of the COERCION measures the absence of bargaining.

We try to discover what things we have that the other party values highly. The best bargain is to offer to exchange for things we value highly things that they value highly.

Bargaining continuum. A geometrical model of the negotiating process where the gains to one negotiator are matched by losses to the other (after R.E. Walton and R.B. McKersie, *A Behavioral Theory of Labor Negotiation*, New York, McGraw-Hill, 1965.)

Consider two negotiators, a union official and a manager in negotiation over a wage rate. Assume that the current rate (CR) is 4.40, as in figure 1. The continuum could be marked off as follows. There is some rate at which employees will quit and seek work elsewhere: this could be 3.40. The employees do not expect to face a wage cut of that size. Indeed, if their bargaining agents (the union) accepted a wage out to a rate of 3.90, they would sack their agents and sign up with another union. This is the lower limit of possible wage rates for the employees (UL in figure 1).

Figure 1

		UL		CR	ML	
3·40		3·90		4·40	4·60	4·80

Conversely, there is some wage rate at which the company would prefer to sack the entire workforce or otherwise go out of business: this could be 4.80. The management side do not expect to have to go as high as this. Indeed, if they went beyond 4.60, the company would replace them as its negotiators (and repudiate whatever they had agreed to pay). This is the upper limit for the management (ML).

The lower limit for the union and the upper limit for the management are where the negotiators offer maximum and indefinite resistance to offers or demands. These points are the lower and upper boundaries beyond which the other party cannot influence the outcome by negotiation.

Figure 2 shows the so-called settlement range.

Figure 2

CR	UR	MT	UT	MR	
4·40	4·45	4·48	4·55	4·58	

Settlement range

Each negotiator has a range of possible rates at which he would be prepared to settle. These run from the most optimistic aspiration, to their most pessimistic aspiration (the MUST GET objective). Suppose the union estimates that the best it can do is to achieve a rate of 4.55; that is the union's target rate (UT). Suppose that it estimates that the least it can settle for is 4.45; this is the union's RESISTANCE PRICE (UR). At management offers below this minimum rate, the union calls for strike action. Conversely, suppose the management assesses its target rate – the one it optimistically thinks it can achieve – as 4.48 (MT) and its pessimistic resistance price as 4.58 (MR). At demands from the union in excess of 4.58, the management prefers to take a strike.

In figure 2, the range from the union's resistance price of 4.45 and the management's resistance price of 4.58 is the SETTLEMENT RANGE. Depending on events a settlement is possible within this range.

Neither party knows for certain the resistance price of the other. To disclose them is self-defeating. If the union disclosed that it would strike if offered a rate lower than 4.45, which is lower than the management's target rate of 4.48, it would induce the management negotiators to revise their optimistic target and offer 4.46; if the company disclosed it would take a strike above 4.58, which is higher than the union's target rate of 4.55, it would induce the union negotiators to revise their most optimistic target upwards and demand 4.57. This is the classic HAGGLE situation.

The resistance prices may not be compatible (see figure 3). If the union's resistance price (UR) is 4.60 and the management's resistance price (MR) is 4.50, there is no settlement range. The most the management is prepared to pay without taking a strike is lower than the least the union will accept without going on strike. Unless the negotiators change their positions, there will be a strike.

Figure 3

CR	MR	UR
4·40	4·50	4·60

The bargaining continuum model can be applied to any system of DISTRIBUTIVE BARGAINING, where the price of something is to be determined.

See USED CAR SALE.

Bargaining language. Some forms of language help negotiators, others don't. The following language does not help:
- 'I'll increase my offer by ten. How about that?'

- 'OK. We'll throw in two extra terminals.'
- 'If I improve the payback period, will that do?'
- 'We'll cover the insurance costs. OK?'

These are UNCONDITIONAL OFFERS. They do not require anything in exchange, except by implication, consent to the deal. Faced with an unconditional offer you accept it as a movement towards an even better offer. If they are moving towards your requirements *at no cost to you* keep them moving, by withholding agreement and asking for more:

- 'Sorry. Ten is not enough. I need at least 20.'
- 'Make it five extra terminals and abate the maintenance charge.'
- 'Not really. Payback is only one of the issues.'
- 'We need more than insurance covered. What are you proposing to do about security costs?'

Use CONDITIONAL LANGUAGE:

- 'If you pay in 21 days, then I'll increase the offer to ten.'
- 'If you buy the standard software, then I'll include an extra terminal.'
- 'If you sign the order now, then I'll improve the payback period.'
- 'If you pay for full security cover, than I'll abate the insurance charge.'

Note the format: If you . . . then I. Tell them what they must do first. This is the price of getting you to do something for them. If they meet your conditions, and only then, do you commit yourself to do something for them. If they respond to reject your conditional propositions, and make additional demands, the conditional format enables you to reply:

- 'If you pay me in advance, then I will supply 20.'
- 'If you buy the full library of software, and take out a five-year maintenance contract, then I will increase the suite by three terminals.'
- 'If you specify all the outstanding issues, then I will consider my response.'
- 'If you meet the full insurance costs, and give me a contract to manage your pension fund, then I will abate the security costs.'

Conditional language protects your offers from being ambushed: it forces the other side into BARGAINING.

Barter. Exchange of goods and services without using cash. A system that pre-dates monetary economies. It also sometimes supersedes them when they break down in times of war, revolution, inflation and other disasters. Anybody with anything to trade can try bartering for what they want. Children barter toys because they have no cash. Allegedly the 'black economy' is full of people trading their labour for food, their surplus food for timber, their surplus household fixtures for whatever they can get for them.

Barter is not confined to depressed rural backwaters and urban ghettoes: affluent people barter too. It could be a tax dodge, or simply because they prefer not to use cash with friends. An architect designs an extension for a restaurant in return for a year's dining; an accountant audits a garage's books for the use of a truck; neighbours swap lawnmowers for sprayers, freezer space for homemade wine, and childminding for use of the pool (they have also been known to swap spouses).

Bartering is less efficient than cash, if cash is available. It takes time to work your way through a series of barter transactions to get rid of something you no longer need for something that you do. The guy with a chain saw for trade might not want your excess tomatoes: he prefers a hedge trimmer. The man with the hedge trimmer for trade wants a shed painted. The painter is looking for tomatoes (get the picture?). If you discover a barter chain that starts with what you have and ends with what you want – and it takes time to do so – you still have a lot of work to do. You must negotiate to exchange each item. Using cash short cuts the problem. You buy the chain saw with the money you get from selling your tomatoes.

Barter requires negotiating skills. Don't forget the basic principle of trade: its not what its worth to you that counts, but what it is worth to the guy that wants it. The broken fridge may be worthless to you if you don't know what's wrong with it, and don't know how to fix it. If the other person does, its worth a great deal more to him than it is to you. Make your offer with this in mind.

BATNA. See below.

Best alternative to a negotiated agreement (BATNA). A standard against which any proposed agreement is measured. Not how a proposal stacks against your pre-determined BOTTOM

LINE, which may or may not be soundly based, but how the proposal matches your realistic alternatives. (After Roger Fisher and William Ury, *Getting to Yes: Negotiating agreement without giving in*, Houghton Mifflin, Boston, 1981.)

The more attractive your alternatives to the proposed agreement the more power you have. The fewer your alternatives, and the less attractive they are, the less power you have.

To develop BATNAS, list all the things you could conceivably do if you fail to reach an acceptable agreement. Now convert some of the most promising ALTERNATIVES into practical options. This eliminates the more far-fetched and unrealizable; it also tests those that are left. What is involved in realizing your short list of alternatives? Can you do anything now to put them into operation, ready for use if the negotiations fail? If 'yes', do it; if 'no' reconsider the viability of your alleged options.

Select, from the best alternatives that remain, your single best option. This is your BATNA. Now judge all proposals and offers against this BATNA. If the offers are better than your BATNA, take them; if the offers are worse, negotiate to improve them, and, if in DEADLOCK, exercise your BATNA.

Bid. A competitive system that puts maximum pressure on a supplier. Buyers' requirements go out to tender; suppliers bid for the business on a one–offer–only basis, quoting their 'best price' for the specified work. Quoted prices contain a minimum of padding, provided buyers enforce a one–offer–only bid procedure and there is no collusion among the bidders (which is illegal).

Allowing bidders to re-bid or negotiate their bids induces them to pad their first bid, until they see what the competition is quoting. If the buyer allows further discussion, he reverts to a normal negotiation and weakens the price squeeze effects of a one-offer-only procedure.

See BID/NO BID: BID LAST: BID STRATEGIES, TWO-OFFERS ONLY.

Bid/no bid. Bidding costs can be high. The use of highly skilled people to prepare a bid is expensive. Research, processing data, surveying the site, testing the sub-soil or sea-bed, plus travel and subsistence for the research personnel involved incur large expenditure. There is the cost of design staff (engineers,

"Nigel's furious. The fake he bid for
has turned out to be an original"

draughtsmen, copy writers, concept developers, media specialists, marketing professionals and such like) needed to prepare a presentation. Finally, managers, including estimators, accountants, contract managers and lawyers are involved. They require expensive presentation aids, travel and subsistence (never cheap for these grades) and back-up facilities. These costs are recouped if the bid is successful. Otherwise they are wasted.

If you don't bid, you don't win business. If you bid unsuccessfully you add to costs. Balancing winning bids with losing bids may not be enough. You must increase the win rate.

There are two considerations: Do you want/need to win the bid? What are your chances of winning? You may not want to win a particular bid. If you are overloaded with work the last thing your need is more work. But failing to bid could cut you out from future work. What do you do: bid high, and hope they say 'no'?

Your chances of success depend on several factors, not all of them in your control. Competition influences the outcome. If they beat you on price, finance, delivery and reliability, you lose.

Winning unprofitable bids is not good for business. Hence, answer the following:

- What happens if you do not bid?
- What happens if you bid but lose?
- What happens if you bid and win?
- What alternative work is in the pipeline?
- How are you placed to meet the terms of the bid?
- Will you undertake special expenditures?
- Is there any VULNERABILITY in the contract terms?
- What is the bid's contribution to profit?

If the decision is to bid, because it is desirable to do so, consider the probability of winning. Bidding for a profitable contract and not winning is a waste of resources. Hence answer the following:

- Who are the competitors for the contract?
- What can they offer in total against:

PRICE
Finance
CREDIT
OFF-SET
BARTER
Quality
Reliability
Availability
Design flair
Technical performance
Specification
Delivery
Service
Training

Marketing of output
PERFORMANCE BONDS
Kick-backs
Other special factors unique to the work.
- What can you offer that is as good, different or better than the competition?
- Where are you vulnerable to competitive pressure?
- How can you influence the client to prefer your bid?

If you are vulnerable on price, including finance and credit, can you:
- Use tactics that emphasize the relationship between costs and price?
- Highlight LIFETIME COSTS not just initial price?
- Re-package finance and credit?

If you are vulnerable on quality, including performance and service can you:
- Use tactics to highlight dangers of spurious specifications ('gold plating' by users)?
- Install new procedures for after sales service?
- Invest in high profile quality assurance systems?

If you are vulnerable on delivery, including completion can you:
- In exchange for a time system that stops the penalty clock if the client causes delays, offer realistic delivery dates and *heavy* penalties?
- Show confidence by high profile ordering of long lead time materials prior to contract?

If the answers are positive, deploy resources for the bid. If they are marginal, compare with immediate alternative bids. If they are negative, or insufficiently positive, don't bid.

Bid last. Tactic to maximize your minimal chances of doing better in a competitive bid situation.

If asked to bid competitively for business, and you eagerly send in your bid early, the buyer uses your bid to encourage others to improve upon it. Fables about 'sealed bids being opened at 12 noon on the 30th of the month' are for the naive. Bids are opened as they come in. The temptation to start an auction is overpowering. A phone call here, a whisper across the bar there, a casual comment in the street, is all it takes. Whatever else is about to happen, you have become a spectator.

If sceptical, ask yourself what you would do if you knew your rival's bid just before you dictated your bid letter. Never mind the ethics of how you found out. What would you be inclined to do if his submitted bid was 393,500 and your TARGET PRICE was 398,000 and your RESISTANCE PRICE was 388,000. No prizes for guessing what most people would send in as their bid!

Hence, bid last. Hand it over, by reliable messenger if necessary, at the very last moment that you can (11.59 am?). If invited to re-bid, find out what the bids are, and then back off. Tell them to contact you last. You trump the best bid, or withdraw. Whatever you do, *never* bid more than once in a bid auction: bid last or not at all.

Bid strategies. There are two bidding strategies: ONE-OFFER-ONLY and negotiate. A one-offer-only strategy is either a tender in a competitive situation and is your 'best price' or it is your pre-emptive take-it-or-leave-it bid in a non-competitive situation. A negotiation strategy is employed where direct contact with the client is possible. Your offer is PADDED with a realistic negotiable margin.

How do you distinguish between the strategies when the other negotiator makes an offer? Is it one-offer-only or has he come to negotiate? Asking him does not help you. Why? Because the answer you want is not the one he is likely to give. You want his offer to be negotiable, but if he says it is he invites you to strip away his padded margin. He is more likely to say that his offer is non-negotiable, which is not the answer you want. So don't ask questions when you don't want to hear the likely answer (see KILLER QUESTIONS). Always assume all offers are negotiable, and, depending on your interests, act accordingly.

Black economy. System of working outside the formal economy.

There are two parts to the price of your labour: what you pay to the state if you work, including licence fees, insurance and taxation; and what value you place on your labour time. Together these are the cost to a customer of hiring your services in the formal economy. Where the State-imposed costs of hiring are significant, you reduce your costs to the hirer by offering to work outside the formal economy and charge only for the value *to you* of your labour time. In the black economy you work without licence fees, insurance and taxation. Implicitly, you undertake not to report your work activities to the relevant authorities.

If it is not illegal, it is probably still unethical. The hirer is absolved from responsibility, for he pays you a fee for doing a specific task, and leaves it to you to meet your formal obligations to the State.

The following would be a typical conversation on the fringe of the black economy.

'How much for painting the house?'
'Six hundred.'
'That's too much.'
'How will you pay me?'
'Money of course.'
'Yes, but is it folding money?'
'What do you mean?'
'Is it cash, or by cheque against an invoice?'
'Er, cash if you like.'
'OK. If its in non-consecutive twenties, its 500 to paint the house.'
'Agreed.'

To foray into the black economy ask:

'How do you want to be paid? Cash or cheque?'

or

'What is the ready cash price?'

Warning: Check the occupation of the person buying your services. Every country employs tens of thousands of tax officials. You might be living next to one.

Blackmail. Influencing another's behaviour by violent threats to something, or someone, they value.

COERCION is common in and around the negotiating process. The essence of the blackmailer's strategy is to credibly threaten harm unless you comply with the blackmailer's demands. As a target you have two choices: comply with, or resist, the black-mailer's demands. As a blackmailer you have two choices:

reprieve or punish. These are represented in figure 4. The target's choices are shown in the vertical columns and the blackmailer's in the horizontal rows.

Figure 4

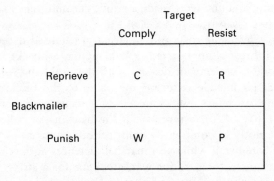

There are costs in complying. These include handing over money, changing a policy, releasing the blackmailer's cronies, or refraining from doing something you would otherwise prefer to do. The blackmailer may punish you out of vindictiveness, though promising to withdraw (W) if you comply. If you choose to resist, there are costs of doing so. The blackmailer implements his threat and inflicts punishment – kills a hostage, destroys property, besmirches your reputation, causes havoc etc. (P).

You also benefit from each choice. By complying you avoid the blackmailer's threat of punishment (net of consequences). By resisting you avoid the costs of complying, and avoid punishment (if the blackmailer is bluffing or is stymied by your resistance).

The outcome depends on the balance of probabilities of the alternative events occurring. This depends on how each party perceives the other's value systems.

Your tactics as a blackmailer aim to convince the target that threats will be carried out if the target does not comply. If the target greatly values the object of your threat (the victim, the business, the state of peace), and believes that the threat is credible, he is persuaded to comply and not resist. As a blackmailer your tactics include: enhancing the credibility of the threat (visibly preparing for war, for strikes and demonstrating a capacity for punitive actions). Credibility is enhanced if there is an inevitability about the threat being imposed – a third party inflicts the punishment automatically if your deadline is not met; you have a record of imposing punishment in similar circumstances; your missile system launches on warning without discretion; and you have made a public commitment to a line of action (see COMMITMENT TACTICS).

Tactics available to you as a target are limited if the blackmailer's threat is unexpected (a kidnapping, a hijack), and you have little experience of dealing with the problem. As a target your tactics include reducing the value to the blackmailer of choosing to inflict punishment, by encouraging belief in a positive pay-off for a reprieve. If the blackmailer believes that you are ready to comply, he holds off punishment.

You could stall while you marshall defences against the costs of punishment (prepare for war, stockpile for a strike, arrange alternative supplies, set the police to hunt the kidnapper etc.).

Under the stress of maintaining vigilance for 'tricks', or merely from reviewing the uncertain pay-offs of the exercise, the blackmailer sometimes reduces his demands to encourage compliance. Experience shows that this encourages resistance, because it increases the net benefits to you the target of non-compliance.

Your willingness to resist depends on the relative pay-offs for compliance (C) and resistance (R). The relative balance between the pay-offs (net benefits) decides the appropriate action: if $R > C$ you resist; if $C > R$ you comply; in both cases you aim for a reprieve (if the risk of P is minimal).

As a blackmailer you have a better chance of succeeding if the cost of compliance to the target is not unreasonable. Blackmail threats fail when the compliance demand is unrealistic: 'Reverse all your foreign policies by 6pm or we shoot the hostages'. Similarly, with unrealistic strike threats: 'Raise our wages by 300 per cent or we go on strike'. Unrealistic compliance demands reduce the net benefit of compliance relative to resistance, i.e. raise the net benefit of resistance.

Blame cycle. Negotiators get bogged down in blame cycles, because identifying the guilty is easier than addressing the problem. You blame the supplier for inefficiency, he justifies his actions by counter-attacking your inefficiency. Each side raises issues of less and less relevance to the immediate problem. The result is a non-constructive ARGUMENT.

Blame cycles are easy to slide into, and once started are time-wasting, difficult to stop and destructive of a relationship. Try a three-step response to anybody with a complaint against you, or your organization. Tell them:

'Let me say three things to you about how I intend to handle this problem:
'First, I am going to apologize on behalf of my people for the problem we have caused you.
'Second, I am going to listen to what you have to say.
'And third, with your help, I am going to put it right.'

In almost all cases, the complainer cools down, and adopts a more conciliatory attitude.

Blocking offer. A disreputable tactic. The terms look good and everything is moving to a conclusion. Suddenly, another negotiator appears on the scene offering much better terms. You drop out of the first negotiation and switch to the new one. Once the old negotiation is dead, the new negotiator becomes difficult. There are 'problems', unforseen 'difficulties', and newly significant 'small print' in his proposal. You have two choices: settle on the now much-reduced 'better' terms, or drop out of the negotiation. If the first choice is tried, you might find he has beaten you to the second choice: he had dropped out on you because he never intended to do a deal on any terms. His was a blocking offer.

Why should somebody make a blocking offer? Often because they do not want you to conclude a deal with anybody else. Consider a restaurant owner with a prime site business, and across the road a shop unit comes on to the market. He does not want a rival restaurant opposite his business, and when he hears that you are about to sell to a restaurant chain, he conspires to spoil the deal with a blocking offer. His offer has to be good enough to tempt you – say, 40 per cent more than their offer. Can you refuse it? Unlikely. His offer is conditional on 'minor' issues but the margin is enough to make these seem unimportant. Once the other buyer is out of the way, he prevaricates, quibbles, drags everything out, stalls, mislays papers, is difficult to contact and generally avoids you.

Counter: sell him an OPTION for a sum at least equivalent to the margin between the bids as a condition of your withdrawing from the market – if he completes on the agreed terms his money is set against the price, if he doesn't, you keep his money. If he is serious about the offer he will agree to buy the option. Prevarication from him on this point suggests he is making a blocking offer. Go over his offer very carefully; watch out for LIFEBOAT CLAUSES; if there is anything unusual in it, especially where he has discretion, insist on its removal or amendment.

Bluff. Much loved by script writers with a passing acquaintance of the works of Machiavelli. It is almost always counterproductive. Bluffing means you live dangerously, which is exhilarating from the security of your arm chair, but it is cold sweat in the real world of business.

Avoiding bluffing does not mean you disclose your vulnerabilities. Confessing that you have not had an order for six weeks hardly induces them to accept your prices. But telling them that you are selling computers like hot cakes, when you are not, is hardly convincing if they ask: 'Could you give me the names of the buyers, as I would like to call them about your products!' (Hence, when you hear verifiable claims, ask for details.)

A called bluff is a killer. Your prospects are dead from then on.

Bobbin' and weaving. Tactic to dodge a powerful assault on your weak flanks.

All positions have weaknesses. The impregnable is still penetrable – somewhere. Other negotiators search for the weak spots. They mount their attacks along lines which you prefer them not to know about. Damage avoidance is called for.

Parry the attack with a promise to come back to that point later ('I could take up that point right now, but I prefer to do so when we have all the facts on the table'). Acknowledge the problems, but deny its importance ('Yes, you are right, we did miss that delivery, but against the entirety of our dealings, a missed delivery is hardly the decisive criterion of our competence'). Refer to time constraints, or NEED TO KNOW assessments, as the reason for not answering the challenge ('I wish we had time to go into all the details and the special circumstances of that case, but if we opened up that discussion we would be here for hours'; 'To answer that point properly, I would need to disclose to you highly confidential details which would hardly endear me to your accountant, or the other people involved, so please do not pursue those matters further without the highest clearance from your side').

See FRONTAL ASSAULT.

Body language. See NON-VERBAL BEHAVIOUR.

Bottom line. A pre–determined limit beyond which you prefer not to go.

Upside: a bottom line organizes your preparation by prioritizing your OBJECTIVES.

Downside: a bottom line is only as sensible as the amount of thought that has gone into defining it.

Example: You decide the bottom line price acceptable for the plant is nothing less than 400,000. Two questions:

1 What happens if you are offered 399,999? If you would accept it, how far below your bottom line would you go, and, therefore, what is your *bottom* bottom line?

2 What happens if nobody offers to buy the plant after six months or a year? Do you revise your bottom line or stick?

Bottom lines are serious if every contingency has been though through before they are set in concrete. Otherwise, they are more dangerous than helpful. Consider the BEST ALTERNATIVE (BATNA) approach instead.

Boulwarism. A version of ONE-OFFER-ONLY applied to labour contracts. Named after Lemuel Boulware, vice president of General Electric (USA), who introduced a negotiating stance that left no room for traditional methods of negotiation. GE surveyed employee opinion, aspirations and attitudes, considered what the company wanted to do in terms of wages and other conditions of employment, and presented a total package to the employees which was effectively non–negotiable.

Boulwarism is a major bogey in union mythology. Because it denies a formal bargaining role to the union, it produces considerable hostility, especially when introduced suddenly.

The spirit of Boulwarism is paternalistic: management knows

best. Management determines what is acceptable to the majority of the union's constituents and offers it as a final package. The union is reduced to the role of trying to persuade management not to make an offer until they have had a chance to influence the contents of the package.

'Boulwarists' certainly consult the union – sometimes exhaustively – before they decide where to open (and settle). The union is an agent – persuader not an agent – negotiator. Having surveyed and sampled opinion, the optimum offered is pitched and you require that it be accepted without further debate. You are ready to go over the heads of the union and make the offer direct to your employees. If faced with strikes, you face them out, encourage employees to cross picket lines, organize 'back to work' breakaways and switch production between plants. Having chosen an offer that you believe is acceptable to the majority of the employees, you know that a strike is unlikely to win enough support to be sustained.

Faced with expensive annual strikes in response to rejected opening offers, which eventually are improved upon, management pitches the final offer close enough to win majority acceptance from the employees and they undermine union attempts to lead a militant rejection.

Boulwarism, or unilateral final offer, is likely to succeed where the union leadership is discredited, the employees are recovering from a prolonged strike, the market has visibly turned against the products and survival as a company can be put to the forefront of a majority of the employees concerns and where management intelligence has correctly estimated where the shop floor is willing to settle. Boulwarism is not recommended for the faint of heart or managements that have not done their homework.

Bribery. Bribery is a crime. It is immoral. It is unethical. It is unfair. It is . . . practised.

Faced with a demand for a bribe that gets you the business, what do you do? Faced with an offer of a bribe that gives them the business what do you do? Consider the following:

1   A person you know tells you she knows of a buyer who might be interested in your services. She gives you the buyer's

name and address. You offer to take her out to lunch next weekend, if the deal comes off, you tell her she can expect a present in return for the introduction. Is this a bribe? Who is bribing whom?

2   Another phone call, this time from a stranger who says he knows of somebody who is willing to do business with you. He wants 5 per cent if the deal comes off. Do you reject the offer, haggle over the 5 per cent, or say 'yes'. Is 5 per cent a bribe?

3   This time you hear of somebody who can introduce you to the buyer of your product in a major foreign country, which you have been trying to get into for years. Do you approach the contact and ask for his assistance? Do you offer an inducement? Do you wait for him to ask for one? Do you tell him he is to do this favour for nothing? Who is bribing whom?

4   You are in the check-in line at a foreign airport. You notice that those who include a 50 quonk note with their tickets get a seat, the rest are made to wait (next flight, next week). What do you do?

"Sam, here, is in charge of ethics. He sees that we don't pay out more in bribes than we receive in back-handers."

5   You are waiting for an interview with a government minister in a foreign country, and you note that those who pin a 2,000 quonk note to their business card get an interview. The rest don't. What do you do?

Bribery is corruption. It taints all who touch it. But in many parts of the world, it is the way they do business. To cynics the boundary between bribery and paying for a service, or permission to do something, is not entirely clear. You know you have crossed the boundary when you are caught.

Do not assume that everybody is on the take: any country's prisons are worse than its hotels. Salve your conscience, perhaps, by redefining the bribe as a commission (after all, your home town is full of guys earning commissions).

Greedy people get sticky fingers. Your GO-BETWEEN pays-off out of what he gets from you. Occasionally, a Very Important Greedy Person gets between you and your deal (see SKIMMERS). It costs you a small fortune to get past him. You either pay up and shut up, or you shop him and run.

Brinkmanship. A high-risk enforcement tactic. Foster Dulles, US Secretary of State during the 1950s, exemplified diplomacy by brinkmanship. Here is a taste of his philosophy:

> You have to take chances for peace. Just as you must take chances in war. Some say we were brought to the verge of war. Of course we were brought to the verge of war. The ability to get to the verge without getting into war is the necessary art.
> ('How Dulles Averted War', *Life*, 16 January 1956, p.78)

See LAST CLEAR CHANCE.

Brooklyn optician. Version of the ADD-ON tactic. Seller adds-on costs until the buyer signals to stop. Supposedly worked to effect by a legendary optician in Brooklyn, New York:

'The lenses are $90 . . .
. . . each
the frame is $40 . . .
. . . for the basic shape, like your grandmother wore,
and $89 for a designer pair . . .
. . . plus $30 for fitting
. . . in the shop, and $50 for a home visit . . .

. . . within four blocks, otherwise it's $5 a block extra
You can have them in 5 days for $10 . . .
. . . a day
Regular brushed steel is $20 . . .
. . . a part
and it's $45 if you want gold . . .
. . . leaf
18 carat gold is $30 . . .
. . . a lens frame . . .
plus state taxes . . .'

And so it goes on and on. Each pause gives the buyer an opportunity to call a halt, which if not taken, tells the seller to keep piling on the add-ons.

You can apply the tactics if you know your variables:

- 'My normal charge is 350 . . . weekends extra.'
- 'That will be 90 . . . plus 30 for delivery . . . tomorrow . . . 35 today.'
- 'The documentation charge is 120 . . . per head.'

Counter: Cut in at the first pause.

See TAKE-OFF.

Buying signals. See them, stop your offers. Send one, and the offers stop.

Why? Because buying signals show a willingness to settle on the terms of the current offer, so why offer more?

Examples of buying signals:

assumptive ownership – 'I'll make this room my study';

issuing instructions for delivery;

disappointment at lead times for possession;

concentrated attention on buying details;

asking questions that relate the product or service directly to your usage;

looking intently at the product (get them to handle it, fly, sail, drive in it, touch, hear, smell it (the 'SIZZLE'), and keep it in their sight (every glance at it is another signal);

asking what their spouse/partner thinks;

showing good humour with their partner (the euphoria of the purchase);

any positive response to an ASSUMPTIVE CLOSE

C

Capitulation. The ultimate CONCESSION.

Car buying psychology. All car salespeople have at least one large advantage over you: they practise their sales technique several times a day, while you try it perhaps once every two or more years.

Apart from experience and skills in playing the ADD-ON, they have other advantages. First, there is the psychology of the model range. With popular models at the lower end of the market the seller must convince you that you can afford to buy, by offering you various inducements to do so. These inducements (TRADE-IN, PRICE) are actually very expensive, but they sound reasonable. If you can afford to buy without the seller's inducements, you are obviously buying a cheap model for your spouse or lover.

With top of the range models, if you have to be convinced that you can afford one, then you can't. The psychology is reversed: you try to convince him that you can afford it, and to prove it, you refrain from quibbling about price, and you order lots of expensive extras.

Car buying strategy. Decide why you want to buy a particular model, new or USED. Substantive are better than fanciful reasons. Any seller can sell you a dream (the SIZZLE); it takes more effort to sell you something that specifically meets your needs. And if he can't meet your needs he is motivated to induce you to compromise by offering concessions.

Decide on your maximum budget and how to finance it. Is it all cash, cash plus TRADE-IN, cash plus finance, cash plus trade-in plus finance, all trade-in, all finance? However it adds up, it is the maximum you can spend.

Don't disclose your budget limit, nor how you are financing it: you would not do so in any other negotiation, so why do it in this one? Look at models; ask QUESTIONS; don't talk price. Choose the model you want to buy; don't let the seller choose for you (he'll SWITCH SELL at the swish of a wiper).

Make a firm offer for the model you want. Your offer is the on–the-road price, inclusive of the extras you specify. Then SHUT UP. Let him try to sell to you; let him say what he likes, but until he agrees to your price and conditions do not fill in any order forms, do not complete any paperwork. If he wants to dicker over the extras, fine. Haggle. If he says 'no', be ready to walk away. If you can't do that, you lose.

If you want a trade-in, see what he is offering after you have agreed a price and terms. He'll try to get something back on a lower trade-in price. Fine. Compare his offers with the market place (private sale for cash for similar models). If you need finance, give him an opportunity to quote. He'll try to get something back on more expensive credit terms. Fine. Compare his offers with the market place (banks, loan offices, finance companies).

Don't feel pushed to buy: there never was a car that had to be bought today, there never won't be another for you to buy tomorrow.

Cash. Instant, perfect liquidity. Also easy to lose through theft, accident and impulse.

Insist on cash:
- Sooner rather than later.
- When dealing with unreliable, untrustworthy, or otherwise suspect people.
- When your banker has closed your account.
- When your creditors have charge of your assets.
- When you need the money quickly.
- When you're unlikely to spend it.
- When the transaction is dodgy.
- When it is a NO-COME-BACKS deal.

Refrain from accepting cash:
- When dealing with reliable, trustworthy and otherwise honest customers.
- When you are paid in dark alleys.
- When you can wait for your money.
- When you have a long journey to make.
- When your banker is happy with your account.
- When you are an impulsive spender.

Pay cash:
- When you don't need a written record.
- When it helps reduce the price.
- When you have too much cash on your person.
- When it gets you additional concessions.

Don't pay cash:
- When you need a written record.
- When you suspect your money is forged.
- When you might need to cancel the cheque before it is presented.
- When you are not sure who you are paying it to.
- When there is a delay between payment and the service.

Cash is normally convertible into different currencies (Hard Currencies). Check for exchange controls at frontiers before crossing with a suitcase full of cash. Ignorance is no defence. Do not accept payment in non-convertible Soft Currencies (generally, currencies of Communist states), or in large denominations of convertible currencies that by the law of their issuers are non-convertible (generally, these countries have exchange controls).

Cash flow. When money rather than promises, materializes in your possession.

A positive cash flow is caused by more money coming in than is going out (not when more money is promised than is to hand). You can be the best seller in the world, but if your customers do not pay for what they 'buy', you go bust. Overtrading causes a negative cash flow – more money going out than is coming in.

Profit results from generating a positive cash flow. At its most basic this means getting cash out of the pockets and purses of customers and into your cash registers (a point often missed by your counter staff, who think their wages come from somewhere else). Positive cash flow boils down to the same arithmetic: taking one period with another, are you taking in more money than you are paying out?

Propositions that conform to this arithmetic are worth considering; those that do not, are not. Hence, propositions that undermine your cash flow should be avoided, for they are self-defeating. Agreeing to price your output at marginal cost, or on a contribution (i.e. unprofitable) basis, or to use up otherwise idle capacity, have a seductive habit of becoming the first steps towards bankruptcy.

CBP. (Cash before performance). System operated by whores, actors, celebrities and comic singers (see HOOKER'S PRINCIPLE). It ensures payment. When they arrive for the show, you pay them, or their agent, their fee in cash, otherwise they do not perform, and you face a howling mob of disappointed customers (see OR ELSE tactic).

Use CBP when you don't believe in credit; your audiences might demand their money back; the producer might scoot off with the takings; you are into high living (including drugs and liquor); you are only hours ahead of your creditors; your agent is ripping you off; you are in tax trouble.

CBP is an opportunity to negotiate a lower fee for a star's performance, depending on how badly they need cash. But note: 'stars' hire heavies to handle their CBP.

If you are the star, use CBP to increase your fee. Back up failure to meet your reasonable requests by a threat not to perform (see BLACKMAIL). Note: professional impresarios are not given to giving in. Confine this technique to inexperienced amateur impresarios; when your career has passed its peak; when your are in a town or country you do not expect to visit again.

Children. The world's best negotiators. Children know how to get what they want. They are utterly ruthless at having their needs met. They have no sense of responsibility, no sense of shame, no feelings of remorse, no notion of guilt, no milk of human kindness and no long-term plans.

Parents know what they want, but lose the art of getting it. They give in to their children, and they give in to each other. They are responsible, they are easily shamed, they are in constant states of remorse, they feel guilty (therefore they are guilty), they are a fount of human kindness (and a bottomless pit for goodies), and they have long-term hopes (pensions, career, retirement, peace, the 'best is yet to come'), and other illusions that everything will eventually work out better in the end.

Result: Children win hands down.

When do children press their demands? At precisely the moment when it is inconvenient to meet them. They train their parents to get up at 2 am for food by wailing. They demand chocolate in the check-out lines at busy stores, when father is too embarrassed to resist. They ask for the car when mother is on the phone, or father is watching a big sports match on TV. They open negotiations on the balance of cabbage and ice cream in their diet with a firm refusal to eat any cabbage at all. You invariably start off by threatening 'no cabbage, no ice cream'. Your futile offers move through 'some cabbage, then ice cream', to 'one leaf, then ice cream', to 'just look at the cabbage for a second, and here is your double helping of ice cream'. Finally, you give in and pass the ice cream.

Children manipulate the strains in the parental COALITION. They know which parent to ask for which of their wants, and which to avoid. If grandparents are about they run a three-ring circus around everybody, and none of the adults is the wiser about what is happening to them.

Their strengths are their determination to meet high ASPIR-ATIONS, to use BLACKMAIL without compunction and to live for their immediate gratification.

You have the last laugh. Children grow up. They acquire a taste for things that can only be got by negotiation (what is courtship but an early attempt at negotiation?). In short, they become conditioned like the rest of us. We win.

Chinese negotiating style. The Chinese are fastidious about detail and nonchalant about time. Adjust your own style to match. Be ready to answer endless questions about your product, to reply to the same questions an endless number of times (particularly those for which your answer is 'no'), and to exhibit great patience. No matter how slow the negotiations appear to be, you still have a long way to go before you are likely to conclude them.

CIF. (Cost, insurance and freight). The seller is responsible for all expenses of delivery, including insurance premiums. The rates for insurance, and the extent of the cover provided, are negotiable.

Circumstances. 'Broken noses alter faces, circumstances alter cases.' Negotiator's litany when faced with a difficult case that is on the margin between being clear-cut and being ambiguous. Case law tries to be tidy. The problem with human beings in relationships is that they never cease to create new cases in new circumstances that the drafters of the rules never thought of.

The negotiator tries to establish that the circumstances are so unique in this case that the ordinary rules do not apply. Whether you agree or not depends on the plausibility of the case, the genuineness of the different circumstances and the relative inevitability of the precedent being set.

Clarification. See SEEKING CLARIFICATION.

Coalition. Almost all negotiations are between coalitions. You rarely negotiate exclusively on your own behalf. Your first negotiation is with your coalition members, defined (nominally!) as anybody on your side with some right to have an interest in the outcome. Their particular interest may not correspond completely with yours.

Basic rules: Consult your coalition partners. If you cannot convince them of the stance you intend to take, even though they are on your side, review your chances of convincing the other negotiators.

If your PREPARATION time is taken up with total disagreement between you and your partners on strategies and tactics, invoke, or call for, a COMMAND DECISION. Appearing at the negotiation with two or more strategies, two or more views on possible traded concessions, two or more 'leaders' willing to air their differing views, and two or more RESISTANCE PRICES, is likely to be disastrous at worse, and vulnerable to exploitation at best.

Should you take advantage of an opposing team in obvious disarray? Yes. Disarray in an opponent is usually a result of a dispute about their negotiating objectives, one lot preferring an accommodation with your view (the 'moderates'), the other demanding a tougher line (the 'militants'). Take advantage of these divisions to achieve your OBJECTIVES by assisting the moderate position to prevail, not by crushing the entire coalition.

How *not* to take advantage:

- By pointedly preferring the moderates.
- By mocking their disarray.
- By personalizing their differences.
- By toughening your demands to the extent that you re-unite the coalition.
- By rewarding or encouraging militancy.
- By undermining the moderates.

How to take advantage
- Support the ideas, not the personalities, of the moderates closest to your position.
- If the moderates are the majority of the coalition, propose accommodating moves to isolate the militants.
- If the moderates are in a minority, demonstrate that the pay-off for being militant is less than the pay-off for being moderate.

Caution: be aware that the militant – moderate 'disarray' may be a talented exhibition of the 'TOUGH GUY/NICE GUY' tactic.

The most difficult negotiation to conduct is one where you disagree with the policy guidelines laid down for your side, usually by higher levels of management. Console yourself that you earn the right to lay down policy by competently applying other people's policies. If this is too much, consider resigning.

COD. (Cash on delivery). The purchaser pays cash on delivery of the goods. No credit is allowed. The cash is collected by the deliverer of the goods, who deducts expenses and passes on the net amount to the supplier. Alternatively, the deliverer pays the net amount to the supplier before delivery, and collects the gross amount on delivery.

Use COD if a purchaser is unknown to you, is a financial risk, is known as a late payer or it is necessary for your own CASH FLOW.

Coercion. Facing a conflict of interest, you have two choices: attempt to coerce your opponent into CAPITULATION, or attempt to avoid capitualation by seeking an accommodation with him. Coercion involves THREATS, accommodation involves negotiation.

Coercion can be a two-way process: each side attempts to win by coercing the other with threats. You risk having to implement your mutual threats and suffer the costs of the consequences: courts, strikes and wars are expensive. Your goal is to win, but you are constrained by the cost of implementing your threats. Negotiation aims to share the prize of agreement without paying too high a price for agreeing. Your goal is WIN-WIN, but you are averse to surrendering too much to achieve your goals (it is not peace at any price).

In figure 5 (adapted from G.H. Snyder and P. Deising, *Conflict Among Nations*, Princeton, NJ, Princeton University Press, 1977 p.208), the matrix illustrates the choices between coercion and negotiation. In the coercion dimension you have a direct conflict of interest – what you win the other loses (ZERO-SUM). You have a common interest in avoiding the cost of implementing your threats. In the negotiation dimension, you have a common interest in reaching a settlement – you both win (NON-ZERO SUM). You have a conflict of interest, however, because each of you wants to minimize your own concessions to achieve a settlement.

Ironically, in attempting coercion you use tactics that imply a willingness to accommodate if the risks of outright hositilities loom large. Likewise, in negotiation you use tactics that imply coercion if the risks of conceding 'too much' loom large. In coercing, you could miscalculate. You don't think they will take a strike and they do (and you find they have prepared secretly to do so); you don't think they will fight for some distant islands and they do; you think you can win quickly against a disorganized neighbour and it leads to a long war because you don't.

Figure 5

	Goal	Constraint
Coercion	Win – lose (Conflicting interests)	Costs of implementing threats (Common interests)
Negotiation	Win – win (Common interests)	Minimize concessions (Conflicting interests)

Coercion involves a commitment to do something unless your opponent does or does not do something else. Once you are committed, your options are closed, your opponent's are open (he can choose to do or not do as you demand). If he complies you win, he loses (the Cuban missiles crisis). He can also counter-commit, forcing upon you the choice to do or not do what you threatened. The fear of the costs of failure drive you both into more accommodating stances. (See COMMITMENT TACTICS.)

You back off from hostilities by reducing the imminence of your threats, by making them less explicit, and by minimizing outright provocation. Peace can still fall apart with one miscalculated move.

See BLACKMAIL.

Collateral. Something you need when borrowing somebody else's money. It can be a title to property you own or a promise to pay from something you expect to own (an inheritance). Almost anything that the lender will accept as sufficient cover for the risk of lending you money is collateral.

It can be something absolutely worthless when separated but valuable when together (the lender holds one part, you keep the other), such as high value notes, or cheques, or bearer bonds torn in half.

Borrowers arrange a loan against an item of equal or greater value than the loan. If you default on the loan, the lender gains possession of the pledged item and makes a profit by selling it at its true value. Thus the economics of the noble trade of pawnbroking.

Foreign hotels require you to leave your passport as collateral until you pay your account. If you are likely to leave the country at short notice carry more than one passport. Duplicates are obtainable before you leave home if you affirm that your original is lost; you can also get a duplicate for travel in the Middle East – affirm that you intend to visit both Israel and Saudi Arabia.

Examples of unusual collateral include: a milking cow (causing a dispute as to who owned the calf born before the loan was paid off); a baby held by a garage as a pledge against a mother's return, while she went home to get her purse, after filling up before realizing she had no money with her (the popular press slayed the garage for 'inhumanity', yet it was enabling a transaction to take place); a dog left as collateral which caused so much havoc on a chicken farm that the lender cancelled the loan to get the dog taken away.

To act as collateral the item must be of sufficient value to you to encourage your compliance with the terms of the loan. If that is not enough, especially if you are offering an unusual item as collateral, the item must be of sufficient value to the lender to cover his loss.

Your risks in accepting items for collateral include the possibility that the borrower does not own them – 'his' house is his wife's; the car is unpaid for, or hired from Renta Wreck (check title to, and other burdens on, them); they do not have the value claimed for them – 'all that glitters', etc. (know your business); and he is not as dependent on the item as he implied (he carries six passports).

Collective bargaining. Jointly determined rules for the use of labour in employment.

The rules are negotiated by agents of the employees (unions, staff associations) either directly with an employer or with an agent of the employer (an association of employers within a locality, or in a line of business). The rules include coverage of the following:

remuneration
hours of work
types of work
holiday entitlements
other entitlements
flexibilities
restrictions
lay-offs
standards
work rates
overtime
retirement
promotion
responsibilities of the bargaining agents
obligations of the bargaining agents
relationships between the bargaining agents
access of bargaining agents to members
definitions of reasonable conduct
disciplinary procedures
procedures for resolving disputes

Agreed rules are operated by the management and monitored by the union.

There are benefits to management in having collective agreements with bargaining agents representing employees – a single negotiation covering all employees is more efficient than a series of individual negotiations which might produce different rules for each employee. Rules agreed with a bargaining agent, rather than imposed exclusively by management, carry a workable moral weight.

There are costs too. The bargaining agent interferes with managerial independence; employees show loyalty to, and accept discipline from, an outside agency, which causes disruption in the company (strikes, go-slows, bans), sometimes on issues that are totally unrelated to the employer (SECONDARY BOYCOTTS, political strikes). External bargaining agents also introduce a division within a company which cuts across, or threatens, a company culture based on excellence, pride, self-respect and mutual goal-seeking.

There is no evidence to show that unions raise their members' remuneration above that of non-unionized employees. Low wages and poor conditions exist in both unionized and non-unionized plants; so do high wages and enlightened conditions. Recent trends suggest that union membership is falling as a proportion of the employed workforce in the United States and the United Kingdom.

Should you subscribe to a bargaining agent, such as a union? As with hiring any AGENT, it depends on the relative gains from bargaining for yourself compared to hiring somebody else to do it for you. The advantage of an agent is the superior detailed expertise they bring to bear on your behalf (they deal with similar issues every day). The downside is their concentration of effort on the collective, rather than the individual's, interests.

Collective contracting. Securing a contract through collective bargaining is different from the normal commercial contract negotiation. As a commercial negotiator you are free to contract for proper purposes with whomsoever you find willing to contract with you. Conversely, you are free not to contract if you cannot agree terms with one person. In short, you pick and choose with whom you do business. Collective contracting is different.

In the main, a failure to agree terms merely postpones eventual agreement. Employees are unable, in most circumstances, to decamp *en masse* from one employer and re-contract with another. Nor, in normal circumstances, can the employer purge the plant of all the employees and hire in another lot (though trying to do so is a common tactic in bitter disputes).

There are exceptions of course. An Australian company terminated a damaging strike by sacking the entire workforce and moving its glass-making operation to Fiji; President Reagan sacked striking air traffic controllers and hired a completely new workforce; News International in London sacked striking printworkers and moved its business to a new plant a few miles away. But set against the millions of annual negotiations between bargaining agents and employers throughout the world, these isolated incidents prove the rule.

In a collective contracting regime you must come to a settlement. You need each other to fulfil your functions as employees and managers. Your mutual dependence constrains your willingness to exact unremitting warfare upon each other.

Command decision. When a negotiating team cannot agree on a tactic appropriate to the circumstances, or cannot agree on the contents of an offer, and have no time to refer the matter to higher authority, the most senior negotiator makes a command decision by virtue of rank alone. As in the military, the decision carries its own authority and the team is expected to fall into line. Command decisions are not necessarily correct decisions, but the wrong decision is often better than no decision, and as the person making it takes full responsibility, reckless use of a commander's privileges carries its own penalties.

Commission. Payment for services rendered, for exceeding sales targets, for introducing clients (see BRIBERY).

Set your commission as a percentage of a GROSS value rather than a NET value. The gross value of an income stream is larger than the net value. Therefore, you get more commission. (Conversely, if you are the person paying the commission.) Gross values keep the negotiator honest. Net value is a trifle ambiguous, usually in their favour. Net of what? Who decides the deductables? Some film studios can produce 'net' accounts for highly successful movies, apparently produced in an uncommon (for Hollywood) outburst of philanthropy, if the actors coincidently are working for 'a percentage of net profits'.

How should you calculate your percentage commission? Ask: 'What is the gross value worth to the buyer?' Then set your commission as a percentage of that value and not on how long it takes you.

Well-placed GO-BETWEENS in the oil states were getting from 2 to 4.5 per cent commission from one-off multi-million deals until the oil boom burst (2 per cent is 20,000 a million – a 20 million deal is worth the jet lag). Commercial AGENTS working in Communist economies charge about 4 per cent for delivering business to exporters. Clients with contracts flirt with second thoughts about paying go-betweens (signalled by becoming extremely evasive at taking your calls). GETTING PAID your commission is as much of an art as earning it. Property agents secure their commission on sales by insisting on written enforceable contracts (competition between agents can drive their commission down to one per cent or less).

As a minimal protection require a commitment on company notepaper to pay commission, signed by the chief executive. Check that it specifies your name, the percentage of the commission (how big) of what (gross value), and when they pay it. Avoid statements offering you percentages of their 'earnings from the contract that directly arise from your efforts'. 'Earnings' has a whiff of their net income about it, which after their expensive accountants have had a go won't amount to much (that's why they are expensive); and 'directly arises' is an attempt to confine you to some small proportion of the total order, or to quibble about how much you did and how much they had to do after you set it up. Go for the gross LIFETIME value of the order: in military aircraft, remember the spares cost, over the aircraft's lifetime, more than its original price; in securing permission for a hotel complex, remember the hotel's capital value is exceeded by the income it earns over the years. A percentage of the future income stream should do you nicely. Beware of tying your commission from future income to the actual performance of the project as an income generator. Not only do you delay your commission, you risk not getting paid (see DRIPPING ROAST). Get paid up front on an estimate of the project's lifetime earnings.

Commitment tactics. Methods by which a threat is made credible. For example, you can bind yourself to an irrevocable course of action that would do immense damage to your opponent, irrespective of what damage it does to you, unless he complies with your demand. The more irrational your commitment (you die too) the more credible your threat, and the more likely he will comply.

Consider nuclear deterrence. The United States is committed to retaliate against any attack on itself, or its allies in NATO, with sufficient force, all the way up to a strategic nuclear exchange with the Soviet Union. There can be no winner in this contest. In these horrific circumstances, concern about the effects of a nuclear winter appear misplaced: a nuclear spring would be bad enough. The United States is actually stating it would choose national, not to say worldwide, suicide in defence of itself and its allies. It is totally irrational on one level, yet perfectly rational on the other. Its willingness to contemplate annihilation leaves the decision whether to go to war to the Soviet Union (likewise, from the point of view of Soviet deterrence, the war decision is left to the United States). Neither, rationally, can contemplate unleashing war on the other because irrationally they would destroy each other. As long as each believes in the other's commitment, there is peace between them.

Consider two teenagers playing 'chicken' with old cars on the public highway. In the game two drivers hurtle towards each other in their cars: the first one to swerve to avoid a head–on collision (and certain death) is 'chicken'. Suppose one of the drivers has himself visibly strapped into the car. He cannot get out, nor can he steer his car other than straight-ahead only. Also, his foot is clamped to the accelerator such that once the engine starts and the car moves forwards, he cannot stop it (which means if the game starts, he dies). If the other driver is made aware of his opponent's commitment just before the contest starts, would he still play? Unlikely. Why? Because he knows he is going to die if he drives and does not swerve. He might as well disqualify himself. The one driver's irrevocable commitment to a senseless death forces the other driver to quit.

Apply commitment to negotiating. First, make known your commitment to your opponent – let him see you strapped into your car. Does he believe what he sees, or does he discount the possibility of you behaving so 'foolishly'. As he does not know for certain he cannot discount it entirely. Prudence dictates non-provocation (he refrains from starting his engine).

Your tactics show how committed you are and that you mean what you say. You invest in strike preparations, call meetings, paint posters, start picket rosters, call for funds. Your opponent's warnings of the dire consequences of your commitment (plant closures, job losses, long strikes etc.) have no effect. These are wholly the wrong tactics (as is propaganda against the horrors of nuclear war). In fact, such warnings reinforce your commitment ('this man is irrational, I had better be more careful').

If your opponent implied that your preparations are futile because the plant would carry on working, that you would not be missed and so on, your commitment would be undermined enough for some of your colleagues to have doubts – who wants to suffer for a lost cause? By finding a way to circumvent commitment it loses credibility. In the case of the US Strategic Defense Initiative, or 'Star Wars', the Soviet Union is so violently opposed to the deployment of the American system because by making its strategic weapon stock redundant, SDI reduces the credibility of the Soviet Union's commitment.

Undermine an opponent's commitment using SALAMI (BAGA-TELLE) tactics. A specific threat to boycott, strike, launch a thermonuclear war unless you comply, is vulnerable to minute challenges to the definition of compliance; they demand a meeting by 10 April, you offer one on 11 April; they demand it starts at 9am, you offer 4.30pm; they threaten war if you attack, you send three drunken soldiers across the frontier in a taxi; they demand progress to reform in six months, you schedule it for fifteen months; they demand no more than 10 per cent penetration of their markets by your exports, you send 10.43 per cent. Salami counters undermine commitment, because their threat is disproportionate to the challenge. By carefully extending the challenge in size and number you widen the credibility gap between their commitment and their behaviour. Of course you could start World War III.

Communication. Message sent from one negotiator to another. If you do not communicate at all, you don't know what they want and they don't know what you want. Even if you are communicating, it is not certain that either of you will find out the other's needs.

Messages are misunderstood, misinterpreted and mislaid. The message you send need not be the one that is received. They may entirely miss the significance of the message you are communicating. They need not believe what you are saying, could doubt the provenance of the message and could be at a total loss to understand you because your message does not make sense.

THREATS, promises and COMMITMENTS have little effect if they cannot be communicated. A strategic non-availability enhances your position at critical junctures in some negotiations. 'Accidentally' cutting off a telephone conversation, for example, could leave your last statement as the only one they can act upon (to do this convincingly, practise cutting yourself off in mid-sentence without pausing). By the time the line is reconnected you have 'left' on urgent business, or already acted on your last statement.

We communicate on several levels: what we say, how we say it, and our 'body language' (see NON-VERBAL BEHAVIOUR). The latter accounts for a greater proportion of the message received than the other two together. If our gestures say something different from the contents of our speech, and this is perceived by the receiver, we have a credibility problem.

A written communication can be re-read many times. It has the benefit of permanence. It has the disbenefit of inflexibility. The written word does not score highly on subtlety, and scores nothing at all on the nuance of the sender's tone. That is why lawyers make a fortune re-drafting contracts and arguing over the meaning of written words. It is also why receivers react negatively to what they perceive to be your written insults, callousness, abruptness and threats, particularly in the difficult phase of a negotiation where the parties are debating the issues closely.

Use the telephone to bolster your firmness. It is far easier to say 'no' on the telephone than to say it face to face. Use the telex or fax to make enquiries, quote FIRST OFFERS or BIDS, and confirm AGREEMENTS (it's not so hot for negotiating complex proposals). 'Answer back' routines guarantee receipt of the message, at least at their telex station, and secretaries tend to place telexes on top of the incoming mail.

Communist negotiating styles. A Communist negotiator is a bureaucrat with a grudge. His bureaucratic outlook is self-protective – if anything goes wrong with the deal, he does not want to be the only person responsible for initiating it. As every other bureaucrat likely to be touched by the deal and its consequences thinks the same, they are included in the negotiation.

As for their grudges, basically Communist negotiators resent the culpability of Western capitalism for most of the failings that have afflicted their countries since before they went Communist. (They see no connection between Communism and their afflictions.) This manifests itself in extremely tight scrutiny of your proposals, constant requests for more data about your product (drawings, specifications, chemical analysis, and all manner of tests, assembly manuals etc.) in an effort to expose your devious scheme to dump shoddy output from your sweatshops (as described by Fred Engels in the 1850s). It is also a crafty piece of industrial espionage on their part. They regard this information as a necessary prelude to discussing prices, which usually induces ritual price objections of a scale and duration that suggest they really believe their propaganda about capitalist 'super profits'.

If you cut prices to get business in Communist countries you don't get more volume, only less profitable business. Pad your prices, and make no moves on them until the technical examinations are exhausted. Wherever your price is standing at the start of the price negotiations (with bureaucrats from another department?) that is where the real price negotiations begin, no matter what concessions you have already made.

Watch a Communist handle the ADD-ON ploy (if they went into the seminar game they'd clean up)! He adds-on extras he wants for the fixed price at every turn. He'll want operating and maintenance manuals, training, spares, warranties, replacement programmes, drawings, parts lists, and in Russian too.

Counter: For your basic package there is one price; for the extras there is another price. If you weaken and throw in the extras free, he'll keep asking for more

see TEACHING WOLVES TO CHASE SLEDGES.

Competitive style. Competitive negotiators win at any cost, which is why they lose. The competitive style is abrasive; it is on the push. The other negotiator ia an enemy, not an ally. Anything he gets is at your expense. It is total war and unrelenting ZERO-SUM.

Suspect the motives of the other negotiator. He's obviously trying a fast one with that proposition. He thinks you'd fall for the dodge of offering you a concession. Well, two can play that game. Demand more, and tell him you've never even seen a banana boat. If he argues, fight back. You are not surprised at the hostility. It always comes down to it in the end; every time you call their bluff and tell them where they can go, they start getting emotional. Amazing!

See COOPERATIVE STYLE.

Compromise. Compromise produces a solution short of CAPITUL-ATION.

If both sides stick to their FIRST OFFERS they DEADLOCK
see SPLIT THE DIFFERENCE.

Concession. Never concede! TRADE.

Concession dilemmas. The gap between the current offers of two negotiators. You are constrained by a desire not to concede everything. You are in conflict with the other negotiator as to the extent of your mutual concessions. You aim to do better than CAPITULATION. Questions with uncertain answers include how much you must move, how far the other party will move, whether your proposals are acceptable or genuinely unacceptable.

Is his refusal of your proposal a genuine inability to agree to your present terms? Naturally, you expect him to try to do better; that is his job. But is his rejection only a test of your resolve?

Look at it from the other side's point of view. Your last offer could have been your final offer. He has no way of knowing what is in your mind. Naturally, he assumes that every move you makes moves you closer to your LIMIT. As you approach your RESISTANCE PRICE he expects you to increase your resistance to further movement. Should he respond to this increasing resistance by moving towards a settlement, or should he continue to press for more movement?

Why should he press for more, when he knows that you are approaching your resistance point? Because he might read your behaviour entirely differently; he might see your last offer not as a prelude to increased resistance but as the ante-chamber of your CAPITULATION.

Concession rates. Pace signals.

Consider a negotiator who moves quickly at first and then stops. The other negotiator is likely to be frustrated because the early movement created expectations and the latter non-movement frustrates them.

Consider a negotiator who moves slowly at first and then quickly. The other negotiator is likely to react to the early slow movement by hardening his own position and to the latter quick movement by hardening it more, because the quicker movement signals that a hard line produces results. This may not be the negotiator's intention.

Consider a negotiator who sometimes moves quickly and sometimes slowly. This has the same effect on the other negotiator as any other form of inconsistency: he does not know whether to apply pressure to get movement, so he applies it anyway.

Consider the negotiator who moves slowly. He does better because his consistency is predictable. If he only moves in response to a TRADE he also signals how to get movement from him.

Concession signals. Size signals.

Consider a negotiator who has a reputation for hardly moving once he places his proposals on the table. Other negotiators learn to delay the appearance of his proposals, until they have influenced the negotiator's decision of where to make his opening pitch.

Consider a negotiator who moves in diminishing steps, starting with relatively large concessions, and ending with smaller and smaller concessions. This creates expectations in other negotiators that a RESISTANCE PRICE is being approached. Indeed, the settlement point is signalled: 17,000; 16,000; 15,800; 15,650; 15,550; 15,500; 15,450; 15,420: what is the signalled settlement price?

Consider a negotiator who moves unpredictably. Sometimes a large concession is followed by a small one, sometimes the reverse. Other negotiators are likely to look for large concessions each time, and to be disappointed if they are not forthcoming.

Conciliation. Alternative form of dispute resolution (see MEDIA-TION). The aim is to reconcile the parties in dispute not to judge between them. Useful in fractious cases where the normal relationship between the parties has broken down and negotiations have deadlocked. Where inter-personal conflicts obscure a proper sense of balance the actual issues in dispute can be lost in a mutual bout of MARTYRDOM. Conciliation (through professional conciliators – more commonly known as mediators in the USA) is an alternative to litigation and mutually destructive sanctions.

Concorde fallacy. So called because the decision-makers involved in the development and production of the Anglo-French Concorde supersonic aircraft argued that though the costs had escalated beyond imagination compared to the original estimates, the project should continue otherwise the previous investment would be wasted. This is a fallacy because sunk costs are forever sacrificed, and decisions should take place on the basis of avoidable, i.e. future, costs. Concorde by any standards should have been cancelled. Vast expenditures of public money have been wasted, given their alternative uses, in pursuit of a fallacy. If the Concorde fallacy were ever generalized, then no error could ever be corrected once resources had been committed to it.

In negotiating, beware of the Concorde fallacy – throwing good money after bad is seldom a sound proposal.

Conditional language/offer. States the negotiator's terms for settling an issue.

'Give me some of what I want, and I will give you some of what you want.'

Effective negotiators use conditional language when making an offer: 'On condition that', or 'Provided that', or 'If you will', do such and such, 'Then I will agree to do so and so.' Language helps to educate the other negotiator in how you intend to settle the issue.

UNCONDITIONAL OFFERS and language undermine the essential nature of negotiation: coming to agreement by trading things that one negotiator wants for things that the other wants.

Conflict. A reason for negotiating; variance of views, beliefs, attitudes, interests, actions, desires, needs, aspirations, intentions, hopes, dispositions, expectations, shares, solutions and behaviours. The competition of parties for a scarce resource, be it tangible (land, money, goods and services), or intangible (power).

Irreconcilable conflicts are resolved by 'live and let live', or the outright triumph of one side. The decision is 'peace or war?'. Reconcilable conflicts are resolved by PERSUASION, PROBLEM SOLVING, MEDIATION, ARBITRATION or negotiating. The decision is 'debate or trade?'.

Remember conflict is not necessarily a bad thing. The essence of a free society is the right to hold differing views about everything. Your rights to differ are constrained by the rights of others not to have your views imposed upon them, except by due process of law or democratic process in government.

Differences are resolved in an orderly society by the rule of law. What worries most people is when individuals, or groups, or even majorities, take the law into their own hands and impose their will by COERCION. The act of attempting to coerce, provokes the acts of resistance. If the coercion is violent, so is the resistance. Disorderly conflict is disruptive of the rule of law, and laws exist to punish those who resort to it. Orderly conflict – freedom of expression, assembly, dissent – and its orderly resolution – persuasion, mediation, conciliation, arbitration, problem-solving, negotiation – is protected under law and benefits those who resort to it.

Conflicts of interests and rights. When parties have differing notions about their relationship, or the terms of doing business together, they are said to have a conflict of interest. When parties dispute the application of an agreed PROCEDURE, such as in a disciplinary case, they are said to have a conflict of rights.

'Interests' and 'rights' are common terminology in collective bargaining to distinguish how the conflict is to be resolved, whether within the terms of existing procedures (conflict of rights), including re-interpretation of clauses (through a judicial or quasi-judicial process), or through fresh negotiations to create a new agreement (conflict of interests).

American terminology distinguishes between a 'contractual dispute' (one involving differing perceptions of 'rights') and a 'terminal dispute' (one involving differing perceptions of a future

relationship when the parties are out of contract). French terminology distinguishes between *'conflicts juridiques'* and *'conflicts
économiques'*.

Constants. Whatever the parties agree is non-negotiable, whether
by convention, custom and practice, lethargy, ignorance,
convenience, or precedent. Contrast with TRADABLES.

Identify the constants in your business. What benefits are there
in having non-tradable constants? Who determined that they are
non-tradable?

Examples of constants include:

scale fees
minimum rental periods
minimum stock levels
minimum re-order quantities
credit terms
use of in-house services
purchase of own company products
compulsory insurance
exclusive dealing through specified agents
single named suppliers

Consider the negotiating advantages gained against the
competition of changing your constants into tradables.

Constant sum. Jargon from GAME THEORY. Where the sum of the
pay-offs to the negotiators remains the same across all possible
solutions to the dispute (see ZERO-SUM).

Figure 6 illustrates a constant sum negotiation. The seller's
asking price is 600, and the buyer's offer is 400. The difference
between them is 200. Consider the negotiation to be about
dividing, or sharing, the 200 between them. If the seller capitulates
and accepts 400, the entire 'prize' of 200 goes to the buyer (he
'saves' 200 from the asking price); if the buyer capitulates and pays
600, the entire prize of 200 goes to the seller (he 'gains' 200 over the
offer price). Any agreed price between 400 and 600 divides the
gains between both parties such that the sum of the gains equals
200. At a price of 550, for example, the seller gains 150 above the
offer price of 400, and the buyer saves 50 from the seller's offer of
600 (150 + 50 = 200). Likewise for all intermediate prices.

Figure 6

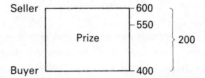

Consulting fees. Why do some consultants make more money than others? Because most do not appreciate why they are being consulted. Consultants are hired for their expertise, yet everywhere they sell their time instead of their expertise. Time costs less than expertise – in fact, expertise is only valuable because it saves time getting to the right answers.

Example: A professor of undersea engineering is asked by an oil company to solve a leakage problem in drilling seals. He obliges and charges his time at three weeks of his professsorial salary. The oil company saved millions by his advice while he still researches in a run-down laboratory and cannot afford good research staff.

How is it that so-called experts do not appreciate the value of their expertise? Because they think in terms of cost-based fees – what it legitimately costs them to provide the advice (which is how they are required to submit research proposals for approval within the academic community). But accountants, architects, lawyers and advertising and public relations executives often think similarly.

Time-based consultancy fees are calculated on a formula: divide annual gross salary costs by the number of working days, add a margin for administrative costs and a margin for profit and charge out services at a daily rate. An alternative method is to establish the gross value of the advice to the client and charge a percentage. If the contract is worth 200,000 and the advice secures it, what is that service worth to the client, not what does it cost to give the advice? It might take ten minutes or ten days, but a time-based fee under-charges the client by thousands.

Why should the client agree to a fee based on the expert's value to him? Because the fee has been negotiated before the expert applies his expertise to the problem. How do you the expert know what your advice is worth? Ask questions. Do some PREPARATION. Either you are an expert, or you are not.

Contingency pricing.Method of pricing an uncertain value.

Forecasting is neither an art nor a science, it is an opinion. Valuations of the future worth of a business are as variable as the parties' interests. Buyers understate future worth, sellers exaggerate it. How to set the price for the business?

Example: The buyer offers a compromise valuation, which is less than the seller is demanding. In addition, the buyer offers a contingency price agreement: if the future conforms to the seller's opinion, the buyer pays an increasing schedule of prices; if the future conforms to the buyer's valuation, the seller receives nothing extra.

Buyer's downside: the future is a result of the buyer's beneficial contribution, and not just the intrinsic worth of future business. The seller depends on the buyer's efforts and not the value of the business when the seller owned it.

Seller's downside: the buyer controls the business and can influence its future performance to understate its true worth. The buyer gains a business worth more than was paid, by treading water until the contingency agreement expires.

Negotiable issues include:
- Is worth based on gross or net income?
- How long is the contingency agreement for?
- Is the seller's price set at last offer, or something less?
- Is the buyer's initial price set at last offer or something more?

Contract. See AGREEMENT; COLLECTIVE CONTRACTING; CONTRACT LAW.

Contract law. Highly technical subject monopolized by lawyers. The advice offered here is not a legal guide to the complexities of contract law; it is a common sense summary of the main principles, which inevitably apply differently in each country. (Check with your lawyer in your own interest, but pay for his time not his expertise! See CONSULTING FEES.)

A contract determines the terms under which a business or personal relationship is conducted. It is enforceable at law (though the law varies in different countries).

Generally, an offer to contract is valid if the parties communicate their intentions to be under contract to one another, and if the bargain is specified (in the jargon, there is a consideration). If the offer is accepted, there is an enforceable contract (providing the subject of the contract is not illegal, for example, a contract to supply heroin). To prevent undue prevarication over acceptance, the offer lapses if acceptance is delayed beyond a specified time. Or an offer can be withdrawn on communicating this to the other party before he accepts.

An offer to contract is accepted if the acceptance is unconditional, is communicated to the offeror by the named offeree, and does not amend the offered contract (a new negotiation?).

A contract is valid whatever the consideration agreed by the parties. There is no legal remedy if you agreed a fee much less than your services are worth. The fact that you negotiated a poor contract is your own responsibility in law (unless you can prove duress, fraud, illegality, undue influence).

Cooperative style. Negotiators are cooperative antagonists.

Your antagonisms arise from your conflicting, or competing, goals; your cooperation arises from the fact that DEADLOCK leaves you both worse off than COMPROMISE.

You do not have malevolent designs, you are not distrustful, nor are you naively open. You understand why the other negotiator is hesitant about openness, but do not suspect his motives. If he SIGNALS, you respond but not recklessly; if he makes PROPOSALS, you search for bridges between his requirements and yours. You expect to TRADE for an AGREEMENT, and you intend to honour that agreement.

You also know how to switch into a COMPETITIVE STYLE if circumstances demonstrate it to be necessary.

Copyright. Do not sell it for a mess of pottage.

Copyright in a book, a play, any creative script, lasts for your lifetime. Your estate earns ROYALTIES after death (of you, not your book). In the UK this lasts for 50 years from when you die; for the first of 25 years your copyright is exploited exclusively by your publisher, and during the second 25 years, by anybody wishing to publish your work for a royalty fee. After this time copyright lapses and anybody can publish your work without paying royalties.

The mess of pottage may look good at the time, but you could regret it if the big money keeps rolling in and you are getting nothing. Of course, not every book sells. Most make next to nothing, but the happiness of those who sell their copyrights at no loss is no compensation for the grief of those whose losses are immense.

Insist on retaining your copyright. Licence the publisher to exploit your work for a royalty. Consider a limited duration licence of five to ten years. Do not give them authority to assign your licence. Insist that if they fail to meet the terms of the contract or go bankrupt, the licence unconditionally reverts to you (saves disputes with liquidators who treat your copyright as a forfeited asset).

Corruption. No way to do business, but in many places the only way to do business and the only way to get into, and around, some countries just to look for business, or simply to stay out of trouble (see BRIBERY).

If you are 'on the take', examine your vulnerabilities: the briber has a row with his lover, she shops you both in revenge; the briber gets caught, and confesses about you in exchange for a shorter sentence; you fall out with your lover, he exacts his revenge; you get caught . . .

Cost breakdowns. Worth getting. They identify the TRADABLES and the padding. Volunteering them is not so hot; it gives the other side ideas.

'To painting of your office as per your specification we have much pleasure in quoting a price of 6,000.'
'How is the 6,000 calculated?'
'Paint and materials, 1,000; labour 4,000; equipment hire 500; making good all defects and clearing up 500.'
'Why is labour charged at 4,000?'
'It's ten men for 40 hours at 10 an hour. This includes an overtime premium.'
'What equipment are you hiring?'
'A paint mixer at 100 and ten ladders at 40.'
'What is the cost of clearing up?'
'250.'
'What paint and materials are you buying?'

'SuperDelux Pale Moon at 400, best quality undercoat at 200, paste 50, silk wallcovering at 350.'
'Thank you.'

You now have useful information to begin negotiating. How much overtime, if any? Is ten men the optimum combination? How much off if you supply the ladders? How much off if you clear up? What savings are there for marginal adjustments in the quality of materials? Is that the wholesale price or is it marked up?

To get a detailed breakdown, ask for one. Show a written policy from your organization, insurance company, local authority or bank, requiring a breakdown before an order is placed (if necessary, form a dummy company and print the policy in its name).

To resist supplying a breakdown, show a written policy prohibiting your organization, or self, from doing so ('proprietary information', 'commercial confidentiality' etc. are useful first line defences). Refer buyer to your competitors' prices, and assert that that is the deciding factor, not how you go about your business. If the buyer persists, consider the consequences of continued resistance.

Counter-trade. A form of BARTER. The United States government sees it as undermining the Western trading system (which is based on hard currency transactions) and giving Communist states access to Western technology without having a ready means to pay for it.

Traders without hard currency offer lists of goods they will exchange instead. The practice is common in Communist and Third World countries. It is also used by some oil-rich Arab states (for example, Saudi Arabia buys military aircraft with oil). China, for example, could pay for the construction of a major processing plant for an agreed amount of the output it processes. If China uses cheap labour to operate the plant, the ensuing product, *after delivery to your markets*, is cheaper per unit than competing sources from elsewhere.

More often, the goods offered for barter are unconnected to the goods supplied. These may or may not have readily obvious uses to you (or anybody else!). Counter-trade lists often include absolutely useless goods that the other party is trying to dump. If the goods have obvious commercial value, ask: 'Why don't you sell the goods yourselves and pay me from the proceeds?' If the answer is unconvincing, you have been warned. If you don't want to barter, say 'no' firmly, and repeatedly. Either they accept this, eventually, or break off negotiations.

Most likely the goods are not of obvious monetary value. You can take it that sellers pad the value of the goods they offer, so challenge whatever price they put on them. Identify the costs of taking barter goods for your services. It is not the 'price' in the country wanting to barter that is decisive, but the net selling price of the goods in your country that counts.

Unless you intend to use the barter goods yourself, you must dispose of them to third parties. What is the money value of the barter goods in your markets, net of transport and associated costs? Disposing of the goods imposes marketing costs upon you.

There are other problems too, which must be reflected in the 'price' you agree on. Does the quality vary? Whose inspection is decisive? Can you use a recognized inspection firm to warrant the quality and quantity of the goods on arrival (not despatch)?

Are you VULNERABLE? Transactions may take place over a period. During that time the 'price' of the barter goods could vary downwards, evaporating your slim profit on the deal. Consider how you can relate the barter 'price' to market prices to cover your risks.

If they spring a barter deal on you after a money price has been agreed, watch out. They could be bluffing to finesse additional discounts from you. You may be persuaded to 'buy' a money deal with a lower price to avoid the complications of disposing of the barter goods. If you fall for this you have been RUSSIAN FRONTED. They never intended to do a barter deal at all; it was only a device to lower your money price.

Never DISCOUNT a barter deal. Never accept a general description of the quality or specification of the goods. Never accept a barter deal to salvage your investment of time, trouble and expense in an apparently fruitless negotiation.

Courtesy. Nobody ever got a worse deal by being courteous.

Credit. Give it, and pay it, when due.

Credit control. It is easier to avoid debts than to collect them.

Know who owes you money. Require them to establish their creditworthiness, and check everything they claim.

Set pre-determined limits on amounts allowed to be outstanding, days allowed to be overdue, time allowed to pay. Rates of repayment, how much each instalment, interest charged and COLLATERAL for the loan are negotiable.

The perennial claim 'the cheque is in the post' is never true (it is one of the most discredited sentences in the English language, and for good reason). See GETTING PAID.

If you are running into credit problems, inform the creditor early. Credit controllers trust debtors who talk to them marginally more than those who are evasive. An unexplained debt excites suspicions and receives most of the energetic attention of credit controllers. Negotiate a re-scheduling of the debt. Your leverage to do so increases with the size of the debt, for a large debt is a shared problem, a small one is yours alone.

Culture differences. They count. In a 'foreign' country you are the foreigner. The negotiators you meet are not foreigners, they have no weird customs, their attitudes and manners are not suspect, and their negotiating styles are not unusual. It is you that is the odd one out. Everything they do is perfectly natural where they live and work. You with your strange ways must adapt to them, not them to you, assuming you want to do business with them.

Considering cultural differences is not an exercise in stereotyping the negotiators you deal with. Nor is it a patronizing attempt to 'understand' their ways. It is only a prelude to taking account of the differences, and accommodating to them where possible.

If the Japanese pace of negotiation is slower than yours, then you had better slow down; if the American pace is faster, you had better speed up. If Arabs are not disciplined by time, then allow for it in the time allocated to negotiating with them, and do not get annoyed because they are not rushing about like commuters in the big cities of Europe and North America. If the Russians are suspicious of Western capitalists, do not behave suspiciously; if the Chinese keep asking the same questions and do not appear to take 'no' for an answer, answer patiently with variations on how to say 'no'. In short, abide by the advice to travellers going to Rome.

D

Deadlines. Can help or hinder, depending on who discloses that they have one.

Deadlines put you under pressure. If you have to get the spares by Friday, your negotiating leverage crumbles on Thursday. If you must terminate the negotiation by New Year's Day, your biggest concessions appear on New Year's Eve. If you are up against your leadtime for ordering materials for a major project, your buying power diminishes. But this pressure is as nothing compared to the pressure you attract if you disclose your deadlines to the other negotiator. Will he take advantage of your predicament? Yes. He cannot help himself. Whatever else the disclosure does it must stiffen his resolve not to move in giant steps towards you; knows that you will soon be leaping towards him. Hence, don't disclose deadlines that the other negotiator has no other means of knowing about.

Deadlines that help you:
- Those that force the other negotiator to decide.
- Those that the other neogtiator discloses.
- Those that the other negotiator does not control.
- Those that impose costs on the other.
- Those that give you options.
- Those that you control.
- Those that they know you will stick by.

Deadlines that hinder you:
- Those that are arbitrary.
- Those that are imposed by your own people.
- Those that they know about.
- Those that are imminent.
- Those that remove your discretion.
- Those that cannot be ignored.

Deadlock. We negotiate because we face the deadlock of disagreement. Unblocking deadlock could be a victory for good sense, or a triumph of bad judgement. It depends on what we concede to get agreement. As many companies go bust because they negotiate unprofitable agreements as go bust because they cannot find enough customers.

If the most the buyer offers is less than the least the seller will accept, deadlock is inevitable, unless one or both change their RESISTANCE PRICE, or trade off some other variable.

Single issue bargaining is more prone to deadlock – you resist conceding when you get nothing back (ZERO-SUM). Widen the issues, increase the agenda, be creative with the PACKAGING of the TRADABLE variables.

Deadlocked on price? Pay in some other way. Pay less now, more later; pay more now, rest later; pay some in cash, rest in kind; pay in another currency in another country; split the invoice across different budgets.

Deadlocked on a single issue? Compensate by movement on another issue; link several issues together; set the issue aside while settling the other issues.

Deadlocked on the value of future trade? Apply CONTINGENCY PRICING – if your estimate materializes, your price applies; if theirs materializes, their price applies.

Deadlocked across the issues? Amend the specification (what are marginal changes in performance worth?); alter the time structure of events (SALAMI?); change the responsibilities (who delivers?; who inspects? who insures?; who secures? who warrants? who risks? who owns?); change the nature of the business (from production to distribution; from home-made to importing; from foreign to local ownership; from ownership to management; from management to royalties; from royalties to buy-out).

See FEAR OF DEADLOCK.

Deadlock tactics. Plays on the negotiator's FEAR OF DEADLOCK. If negotiators 'fail' to agree, they anticipate pressures from the people behind them. Hence, they move rather than lose.

Threaten deadlock by talking up the difficulties of reaching agreement; introduce phoney deadlines; stage phoney WALK OUTS; exhibit phoney temper; become unavailable; demonstrate pessimism; accuse them of not wanting an agreement; make 'final offers'.

Counter: Show no concern about deadlock.

Debt collecting. Not for the squeamish, the gullible or the saintly.

Some people don't pay and never intended to pay; some people intended to pay but find it convenient not to pay; some people don't pay because they can't pay; and some people only pay if you make them pay. (See CREDIT CONTROL.)

Legal remedies are almost always more expensive than they are worth, especially in countries with relatively informal legal systems. The only certain gainers work in the legal profession or for it.

Letters and phone calls are useful to a point, but hard nosed debtors who owe everybody money develop wonderful imaginations: 'the cheque is in the post'; 'I am in conference with my accountant and will ring you back'; 'That invoice was paid weeks ago;' 'Check with your bank, our cheque number was . . . ., dated the 20th of last month,' and many more you should hope you never become familiar with.

What leverage do you have? Can you run up debts using their services to the value of the money they owe you? (This works with hotels, printers, hire companies and service organizations, if you can use their services, and with anybody who will supply against a letter from a company.) When they try to collect, reveal the net balance and offer to call it quits.

Collecting debts is best done in person, your own or an agent's. Invariably you can collect something towards payment (do not be snowed with a promise). If you are thrown out, decide whether to pursue the matter or forget it (all companies experience some bad debts, and mark-up their prices to cover themselves).

No debt is ever a matter of principle. If you find yourself believing that it is, reconsider you priorities: how much can you make while you are tied up with an obsession about principles? No debt should dominate your working hours. Keep the emotion out of it. A bad debt is no different from theft, except you know the name of the thief.

Remember the fundamental principle of debt collecting: any payment is better than none, including in kind. Collect what you can and run. If necessary, agree for part payment in final settlement. Take your money and get back to minding your business.

Debt swamp. Swamps are not just messy, they can kill you. A debt swamp has an inevitability about it. The more you struggle, the deeper you sink. Unlike nature's swamps, nobody ever fell into a debt swamp accidentally. They might get there by ignorance, but mostly they get there by carelessness.

In the debt swamp you borrow money for a purchase (a house, a car, a yacht). Land and house values appreciate, cars and yachts depreciate. All of them have costs (rent, taxes, repairs, maintenance etc.) as does the loan (interest and principal). If the costs of the loan cost more than the goods, you get your feet wet in the swamp.

Suppose you borrow to buy a house as an investment. If the rental income, net of your expenditures (repairs, maintenance, taxes), is less then the loan charges, you must supplement these out of your other income. If land zoning changes take place and reduce the resale value of your plot below the value of the loan, you must make up the difference out of your other income. If the car, or yacht, depreciates faster than the loan is paid off, you must make up the difference out of your other income.

What happens if you have insufficient other income? You can always borrow the difference and get more than your feet wet. As the debt swamp rises, your insufficient income is squeezed. In desperation you turn to a lender and borrow to keep the swamp down; but borrowing more puts you further into the swamp. And so it goes on until you are bust.

What do you do? Avoid unsound investments; avoid paying silly prices for things you think you need; avoid staying with a bad investment when you should get out and limit your debts; avoid becoming emotionally attached to the objects of your ego – a set-back is better than a total rout.

Decision analysis. A negotiator's PREPARATION tool.

To choose a course of action (whether to offer or not, whether to go in high or low, whether to take what is on offer or not etc.), estimate the value of the competing outcomes and their probability of being realized. Obviously, choosing an action with a very high value for you means simultaneously reducing the probability of achieving it, if only because your opponent resists your endeavours, while increasing the probability of success (making offers more likely to be acceptable to your opponent) means reducing the expected value of the outcome.

Set an objective to assess the probable outcomes against. Calculate the expected values of each option: value of the outcome multiplied by the probability of the outcome materializing. For example, if the value of the contract is 200 and your estimate of the probability of your proposal being successful is 0.6, then the expected value of the outcome is 200 × 0.6 = 120. But you have negotiating costs too, and the probability of your proposal being unsuccessful is 1.0 minus 0.6 = 0.4. The expected value to you of being unsuccessful is your negotiating cost (say, minus 20) times the probability of this event occurring: − 20 × 0.4 = − 8. Now the expected value to you of negotiating for the contract is the sum of the expected values of each event: 120 − 8 = 112.

You now have a basis for comparing whether to negotiate for this particular contract as opposed to any other one that is available. Choose the negotiation with the highest expected value, or, if your resources permit, choose to negotiate for those contracts that have expected values that are better than the cut-off expected value you set for your business, and reject all those that fall below it.

The analysis can be extended to cover more complex decisions, though the principle is the same. Each decision is framed in an 'either, or' mode, and each outcome is given a value and a probability of its occurring ($V \times P = EV$). The probabilities are estimated on the basis of your experience. True, you can 'massage' your arithmetic to get any result you want, but this implies you have already made a decision and therefore you do not need decision analysis!

Delaying tactics. Time changes the balance of power. Tactics to avoid a decision.

Take two belligerents reconsidering the future of their war. When should they sue for peace? When there is a stalemate. But the fortunes of war often swing from side to side. One side's forces are pressing ahead in a devastating offensive: will the losing side be amenable to negotiations for peace? Not if it believes it can stem the enemy's offensive and can redress the power of imbalance. What of the side whose armies are poised for final victory. Should it sue for peace and rob its forces of their triumph? Negotiations are unlikely while each side has different opinions of their fortunes.

Consider a war where each side recognizes that continued conflict is unproductive. Suppose peace negotiations begin on neutral territory, either directly between the delegations of the belligerents or under the mediation of a third party. What do the negotiators do if there is an unexpected military reverse for one of the parties? At the very least, the winning side has a strong incentive to slow down the negotiations, for each day's delay strengthens their bargaining power. Their delaying tactics include:

quibbling about details
taking longer adjournments
seeking further instructions
'diplomatic' illness
abiding by national holidays
provoking rows
changing the delegation
raising old issues
insisting on full translations
requesting venue changes
cancelling meetings
starting late
finishing early

"For heaven's sake, Alice, you've got to be firm with these salesmen"

Similarly, in labour disputes, the fortunes of the strike swing one way and the other. A 'back-to-work' movement gets under way, stockpiles run down, public pressure to settle intensifies, violence weakens solidarity, intimidation breaks the back-to-work movement, the leaders become disunited, some employers settle individually, the government intervenes, and the economic costs mount disproportionately.

Negotiations may begin to end the strike, but they can be strung out by each side depending on how they perceive the balance of power. It is not difficult to cause delays by spurious means, and it is frustrating having to deal with them when you are the victim, much as soccer players get irritated by time wasting near the final whistle. But unlike soccer, where the delays occur where the game is decided, negotiators faced with delaying tactics while the balance of power shifts elsewhere have only one option: return to the war, strike, or fight and stem the tide, and come back to negotiations at the next stalemate.

Delivered at frontier. The seller's obligations are met when the goods arrive at the frontier, short of the custom's hall.

Delivered duty paid. The seller's obligations include delivery to the named destination free of all duties. Can be modified to 'Delivered duty paid, exclusive of Valued Added Tax' (or any other tax).

Delivery. Charge for it as an ADD-ON; demand it as a DISCOUNT.

Devil's advocate. PREPARATION tool. A negotiator takes the role of expressing directly contrary positions to the ones prepared by the team. Assuming you are on the side of the angels, the devil's advocate tests your arguments for soundness and consistency. Thinking through your proposed responses to the arguments advanced by the devil's advocate tests their credibility (if you don't convince your colleagues with your answers, you won't convince the opposition), and also exposes deficiencies in the data or preparation, which allows you time to fill in the gaps.

But be careful: there is a risk that you become 'word perfect', and slightly wooden in your presentation; or you feel that you must have an answer to everything.

Dicker. See HAGGLE.

Discount. A deduction from a price.

Discounts are given for all kinds of reasons. Some are common in particular businesses and do not require individual negotiation. For example, construction firms automatically deduct 2 per cent off an invoice for early payment (which means the supplier automatically adds 2 per cent to every invoice in case payment is delayed).

Discounts have a habit of growing into permanent features of an invoicing system because they set precedents. An invoice is discounted to encourage a client to pay on time, to order large volume, to pay in advance, to pay something on an overdue account, to maintain loyalty, to accept point of sale displays, to place an order before a set date and so on. After the event, the client expects the discount to continue. Rival suppliers respond to price discounting by offering discounts themselves. The result is a PRICE WAR.

Negotiators facing a price quotation should always ask for discounts, and should be creative about the reasons they require them. Discounts can be demanded credibly for: early payment; advance payment; payment of a deposit; large volume; purchase of several items; right to use your name in supplier advertising; end of stock purchase; first of stock purchase; reward for recommending other customers to supplier; loyalty to supplier over the years; first time use of supplier; placing all your business with supplier; placing some of your business on introductory basis; seasonal purchases; delivery at awkward times; re-scheduled deliveries; instant delivery; delayed delivery; collecting from supplier ex-works with own transport; missed delivery; incomplete or mistaken order; any inconvenience caused by supplier, and so on.

Discussion. See ARGUMENT.

Disposal. See GETTING OUT FROM UNDER.

Distributive bargaining. Examples of distributive bargaining include:
- A wage negotiation.
(A wage rise increases employees' incomes and employer's costs.)

- A price negotiation.
  (A fall in price benefits the buyer and reduces the income of
    the seller.)
- A boundary or territorial negotiation.
  (A gain in territory by one country reduces the territory of its
    former occupier.)

The algebraic sum of the gains and losses produce ZERO-SUM
outcomes (contrast with INTEGRATIVE BARGAINING).

Distributive bargaining assumes a CONFLICT OF INTERESTS. If we
divide a scarce resource between us, what you gain I lose. But
conflict is not unbounded. Neither of us can get our own way
entirely (if we could we would not bother negotiating). We
negotiate to divide the available resource between us.

The union cannot force up wages indefinitely – the employer
would go bust; nor can the employer force wages down indefinitely – the employees would quit. The buyer cannot force down
the price to zero – the seller would seek another buyer; nor can
the seller raise the price indefinitely – the buyer would take his
business eslewhere. Neither country can extend their boundaries
indefinitely without a high risk of war.

See USED CAR SALE.

Don't negotiate. When you are:
    in a hurry
    exhausted
    emotionally involved
    sexually aroused
    busy with other tasks
    late for an appointment
    bored
    angry
    under pressure
    meant to be elsewhere
    desperate
    under the influence of drink and drugs
    euphoric
    suspicious
    jet lagged
    hungry
    need a visit to the rest room.

Doubling time. The most powerful tool in the box: how long does it take a sum of money to double in size for any given rate of growth? Approximate answer: divide 70 by the rate of growth.

Growth rate (%)	Doubling time (years)
1	70
2	35
3	29
4	17.5
5	14
6	11.9
7	10
8	8.9
9	7.7
10	7

Remember the simple rule when they make offers about commission, profit, earnings, rents and similar rates. Ploughed back into the original sum, and left to grow, the rule tells how long it takes to double your money and helps to keep the relative merits of offers in perspective.

Dripping roast. Sweat once, benefit many times.

Win an order and bask in the income from the repeat business; earn a continuing commission once, spend it many times; write a best seller, bank the royalties earned even while you are sleeping; take a small percentage of a large volume supply contract, and join the gravy train.

Dripping roasts are sound business, if you can get them. Your small percentage (the BAGATELLE?) turns over regularly, for no additional effort. One deal in the 1970s was worth $120 million a year as a percentage of an oil contract for the go-between. But don't knock the small dripping roasts – they pay the rent.

Dutch auction (so-called). If you have two or more written BIDS or TENDERS for the same item, instead of selling to the highest, or buying from the lowest bidder you contact each bidder separately and offer them an opportunity to improve on their offer by quoting them their rival's last bid. This is popularly and mistakenly called a 'Dutch auction'. Keen buyers re-bid just above their rivals, and keen sellers cut their prices to just below their rivals, in the hope of winning. Try several rounds of quoting and re-quoting the last bid to the rivals – and why not if the bidders want to keep bidding? – until only one bidder survives, having beaten the others (some of whom might drop out in disgust at your tactics).

Faced with an invitation to re-bid in these circumstances have nothing to do with it on the grounds that it is unethical, or because it means you lose if you win (your final bid is worse for you than your original bid). Alternatively, you could win if you lose: at least you force your rivals to pay more/earn less than they intended. It is normally best not to play a re-bid game.

If you decide to play, insist on bidding last. Make only one bid and make clear that you will only make one bid. When the auctioneer has been round everybody else and fixed a new price, you can offer to better it or quit. Do not rejoin the game having declared you will make only one bid.

E

Eight-step approach. Method of analysing negotiation as a process that goes through eight common steps, no matter what the negotiation is about, how big or small are the stakes, who is conducting it, or where it is taking place. First developed in 1972 – 4 as a training aid for negotiating skills courses for industrial relations managers, it was applied to commercial negotiating skills training in 1975. It is widely used throughout the world in its original form and numerous versions ('four phases'; 'five steps'; 'six steps', etc.). (After Gavin Kennedy, J. Benson and J. McMillan, *Managing Negotiations*, London, Hutchinson, 3rd ed. 1987 (1980).

The eight steps are:

Prepare
Argue
Signal
Propose
Package
Bargain
Close
Agree.

Negotiators spend varying amounts of time in each step, they pass back and forth between the steps and they use different combinations, techniques, behaviours and tactics for each step. The analysis does not imply that negotiators rigidly make orderly progress through the steps, nor is there a prescriptive inference that they should do so. Based on observation of and participation in actual negotiations, the approach identifies the main activities of the process of negotiating a settlement, assesses the contribution of specific tactics and behaviours to the progress of the negotiations, and forms the core material of a negotiating skills training programme.

Emotion. Used sparingly, emotion can help a negotiator express commitment (see COMMITMENT TACTICS).

There are emotional possibilities in: sending messages, signalling EXPECTATIONS, underlining THREATS or PROMISES, establishing RAPPORT, overcoming obstacles, reinforcing TRUST and altering PERCEPTIONS.

Conflict generates emotions, sometimes overpowering in their

expression. Emotion can be an obstacle to progress; it can inhibit judgement of self-interest; it can cement a DEADLOCK and protract the negotiation. Tactics to reduce emotional tension, include:
- Refraining from exciting INHIBITIONS.
- Refraining from mocking opponent's weaknesses or setbacks.
- Demonstrating willingness to understand, if not to agree with, opponent's views and INTERESTS.
- Refraining from emotional attacks on opponents or challenging their motives, integrity and legitimacy (in both position and parentage).

Faced with an emotional outburst, either in attack or defence, remain calm and apparently unmoved. Emotion is fed by the emotional reaction it provokes; it calms quicker if not fed. When interrupted, wait for the interrupter to finish, then re-commence after a small pause. When threatened in the heat of the moment, do not counter; either ignore the threat as an embarrassment best forgotten, or express disappointment, in sorrow not anger, that he thinks it necessary to introduce a 'negative tone' (try not to call it a 'threat') into your discussions 'at this juncture'. (See TIT-FOR-TAT).

It is sometimes difficult to eliminate emotions when you have a strong feeling for or against the other negotiator for some reason (family, friendship, love, sympathy, likeability, solidarity, suspicion, distrust, 'dirty tricks', duplicity, unfulfilled promises, and such like). But deals that get clouded with emotions, positive or negative, are worse deals than those that you remain clear-headed about. Remember: business is business!

Equity. A much underused asset. If the essence of raising your NET WORTH is to use other people's money to do so, your equity is a useful instrument for LEVERAGE. You borrow multiples of your equity to purchase or fund wealth-creating investments.

Equity is the difference between the value of an asset and what you borrow to acquire it. If you own the asset clear of all borrowing, then you have 100 per cent of the equity at your disposal. Your house, less the mortgage, is a source of appreciating equity (and you need not leave home to utilize it); your car, less the finance owed, is a source of depreciating equity;

your pension could be a source of equity (borrow now, pay back on retirement); and almost any item of property that you own can be a source of equity (borrow against its value, and pledge it as COLLATERAL).

Equity is also your share of a business, usually with a right to a share of the net profits. The value of business equity at any time is variable. For quoted companies the shares have a market price, which is prone to sudden panics, rumour, speculation and subjective evaluation (by yourself, as well as potential buyers).

In considering the making of an investment, or any undertaking involving risk of loss, does offering/taking an equity stake improve the acceptability of the proposal? If so, how big a stake as a proportion of the total equity should you propose? There is a negotiable conflict on this point: the larger your share, the greater your influence on decisions within the proposed undertaking; the smaller your share, the less your risk of loss is covered and the less your influence. Conversely for the other party. Borrowers prefer to limit the lender's equity; lenders prefer to extend it.

Apply the principle of equitable contribution: allocate shares on the basis of what each contributes to the undertaking, and throughout the life of the project not just at its start. This limits the equity of the person putting up most of the money, if their subsequent contribution is much lower than that of the other contributors who perform the work or create the sellable concept. Without money the sellable concept cannot become a reality; without the sellable concept, there is no point borrowing the money. This a common situation at the start-up of high technology ventures, where you have the key abilities and someone else has the money (see PARTNERSHIPS).

People with money have more bargaining leverage than people who need it, but conceding too high an equity stake to the people with money and little else to offer is an avoidable mistake. Certainly never concede a majority share in a venture where you will make the largest post-funding contribution. You end up working for somebody who contributes little to the burden of the venture, or have your creation sold over your head to unwelcome strangers, while you are elbowed aside to your inconvenience, humiliation and angry regret.

If those lending the money insist they they need the stake to cover their risk, offer them a share arrangement that reduces their equity as the business produces the income to repay their monetary contribution, thus reducing their risk. This tests the genuineness of their 'cover the risk' argument, for if they refuse, then they are after more than risk coverage.

Insist on an exclusive and unconditional unilateral right to buy their equity back as you repay the money; insist that they cannot assign their equity to a third party without offering it to you at a price determined by formula (such as the agreed terms for repaying the loan). This 'locks them in' and prevents the appearance of unwelcome surprise partners (a multinational that freezes you out?)). Alternatively, insist that their equity is automatically diluted in future years by the issuing of new shares to the working contributors only.

Escalation. Measured pressure tactic, sometimes used unethically.

Jumping from peace to all-out war is an unusual act. The alternative is to raise the stakes gradually in a measured sequence of events. First, a little pressure is applied, then some more, and eventually full pressure is imposed. The other negotiator is given the option of arriving at a mutually acceptable solution, and warned each time he refuses that the pressures will be increased a few notches. If the reason for DEADLOCK is the other negotiator's unreasonable obstinancy, the escalation might work. On the other hand, the other negotiator's 'obstinancy' might be due to your unreasonable demands, as he perceives them. Far from your escalating pressure convincing him to negotiate, it only convinces him that you are being unreasonable. You risk a mixture of indignation and MARTYRDOM, which results in stiffening resistance rather than surrender.

Typical escalation tactics include a seller reversing his view of the price he is seeking from you. Instead of settling for 2,000 as you agreed, he now finds a reason for wanting 2,500. If you are very keen, you pay up; if you have options, you walk away. One thing you can do is be ready to respond to the escalation of the selling price with a counter: 'I'm glad you have raised the question of price and suggested that our agreed price of yesterday is no longer acceptable. I too have thought about what I hurriedly agreed to yesterday, and I concluded I offered too high a price. Now that the price is back in discussion, I wish to lower my original offer to 1,600'. He has the choice: return to yesterday's price or face a new negotiation in view of your determination not to be intimidated by his escalation.

Escalator schedule. Formula to maintain agreed share in uncertain future income streams.

Publishers normally agree to escalate an author's percentage royalties as total sales of a book reach specified quantities. Similarly, anybody owning rights to a product should negotiate escalator clauses in their licencing agreements.

Tactically, your aim is to increase the percentage royalty or fee and decrease the qualifying amount which triggers off the increased royalty (and in reverse if you are acquiring the licence). For example, if the offer is 10 per cent royalty on the first 6,000 copies sold, 12.5 per cent on the next 6,000 and 15 per cent thereafter, counter with a demand for 10 per cent on the first 3,000, 12.5 per cent on next 3,000 and 15 per cent thereafter.

If negotiating commission terms (or salary) in a market where there is a direct link between performance and results (stocks and shares, pension and insurance sales, turnover of a branch office, sales of all kinds, estate agents' fees, new clients added to the firm's books, and such like), go for a escalator clause in your contract: so much for reaching current performance levels and extra amounts for exceeding them. It is better to negotiate this before improving performance, as trying to do so after you have made the improvements is vulnerable to an argument motivated by the HOOKER'S PRINCIPLE.

Ethics. Don't preach to others about your ethics. If a proposal is contrary to your personal standards, decline it without sermonizing. There is not a lot to choose between the unethical and the sanctimonius.

Is there a code of conduct for negotiations? Not in a formal sense. Much that applies to general business behaviour applies to negotiating. If your ethics are in doubt on any issue, apply the quantitative test: are my short-run gains at the expense of longer-term costs? Frame your longer-term gains as a net gain that takes account of potential costs, including the attention of the law, public contempt and damage to your reputation. Sacrificing positive long-term net gains for immediate but smaller short-term gains is an expensive way to do business. See PRISONER'S DILEMMA.

Exchange. How decisions are made by negotiation. You exchange things you have for things you want; you exchange your consent for a consideration; you exchange something you value for peace; you exchange your willingness to negotiate for a better deal than would otherwise be on offer.

See TRADE.

Expectations. You have them: they help determine your strategies and your OBJECTIVES. If your expectations are unrealizable, or you come to believe that they are, you adjust them or pursue a hopeless quest. The same is true for your opponent. Legitimate tactics include attempts to undermine the other side's confidence in the realism of their expectations:

- They aim for 20 per cent, you show that only 10 per cent is possible.
- They arrive expecting a quick settlement; you show them that deals take longer on these issues.
- They are ready to bid money; you show them that money is not the only issue.

Experimental negotiations. Thousands of experiments in negotiation have been simulated by psychologists, sociologists, economists, anthropologists, political scientists, game theorists and mathematicians. The published literature on experimental negotiation is huge, and growing. The experiments vary in sophistication, from full laboratory conditions where every facet of the experiment is controlled, to more relaxed experiments in class with MBA students. In addition, mathematical models have been devised using simple algebra to high level equations. Complex computer simulation has been tried and so have verbal interactive games ('role plays' etc.).

Given the wide-ranging applications of negotiation, the study of negotiations encompasses a variety of academic disciplines. To keep up with the literature, scan two academic journals: *Journal of Conflict Resolution* (Sage: Sage Publications Inc., P.O. Box 5024, Beverly Hills. CA 90210 USA.); *Negotiation Journal: the process of dispute settlement*, (Plenum: Plenum Publishing Corp., 233 Spring Street, New York, NY 10013 USA.).

Expected value. See DECISION ANALYSIS.

Exports. Without these we would all be poorer, yet everywhere the myopic seek to curb each other's.

Exporting may be 'fun' (to quote a recent exhortation) but it is also complicated. Frontiers are jealously guarded and they make no exceptions for goods crossing them; legal systems differ across the world and disputes between people in separate territories – with goods, perhaps, in a third territory or in transit between them – add to the normal complexities (and costs); and the number of intermediaries involved in shipping goods imposes heavy demands on comprehensive documentation, title to ownership, transfer of ownership and proper payment as agreed between seller and buyer.

In theory, customs unions abolish tariffs between members and eliminate non-tariff barriers too. In practice, this does not lead to fewer formalities. The customs authorities have three roles: collecting revenues; restricting certain goods; collecting statistics. All are intrusive on trade. At a minimum customs officials must know what is being exported (and imported). Documentation is required to describe the goods, to value them and to authenticate the declaration. In addition, the shipper (vessel, vehicle or aircraft) has numerous formalities to complete before being allowed to leave. These formalities, and their associated costs, incline the prudent seller towards an EX-WORKS or FOB price for the goods rather than CIF, which a buyer might prefer.

Export credit. It is not enough to compete to export goods on the basis of quality, price and delivery alone. Increasingly, world trade must now be financed by credit to the buyer, and, also, credit to the seller waiting for payment.

Your options for ensuring payment include:
- Cash with order: if you can get it!
- Documentary credit: payment on presentation of shipping documents to buyer's bank (insist that the credit is 'irrevocable', and 'confirmed' so that you can receive payment at your local bank).
- Transferable credit: when you are selling as an agent. Your supplier wants payment when you order the goods for your buyer, but you do not get paid until the goods are shipped to your buyer. Solution: arrange a documentary credit from your buyer in the normal way, but get his bank to pay your supplier

his price to you on proof of shipping the goods to you (this money is deducted from the documentary credit held in your name). When you ship the goods on to the buyer, you receive the balance of the credit on presentation of your shipping documents.

● Back-to-back credit: use of the documentary credit in your favour from your buyer as security to establish a credit in your supplier's favour, paid when he ships the goods. Less favourable to you than a transferable credit.

● Revolving credits: for regular routine transactions that permit a cycle of credit to operate – as one transaction is paid on presentation of the appropriate documents, another is opened.

● Acceptance credits: a bank credits you with an amount, which you can draw against and the bank places your bills in the money market; as the buyer's credits to you become due, these are collected by the bank to cover the acceptance allowed to you on the strength of your transaction with the buyer.

You can use expectations of getting paid by a buyer (the credit system you negotiate) to raise finance for your own operations. The credit is an asset, albeit a paper one. You can sell the credit for a discounted price, the purchaser collecting the difference as his gross profit when the documentary credit is paid. Your obligation to ship the goods remains; indeed, the purchaser of the bill can sue you (recourse) if you do not. Another version is FACTORING: the factor credits you for the agreed proportion of your invoice, collects your invoices in the buyer's country, and keeps the difference, net of costs of collection.

Ex-quay. Seller bears full cost and the risk of making the goods available at the destination named in the contract. 'Ex-quay duty paid' means the liability for customs duties is paid by the seller; 'ex-quay duties on buyer's account' means the liability for customs duties in the buyer's not the seller's.

Ex-ship. Seller bears full cost and risk of bringing goods to the ship's destination named in the contract.

Ex-works. Goods are available at the seller's factory. Buyer is responsible for loading of vehicles and for full cost of transporting them, including insurance, to the buyer's destination.

F

Factoring. Arrangement by which a supplier can improve CASH FLOW. The supplier's invoices to clients are 'bought' by a factoring agency which collects from clients and pockets the difference between what the supplier is paid and what the agency collects from the clients. The supplier gets his money immediately for sales to clients; the factoring agency collects within the normal credit period. As the agency specializes in collecting on invoices its administrative costs per invoice are controllable, and therefore its operations are profitable.

Not all invoices are accepted by a factoring agency. They eliminate known bad payers, or those likely to be bad payers, and can require a larger margin on some others. As most businesses deal with reliable payers most of the time, factoring can be mutually profitable. Some agencies arrange to handle all invoice payments using the supplier's own notepaper, so the clients are unaware they are dealing with a third party.

The spread between the factoring price and the invoice's face value is negotiable. Whether the factoring agency has recourse to the supplier in the case of a bad debt is also negotiable.

Failure to agree. Formal declaration required in collective bargaining PROCEDURE agreements when negotiators cannot settle the dispute at their level. The issue is referred to the next level for further negotiation, often with a different set of negotiators. Sometimes, negotiators fail to agree on the 'nod', so that an important issue can reach an appropriate level more quickly.

Fair. A sense of fairness influences negotiators (see NASH SOLUTION) – in theory. This is shown in EXPERIMENTAL NEGOTIATIONS where the beneficiaries of a distribution are not yet identified. For instance, if you were asked what you would regard as a fair distribution of an estate between you and a colleague, and you were given no additional information as to your likely share, or what you 'deserved' etc., there is a very high likelihood that you would opt for an 'equal' distribution. Some people have suggested that this 'proves' that equality is closer to natural justice than inequality: in fact, it proves how careful we all are to hedge our bets.

If the fair solution is the equal division, it complicates the process of negotiation to find an acceptable division. Consider the case of a negotiation over an as yet undetermined amount, such as a wage or price increase. If you knew the rule was 'fair means equal', you have an incentive to open with a high demand or low offer. Why? Because an equal division between a demand for 10 and an offer of 2 is 6 (you come down 4, I go up 4). You can improve upon your claim by asking for 20, because against the offer of 2, the fair means equal solution is 11 (you come down 9, I go up 9). The result would be unstable if each tries to manipulate the division by moving out the numbers (100, -100 = 0; -100, 200 = 50).

Fairness as a settlement option is popular with economists, because their negotiation models do not incorporate pay-offs for non-economic factors such as bargaining skills, the power balance, perceptions and expectations. Indeed, by eliminating all consideration of such things, or, what amounts to the same thing, assuming that neither negotiator has an advantage over the other in any of these respects, thus neutralizing their influence, the logical conclusion is that the settlement position must end up at the mid-point because there is no economic reason why it should end up anywhere else.

The world as it is, not how we wish it to be, has not distributed any resource equally across its physcial or societal features. Fairness is not a principle of nature, it is a construct of the mind.

Fait accompli tactic. The deed is done and you defy them to undo it. Fait accompli tactics shift power to the doer and raise the stakes if counter sanctions are applied.

Armies seize territory and then offer to negotiate; Israel sets up settlements and then offers to talk about the West Bank; a developer knocks down a unique building and then applies for planning permission; managers introduce new work schedules and then agree to negotiations; publishers send printed and signed contracts and ask for the author's agreement to their terms; buyers send a cheque for a lesser amount than the disputed invoice; a spouse changes the house locks and demands a divorce; a buyer returns goods outside warranty and refuses to pay; a buyer retains goods and refuses to pay; a department occupies disputed office space and offers talks; a hostile bidder builds a shareholding and demands a seat on the board; you eat a meal in a restaurant and demand a discount for poor quality.

Counters: Undertake costs of undoing what has been done; demand return to status quo ante before negotiations continue; do not sign a contract until you are happy with it (cross out unsuitable clauses and return in a reverse fait accompli); send a lorry to buyer's premises with order to uplift the goods (many despatch and stores departments are glad to get rid of excess stocks, and buyers forget to warn them); order materials from the debtor and offer to swap them back; cut off services to disputed offices; inform new board member of changes to meeting venues too late for attendance, miss papers out of his folder, meet with loyal colleagues earlier to sort out positions; retain diner in small room for long hours while you haggle.

It is best to write into your contract firm rules on what cannot be done without invoking heavy legal penalties.

Fall back. If you have not got one, then you stand and fight where you are. Best to think about developing an alternative to fall upon if the negotiations do not work out as you expected.

See BEST ALTERNATIVE TO A NEGOTIATED AGREEMENT (BATNA); RESISTANCE PRICE; OBJECTIVES.

FAS. (Free alongside ship). Seller's obligations end when the goods are placed alongside the ship, either on the quay or in a lighter. Buyer's risk commences at this moment and buyer is responsible for clearing the goods for export.

Fear of deadlock. Extremely common among negotiators. Partly to do with the 'success culture' of open societies. Deadlock implies 'failure'. Successful negotiations credit the personnel involved with high self- and peer group esteem.

Junior sales staff are judged by the quantity of orders gained, and not necessarily their profitability. Not getting an order is a failure that is felt sorely. Given the number of occasions when they must get 'no' for their trouble, compared to the times they hear 'yes', deadlock, and the process leading up to it, is a disheartening experience.

It is no less so for negotiators in other fields. The more public the failure (international summits, closely contested issues, such as European Community meetings) the more embarrassing is deadlock and the more negotiators seek to avoid it. This enables governments without independent media to offer critical comment, to manipulate the fear of deadlock to produce otherwise unobtainable concessions from countries with a free media. For example, Western opinion favours a negotiated reduction in nuclear weapons involving verification, balance and security. When summit meetings occur, extremely high hopes are generated of something coming out of them. Past experience shows that failure is a political burden for democratic governments. This burden is avoidable if they make sufficient concessions to the other party. Given that people are less skilled in evaluating the details than they are in judging whether deadlock was avoided, there is a temptation to trade larger concessions than those governments without these pressures.

See DEADLOCK.

Final offer. If you make one, mean it, otherwise, don't make one.

Declaring an offer to be 'final' is risky. Turning a final offer into a 'final offer but one' (or two, or three) is disastrous for credibility. A called 'final offer' bluff is a stone cold killer.

To handle final offers, pay attention to what you are doing. If no more movement is possible – when you prefer no deal to a deal on worse terms – convey the message to the other side, but carefully. A badly phrased final offer close is provocative because of its implied ultimatum. Tell them that you can go 'no further'; that you are at the 'end of the road'; that it is 'decision time'; that you 'consider the offer on the table to be the best that is available'. None of these statements uses the words 'final offer', but that is how it will be perceived.

They might ask: 'Is that your final offer?' Do not be afraid to answer 'Yes', if it is (see KILLER QUESTIONS). They must consider whether to call what they perceive to be your bluff, by testing your resolve, or to settle on the final offer terms.

First offer. Never accept a first offer. Negotiate.

The first offer is where you open; it is not where you expect to end up. If it is, either you expect your first offer to be accepted immediately, or you are in such a powerful position that you feel there is no need to negotiate. If the former, why not open with a more favourable stance and see if you can improve your position (if they accept your present offer, what other offers would they accept?). If you are so powerful that negotiation is unnecessary, then it is not an offer but an ultimatum.

What is true for you is true for them. Their first offer is not where they expect to end up. So why disappoint them? What other offers, which are better for you as they move towards your position, are they willing to contemplate?

Choosing where to open is a problem. To improve your choice, consider the BARGAINING CONTINUUM. You have a range of possible openings from your RESISTANCE PRICE, beyond which you prefer not to do business, to your TARGET PRICE. Pitch your first offer between your reservation and your target prices and you automatically concede your target price, because it is not normal for a seller's first offer to move upwards, after it has been announced, unless there are major changes in the circumstances of the sale (see ESCALATION; RULES).

What kind of negotiation, if any, follows your first offer? If it is a ONE-OFFER-ONLY arrangement your price will be higher if you believe the buyer has limited options, or lower if the buyer has many options.

Consider your offer probabilistically: the wider the gap between targets, the less probable an early, or any settlement. Negotiations fill the time available for them. The longer the available time, the more ambitious the goals of the negotiators (bear this in mind when negotiating with Communist governments who take years to come to a decision). You can, therefore, influence your opponent's first offer by manipulating the time pressure. If he believes that time is short, and that you have options, his first offer will be closer to, or inside, the settlement range (see BARGAINING CONTINUUM).

Fisher, Roger. Co-author with William Ury of the seminal *Getting to Yes: Negotiating agreement without giving in*, Boston, Houghton Mifflin, 1981 (UK, London, Hutchinson, 1983).

Professor Fisher teaches negotiation at Harvard Law School and is a leading member of the Harvard Negotiation Project. His approach to negotiating was first made apparent in his *International Conflict for Beginners*, New York, Harper & Row, 1969.

His work reflects his experience of litigation and international diplomacy. He searches for the 'rational' solution to a negotiating problem and in doing so he provides many insights into the process by which opponents can be brought to a common solution, separate from their emotional attachments to preferred but incompatible solutions. Broadly, an inadequate summary of his method would include:

- Don't bargain over positions.
- Separate the people from the problem.
- Focus on interests.
- Invent options for mutual gain.
- Insist on objective criteria.
- Develop your BATNA.
- Work to a single-negotiating text.

See BEST ALTERNATIVE TO A NEGOTIATED AGREEMENT; INTERESTS; POSITIONAL BARGAINING.

Fixed prices. Sellers love fixed prices because they preclude bargaining. That is why they write prices on large tickets, print price lists, have standard terms for doing business, issue price catalogues and generally imply that the price on the tag is written in cement.

And why not? Most people accept fixed prices. Few challenge them, fewer still persist after the first 'no'.

But the price on the tag, or printed on the list, is their FIRST OFFER. Whether it is their FINAL OFFER remains to be seen. If thousands are ready to buy off the shelf for the prices on the tags, it is difficult to negotiate a discount. But more often than not, the aversion to negotiating a better price has nothing to do with the buyer's relative power. It is purely contextual; it is a part of the business culture you live in. Ninety-seven per cent of people in Britain accept the buyer's first price; in the United States its down as low as seventeen per cent in some commodity groups; in Australia its in between.

In business, however, most people do not accept the price they are first quoted. They HAGGLE; they attempt to negotiate. Apply the same methods to fixed prices in stores. Open up their first offers to discussion. See what other offers are lurking in the background. (See DISCOUNTS).

Flexibility. In short supply among average negotiators. When their strategy isn't working they keep on with it instead of adjusting to events. They apply 'rules' rigidly, instead of with discretion. They cannot think beyond their emotions. They curtail usable options because they have limited imaginations. They certainly cannot cope with negotiating cultures outside of their experience (don't send them abroad!).

Flexibility in approach, not interests, comes from thorough PREPARATION. The above average negotiator is armed with options, both as to goals and methods of achieving them.

FOB. (Free on board). Buyer pays all costs from the moment the goods cross over the ship's rail. Seller's price does not include costs of freight and insurance from the ship's rail onwards.

FOR/FOT. (Free on rail, free on truck). Similar to FOB. Goods pass to the buyer when they are loaded on to the railway wagon or truck.

Force majeure. Events that are outside the control of the contracting parties which prevent a contractual obligation being met. Revolutions, war, seizure of assets, embargoes, economic sanctions, geological and climatic disturbances and such like can make fulfilment of a contract impossible, or severely delay completion. To penalize the defaulter in these circumstances can be unfair. Include *force majeure* exemptions in your contract.

Force projection. Indirect pressure tactic.

Naval ships are visible. Sailing up and down a foreign coastline, they project their power without using it. Knowledge that a submarine fleet is lurking unseen, below the surface close to a major port, projects power but not by as much as a visible surface fleet.

Unions use force projection in contract negotiations. They hold a mass march and demonstration close to the plant, or even somewhere else as long as the publicity is seen by the managers. A disturbance, a few arrests, TV coverage of a police baton charge or a fiery speech, all contribute to force projection (in this case, of determination).

Buyers' force projection measures include:
- Open contact with competition.
- Competitors' notepaper visible on desk.
- In-house costings in 'make or buy?' report.

- Circular letter calling for tenders.
- Glossy purchasing policy document.

Sellers' force projection measures include:
- Surcharges on small orders.
- Lengthy delivery dates.
- Publicity about growing market share.
- Glossy catalogue without prices.
- Acquisition of, or merger with, rivals.
- Early warning of price rises or less attractive credit terms.

Pressure groups engage in force projection in demonstrations, publicity and media stunts and spoiling tactics at unrelated events (sporting fixtures, concerts, political rallies). All force projection measures aim to influence the negotiators.

Foreclosure. An unhappy and avoidable event. The final slide into the DEBT SWAMP.

True, circumstances can move suddenly against you: the bottom falls out of the tin market just as you go long on the price of tin; a new highway can take your custom elsewhere; your colleagues can abscond with the funds; you can get plain unlucky with the company you keep. But most foreclosures happen because you lose sight of what you are doing, and you ignore your VULNERABILITIES.

Some debtors refuse to take responsibility for their own actions – they sue their creditors for lending them the money in the first place! If you can't pay, don't borrow. If you are taking a large chance – the gamble of the courageous entrepeneur – fine. Just don't start weeping when the gamble does not come off. If you throw all you have on the chance of a lifetime, remember you may spend a lifetime regretting it.

Borrowing for income is disastrous. Covering your borrowing with your capital, and without CASH FLOW to service the debt is as courageous as free-fall parachuting without a parachute.

Slow down the day of reckoning by all means. If your country owes the world's banks billions of dollars, and can't pay the interest, demand a rescheduling of the debt; if you owe your local bank 10,000, be less strident while demanding rescheduling. Evidence, not hope, of a sound repayment system is a great persuader with bankers. Evidence of rapid action to stem a negative cash flow is also sound. Doing nothing wins no concessions. If the situation can be stabilized (cash flow that stems the swamp), and then reversed, nobody will foreclose. If it gets worse, they will.

Desperation drives debt swampers into quick sales of assets. Look for good bargains among debt swampers. They need cash faster than they need good advice. Your risk is the status of their title to the property. If they are selling to stop a slide into the swamp, and not just to up and run with their creditor's assets, you get a bargain; if the latter, you get a legal tangle.

Forfaiting. Subject to certain conditions, a bank forfaits an invoice for an exporter by paying direct to the exporter an agreed proportion of its face value. The bank then assumes total responsibility for collecting the money from the importer, and usually does not have recourse to the exporter if his customer fails to pay. The exporter get its money quicker, which has obvious advantages. The difference between its income from the bank and the face value of the invoice is regarded as justified by the certainty of payment compared to the usual risks faced by exporters. The terms of the forfaiting facility are negotiable. The bank forfaits against good quality contracts, reducing its risks to an acceptable level.

Formula bargaining. An analytical approach to international diplomacy that divides negotiation into three phases: pre-negotiation or 'diagnostic' phase; defining the appropriate 'formula' phase; and the 'detail' phase. Based on structured interviews with diplomats and studies of major international issues. See I. William Zartman & Maureen R. Berman, *The Practical Negotiator*, Yale University Press, New Haven, 1982.

Negotiators are advised to pay attention to the facts, the history of the problem, and how it has evolved, and to look for precedents and how referents governing similar situations have developed, and to know about the specific contexts and percep-tions of the disputants and how they perceive their interests.

If this phase is completed satisfactorily (itself a major assump-tion given the emotional investment of countries in their own interests), the negotiators can engage in a search for an agreed 'formula', by which is meant a mutually agreed perception of what the dispute is about. This formula could refer to an agreed definition of the conflict, to cognitive referents that imply a solution or to some criterion of justice.

For example, a dispute over territory can be transformed from zero-sum ('if country A acquires it, then country B is denied it; and vice versa) to a neutrality of gains and losses such that neither country acquires it (perhaps applicable to Afghanistan after Soviet withdrawal?). Or, in the case of the Israeli-Arab dispute, each party redefines the history of the territorial issue to one of a formula based on the principles of 'security for Israel and territory for the Arabs'. This implies its own solution.

The search for a criterion of justice echoes the prescriptive advice of ROGER FISHER and William Ury. Indeed, the advice of Zartman and Berman in the formula phase is supportive of 'Getting to Yes': 'remember that the problem, not the opponent, is the "enemy" to be overcome' (p. 144).

The detail phase of the negotiations encompasses all the hard slog through the itemised applications of the formula. Care is needed to keep the 'big picture' in focus while negotiating the details, and in being able to match flexibility with steadfastness in pursuit of clearly defined objectives (the 'eye-ball-to-eye-ball' moments in major international negotiations where there is a knife edge between success and seeking other options).

Free carrier. Seller's obligations end when goods are delivered to the specific identifiable place named by the buyer. All risks are transferred to the buyer at that place, and the bill of lading is proof of compliance.

Freight carrier. Seller pays freight and carriage to the named destination, but the buyer is at risk for loss or damage once the goods are passed to first carrier (the truck lifting the goods for shipment to the docks etc.).

Friendship. Neither necessary nor sufficient to get agreement, but seldom a hindrance. The personal relations of the negotiators can be warmer than the relations between the constituents they represent. This is not an uncommon experience in difficult (peace treaty?) negotiations (and in hostage situations between the victims and their captors).

Working on the interpersonal relationship can help, but in some contexts it can hinder. For example, negotiating with officials from a bureaucracy can lead to misunderstandings if your friendly gestures are too overt (are you enticing them into corrupt or disloyal stances?). Certainly, if you are on good terms with the other side it is better than being hardly able to speak to them, but remember, the exploitation of the friendship is not all one way (they get to you too!).

Frontal assault. High-risk tactic to compromise the other negotiator's credibility.

- 'That is not what your predecessor said to us last time we met'.
- 'Your predecessor, bless him, never took that line with us.'
- 'Are you sure that your people upstairs support what you are trying to do?'
- 'Perhaps you should adjourn and consult with your people in more detail before you dig in too deep on this issue?'

The other negotiator is irritated by this tactic and may 'blow his or her top'. It could sour your relationship for good. Use rarely. Remember THE SOMME FALLACY.

G

Game theory. Mathematical formulation of conflict dilemmas and thus eminently suited to abstract presentations of the bargaining problem. Developed by John von Neumann and Oscar Morgenstern in their classic *Theory of Games and Economic Behavior*, Princeton, NJ, Princeton University Press, 1944. It has its origins in games of strategy and prescriptions about how to gamble in games of chance.

Essentially, game theory, applied to modern conflict or bargaining problems, rests on certain assumptions: the identity of the players and their number are fixed and known to everyone (you are not playing against the anonymous 'market'); all players are assumed to be rational and everybody knows they are rational; the pay-offs to each player are known; each player's strategies are known and fixed; STRATEGIC INTERACTION (the manipulation of available information for personal advantage) between the players is limited, but not excluded, by the assumptions.

Though game theory originated in the search for a determinate solution to the bargaining problem (where will the price settle?), it developed by conceptualizing all kinds of conflict problems that competitive price theory did not address. Two person ZERO-SUM games were analysed by Neumann and Morgenstern and they discovered that players in a pure conflict game assumed that the other person was malevolent and therefore disposed to 'do his worst' whatever strategy was selected. It followed that a player did best by adopting a 'maximin' strategy: select the strategy that assured the 'best of the worst outcomes'.

Two person non-zero-sum games are more complex. The degree of strategic interaction increases dramatically as they explore opportunities for mutual gain. This can be handled by eliminating it by assumption or device, or by transforming it into a quantifiable probability.

See NASH SOLUTION; PRISONER'S DILEMMA.

Gazumped. You think you have a contract. The other party considers it to be an intention. Somebody else offers them a better deal, so they drop their intention to deal with you and sign a contract with them. You have been gazumped.

Gazumping is expensive because you must start all over again with another negotiator. It can also be inconvenient if you were relying on the transaction to go through. Looked at from the other side, gazumping may be the only option you have if the other party is unable to close the deal within a reasonable space of time, and you need the deal more than you are concerned about the ethics of gazumping. Hence, gazump.

To avoid gazumping, negotiate an OPTION.

Generosity. Not contagious without a high degree of TRUST between the negotiators. Being generous – in the shape of making unconditional conditions – does not promote reciprocal gestures. Quite the reverse. The other negotiator perceives your actions as a reflection of your weaker negotiating power, and revises his initial demands accordingly.

Unless, and until, you develop a strong relationship with the other negotiator, in terms of generosity, err towards the behaviour of Scrooge, rather than St Francis of Assisi. Like Scrooge, you can let events in the relationship teach you to be more generous, rather than wait for your generosity to teach the virtues of cooperation to the other negotiator (see TIT-FOR-TAT).

Getting out from under. Deals go sour. If you are in the pit, stop digging; get out from under.

We hang on in the hope that something will turn up. Our egos are welded to our projects. To give up is a defeat, a sign of weakness, a confession of failure. Right? Wrong.

Digging in when we have clearly made a mistake is for dumbos. Throwing good money after bad has never been prudent or profitable. It is always senseless to abide by the CONCORDE FALLACY.

If you can't avoid the occasional lemon, get rid of it when you realize you've got one. Study why you got into the mess in the first place, after you have got out of it, and avoid similar mistakes in future. Experience is the best university to graduate from.

Once you decide to quit a deal, settle on an unbeatable price and stick to it. The more people you can bring into the market for your disposal the better. Use your imagination in finding buyers. Keep to a realistic price and do not be tempted to hang on for a 'magnificent' profit (if you could do this, why are you disposing of it?) Remember, the basic rule of the market: the lower the price, the more people are interested. Once the hunt is on for your disposable deal, bring it to a conclusion, don't hang about dithering about your losses – cut them and get your money working somewhere else for a profit.

Getting paid. Not everybody gets paid what they are due. Getting paid is sometimes more difficult than getting the work in the first place.

There can be genuine differences of opinion as to how much is owed, what the agreed price was, who was responsible for the revisions and variations, and whether the completed work was of sufficient standard to warrant payment at all.

Cutting through these difference of opinion, there are also failures to pay based on attempts by the debtor to avoid payment for wholly unscrupulous reasons. Deciding which is the case is a matter of judgement on your part.

Apart from having well-structured and disciplined invoicing systems to collect money from clients, and keeping a firm grip on CREDIT CONTROL, you may have to ensure payment by more vigorous means, including physically collecting it yourself or through an agent.

The basic advice about getting paid includes: some payment is better than none; punitive litigation to collect debts punishes you too in what it costs in legal fees, time and stress (litigation is nowhere cheap); separate the emotion about the debtor from the debt; go and collect it yourself and be ready to take payment in kind as well as cash (think creatively).
DEBT COLLECTING; FACTORING; FORFAITING.

Give and take. Useful description of the negotiator's trading behaviour. A caveat: 'giving' does not cause 'getting' (see GENEROSITY); 'taking' does not cause 'giving'; trading requires simultaneous 'give' and 'take' – one goes with the other – and therefore the safest move is only to offer to 'give' if you can simultaneously get something back in exchange.

Establishing a negotiating relationship based on mutual trust and respect induces a proper atmosphere for 'give and take'.

Go between. Slang trade name for someone akin to an AGENT, particularly in the Middle East. Usually a national of the importing country who acts as the contact person between the exporter and the importer. It is not always clear exactly which party the go-between acts for but several countries insist that foreigners make all their business contacts through a local go-between. In exchange for handling all of the transactions between the parties, the go-between receives a commission paid by the foreigner out of his share of the transaction.

As go-betweens often also act for the other party, or at least are candid with them about the foreigner's real negotiating positions, they can hardly be described as bona fida agents. Their actual status in any one transaction is inescapably ambiguous. Effective go-betweens build a reputation for smoothing a deal to a satisfactory conclusion, hence too casual a recruitment of an individual to act in this role can prove expensive. Consult local 'old hands', or your embassy's commercial attache, before embarking on a contract with anybody offering their services.

Goodwill. Earned, not given automatically (scc GENEROSITY).

Conceding something – no matter how little – in order to 'create goodwill' is almost always futile. The other negotiator stiffens his positon when you make UNCONDITIONAL OFFERS. Also, the 'little' things you give away may acquire considerable leverage potential later in the negotiation – they could even clinch the agreement if offered at the right time – and throwing them away in the futile hope of creating goodwill is extremely costly in retrospect when the result is that you have nothing left to close the deal.

Greed. More than one negotiator has snatched DEADLOCK out of the jaws of compromise by being too greedy. You do not intend to be greedy, only ambitious, but the other negotiator perceives it as greed, and resents your behaviour. Resentment provokes resistance. Your price is just too high, and the project is dropped, leaving you with nothing; or they agree to pay, acquire your property and then don't pay up.

Grievances. Don't just state a grievance, propose a remedy.

Concentrate your attention (PREPARATION?) on your grievance and you are likely to enjoy an ARGUMENT. Think about what you want done about your grievance, and select a remedy within the other negotiator's gift (beware of GREED), and you are likely to enjoy the remedy sooner than you will settle an argument.

Gross. The gross of anything is larger than the NET, hence, go for the gross, not the net.

A percentage of gross income is worth more than a percentage of gross profit, and both are worth more than a percentage of net income or net profit respectively. Especially true when the other negotiator controls the calculation of the 'net'.

Creative accountancy is an expensive art form, precisely because its application to your accounts saves the other negotiator large sums of money. Nobody understands this more than the accountant creatively adjusting the books for your 'partner' – he sees all the arithmetic!

Guarantees. Assurance is of great value in situations where the risks of non-compliance are high. Banks like guarantees to cover their loans; clients like guarantees to cover your performance (see PERFORMANCE BONDS); you like guarantees when its your money crossing the table.

Make sure, when giving guarantees, that you can cover the situation if things go wrong ('Murphy's Law' is not a joke in real life). Extravagant guarantees ('this product works in sub-zero temperatures – you could use it in a deep freezer') are dangerous.

Ask for guarantees. If they can't guarantee something, adjust the price accordingly; if they guarantee something as a matter of course, ask for a price without the guarantee (you are probably paying for it in an insurance premium anyway). If the guarantee needs to be invoked, consider a payment in lieu of litigation to collect it.

H

Haggle. (United States: 'dicker') A noble art. Consists of a seller discovering the maximum a buyer will pay, without disclosing the minimum he will accept (and vice versa, which makes it interesting).

Haggling is part theatre:

- 'Are you trying to starve my children?'
- 'Your price for my home is 60,000; have you no shame?'
- 'I'm making nothing on this deal at all, but because I like you, I'll accept 3,000.'

Hagglers find plausible reasons for amending offers. The reasons can relate to the product ('It's got great potential'); the relationship ('Would a brother take from his own? Only 350 and it's a deal'); the situation ('Seeing it's your birthday/our first meeting/the end of the war, make it 2,000'); or to anything at all ('OK, I'm feeling daft, I'll swap the utility for the caravan'). Hagglers also find plausible reasons for sticking to their demands: 'My wife said I must not take less than 2,500'; 'Take my price and save yourself the effort of taking it away'; 'You must be kidding! This diamond is worth twice what you're offering'; 'I haven't just got here in a banana boat. Nobody will pay a cent more than I've offered, and most won't even offer that'.

Having it both ways. Negotiators often do, if you let them. The capacity for the human mind to accept inconsistencies that suit their interests is almost unlimited. For example:

- An increase in rents of 100 is an 'intolerable burden to impose on me'; an offer of 100 as a pay increase is a 'mean spirited offer not worth collecting'.
- 'The Soviet people regard your attempt to discuss human rights as an intolerable intrusion into their domestic affairs'; 'The Soviet forces in Afghanistan are heroically defending the people against the imperialist interventionists from Pakistan'.

Counter: Draw attention to the inconsistency, but do not entertain high hopes of its having much of an effect. Negotiators believe what they want to believe.

Heads of agreement. Useful device to break DEADLOCK, or to get stalled talks re-started.

Your differences with the other side could be sharp. You find it impossible to handle all the differences, or to decide which issues should be tackled first, or whether some issues should be tackled at all. Can you agree a set of headings? What issues can you discuss? These need not be placed in any particular order at first. You are setting up an AGENDA. If you can agree on even a restricted list of headings, the act of agreeing to this could precipitate enough momentum to allow the negotiations to re-commence.

In dealing with certain cultures, the Western preference for detailed contracts can prove to be embarrassing. For instance, the Chinese, and to some extent, the Japanese, prefer to build a relationship based on trust. A detailed contract is a statement of the legalistic distrust of each party for the other. It assumes that dishonourable actions are possible and therefore likely. Work your way round this problem by a heads of agreement tactic. This lists what you have agreed by headings only, with a minimum of explanation. This meets your needs and theirs.

Hooker's principle. Applies to services valued more highly before they are performed than they are afterwards.

A bank telexes and asks you to act as liquidator of a major business for the benefit of the creditors. It is a multi-million dollar operation with sellable assets, including subsidiaries. What is your fee? Do you quote a fee to the bank, or do you get on with the liquidation (it being a time-critical assignment) and bill them later? Do not be surprised if your client expresses doubts about the size of your fee after all the hassle of the liquidation is over: people's views of a crisis depend on where they were standing when the crisis hit somebody else. When does a plumber's fee look reasonable? When the client is up to her knees in water!

Counters: Accept assignments, but state immediately the basis under which you expect to be paid: 'Sure, I can handle the assignment. Do you want me to charge my daily rate or the standard percentage of the gross value involved?' Or 'cost plus usual margin'; 'standard rate'; 'notify you when costs exceed 100,000'; or whatever.

When costs rise towards 'high' numbers, do not hide them from the client, otherwise you are vulnerable to the 'we should have been told' ploy. Inform them in writing of the current costs each month, and request payment on account. They are more likely to push their people hardest to get these paid while they feel the pressure of the crisis than they are when it has passed.

Arrange for PROGRESS PAYMENTS; if possible go for regular payment by dates (total fee/time); if necessary accept payment for demonstrated progress.

See CBP.

Hospitality. Welcome but dangerous. Hospitality exposes you to concession by obligation.

Lunches, dinners, accommodation, services and facilities are widely used in business and diplomacy. They are a natural part of the furniture of social relationships. To refuse hospitality could be unhelpful, insulting and a cause of suspicion; to partake, especially at an overly generous level (and your host controls the level), could imply obligations that you feel, though they did not intend, and raise questions from your own people as to how objective your judgement is likely to be under a barrage of high living.

Hospitality can be used to weaken your resolve; to undermine your stamina (late nights, heavy drinking); to entrap you into indiscretion (and BLACKMAIL); to destroy your reputation. It can also be a genuine expression of a desire to do business together.

How do you know which it is? Follow some 'rules'. Insist on a reciprocity of equivalents – each side is hospitable to the other on the same basis. Tend to a lower level of hospitality than you are tempted to display. Do not socialize late at night, every night (they have an inexhaustible supply of people to keep you at it, while their negotiators rest). Strictly limit your consumption of food, drink and tobacco. Schedule your own meeting sessions for most evenings, so that you can refuse an invitation without offence because your habits have been established from the start. Insist on each negotiator meeting their own expenses in all matters ('both sides bear their own costs'). Cut down business lunches. They are mostly unproductive, expensive and disruptive of the afernoon's schedules. See people in working hours only.

Hostage negotiations. Terrorists take hostages either for material gain (cash) or political influence (publicity, revenge, humbling of an enemy, recognition, release of prisoners, change in policies). Each extortion aim has its own version of a common dilemma: if the demands are conceded, a spate of imitations can be expected; if the demands are not met, the hostages could lose their lives.

Governments are less likely to negotiate over conceding demands from terrorists for political influence than they are over demands for material gains. The former jeopardizes the political fabric, especially in democracies; the latter is mere criminality. Governments can tolerate a degree of criminality without collapsing, especially as the pay-off to the terrorists is with other people's resources (taxation), but extorting influence from a government trespasses on the most sensitive possession of a political elite – its monopoly of power.

The parties to a hostage incident have different preferences. The terrorist had different values from the government. The terrorist concedes that his opponent has higher humanitarian standards than his own, irrespective of the rhetoric used to justify their actions, for terrorism is only 'successful' if the target is more concerned about the welfare of the victims than is the terrorist. This is a paradox for those terrorists who are motivated by moral anger towards 'evil' targets; the more 'evil' they believe the target to be, the less they can hope for success, for if the target is likely to be 'soft' on the plight of the victims, it can hardly be all that evil.

The government is constrained by public reaction to its behaviour during a hostage incident. If it gives in to save lives, it is condemned as unfit to protect society from anti-democratic violence; if it refuses any deals with the terrorists, resulting in death or harm to the victims, it is condemned as unfit to protect its own citizens from the consequences of its own policies. In both cases, the government is on trial not the terrorists. The spectrum between the extremes of 'no surrender to terrorism whatever the cost' (Israel) and 'instant capitulation whatever the terms' (Austria) has been well covered since the modern spate of terrorism started in the 1960s. The dilemma for governments perhaps explains why increasingly they opt for military solutions (some successful – Entebbe, Mogadishu – some less so – Nicosia, Karachi).

The interests of the victims differs from those of both the terrorists and the government. Their immediate interest is in survival. Behaviour conducive to survival is also their best strategy: a victim has no option. Advice about handling the role of victim includes: keep a low profile, show no dissent, do not argue with their beliefs, do not attack them, express no views, do not cause offence and show no impatience at all. If the hostage group is small enough (a dozen or less) there is a possibility of the 'Stockholm Syndrome' emerging, i.e., a bonding relationship between the terrorists and the victims. This can save lives. Making 'friends' in a larger groups risks identifying yourself as a sacrificial victim if the situation turns sour (needing somebody to execute they increase their commitment, and frighten a large group, by shooting you, for if they shoot their 'friends' they clearly will shoot anybody else).

Choosing to negotiate with hostage-takers involves agreeing on objectives: the release of the victims unharmed, the failure of the terrorists to extract concessions of substance, and dissuasion of imitators. In all of this prevention is better than cure.

Failing prevention, what are the options? Does having a public policy of 'no surrender' dissuade terrorists? Not on the evidence. Indeed, the very policy itself could attract hostage-taking, because if an incident can be devised that would shake even the most stubborn of enemies into producing concessions, the pay-off from breaking the 'no surrender' commitment is worth the risk (and the 'glory'). This creates a cycle of escalating incidents, as each horrific incident feeds the rationale of 'no surrender', and 'no surrender' attracts ever more fearsome challenges.

The tactical plays of both sides have become well established. The terrorists reinforce commitment by threatening to kill hostages. Initially, they set out their demands (which if ludicrously 'high', implies irrational and probably unstable people; if very 'low' implies media manipulators). They demand to communicate with high officials, they demand publicity, they set deadlines. Either, the deadlines are extended or they implement their threats.

The government can conduct the 'negotiations' (always a mistake) or leave it to the security forces (best if the rank of the official in communication with them is lowly). Time is required to find out about the hostage-takers (to choose the most appropriate psychological approach), and to plan intervention by force. The terrorists know this, but do not know for certain which policy the government is pursuing, so they impose short deadlines. They are constrained by the fact that shooting victims reduces the value of their threats (and gives the security forces a publicly acceptable reason for intervening by force at risk of other victims' lives).

Government tactics, operated by its security forces, include using time and isolation in tandem to undermine the terrorists' resolve to continue. Nothing should be done in a hurry, no matter what the threat, right from the start. Everything possible should be done to increase the feeling of normality in the immediate vicinity (don't close the airport, its continued functioning helps undermine the terrorists' feeling of self-importance). Here, the media could help (but seldom do). Batteries of TV cameras, news reports on radio, and general attention focusing on the area of the incident fuel the hostage-takers' sense of success and self-importance. It is also dangerous: long distance camera apparatus can be mistaken for a sniper's rifle. Only mentioning the incident on every other bulletin would help, rather than saturation coverage (not mentioning it at all for a day or so would be best).

Democracies are vulnerable here. Appealing to the media would help if government ministers refrained from commenting on the incident while it is under way; prime ministers with an urge to condemn the incident in public undermine the tactic of isolation. Making the hostage-takers important with ministerial statements can undo hours of careful work ('We never comment on incidents while they are happening' is a better public policy than 'No surrender'). Visiting the scene is absolutely counter-productive; announcing the US president's permanent residence in the White House until Iran released the embassy hostages removed what slim chance there was of an early release.

In summary: isolate the incident, downplay its significance, curtail (by self-denying ordnance) media coverage, engage in negotiations with the terrorists at a low level, make no moves in response to acts of violence, maintain flexibility of means to achieve firmly set goals. Remember, winning a hostage crisis is seldom an option (the fact that it occurs is a victory for the terrorists), and your overall objective is to minimize the costs of concluding it without encouraging repetition.

Hotels. No hotel in the world is always perfect every time. If the incident is serious, consider your remedy: what do you want done about it? Choose a remedy that is proportionate to the incident, within the gift of the management level you are dealing with, and present it without emotional outbursts or threats.

The remedy is your solution to the problem, not an alternative to taking your business elsewhere. This latter is not a devastating blow to the hotel (unless you have extraordinary bargaining leverage), for one person's lost business is hardly noticed. It is more productive to persuade management to agree to your remedy from a positive motivation to 'put things right', than from any fears they must disclose about losing your custom. People resist being seen to give into COERCION, doubly so when the expected damage of not doing so is minimal.

A missed morning call is worth a free taxi (going a reasonable distance); a long wait is worth a free drink; a poor meal is worth a brandy or port, or a discount; a broken TV is worth something off the bill (also check that the video is working, you pay for it even if you don't watch it); a lack of hot water is worth a discount; missing laundry is worth a replacement shirt/blouse/socks/stockings from the shop; noise in the corridor, or next door, is worth a discount. Note that the marginal cost of a hotel room is quite low compared to the room rate, and remedies that take money off the room rate are not difficult for the hotel to concede if they produce a satisfied customer.

Hotel purchase. Rule of thumb valuations of hotels are generally based on their proved income-earning capacities. One guide to value is the annual turnover (gross if selling; net of taxes if buying). Turnover shows the recent trade of the hotel, what it actually does, not what it could do under better management. If there are unusual considerations producing recent turnover, these influence the price.

If buying a hotel from a conglomerate, be wary of inflated turnover figures. Other divisions of the conglomerate could be under instruction to use the company's hotel services (overnight business trips, conference room and banqueting facilities, purchases of consumables through the hotel chain's central buying services and such like). Once sold to you, these purchases are no longer available.

When buying a hotel from a liquidator be wary of the trading accounts. The liquidator keeps the hotel open to sell it as a 'going concern', and therefore slashes all expenditures to the bone. This reduces cost of sales, and makes the potential profit look better than it is. Much that needs to be done to maintain a hotel in shape (repair and maintenance; cleaning) can be suspended for a short period. Once you acquire the hotel and take on these necessary tasks, their costs reduce the profits.

Be careful of taking over expensive equipment on lease and rental agreements undertaken by the previous owner. A liquidation is a liquidation; all bets are off. If you don't want the agreements, require them to be cancelled before you take over (and certainly refuse to pay for any money owing from the previous owner). The leasor can take his kit away (if he leaves it, you acquire it for nothing).

Your offer price is based on annual turnover plus stock at valuation (SAV). If you do not want the stock, or any part of it (check all 'sell by' dates on booze and supplies), separate it out and require its disposal. Consider changing brewers to avoid paying for unsold previous stocks. This reduces the cash price you pay. Try for a CONTINGENCY PRICE if you doubt the figures. If there are disposables (valuable furniture, spare land, spare buildings, associated rights) can you sell them to reduce the cost of purchase? (Don't disclose your intentions – the seller could apply your ideas.)

Hustle close. Pressure tactic.

- 'If you don't accept these terms, I will be unable to offer them again.'
- 'This plane is leaving right now. It costs 4 ounces of gold for the last seat, or you learn Vietnamese.'
- 'You know you'll never get a better deal than this one. If you don't take it right now, I'll ring off and call my lawyers.'

Counter: Compare the offer against your options: if better, take it; if worse, don't (see BEST ALTERNATIVE TO A NEGOTIATED AGREEMENT).

I

If. Most useful two-letter word a negotiator can use. PROPOSALS that begin with the words, 'If you . . .' are CONDITIONAL, and the conditions (what you require them to do) protect your proposal from being ambushed. If they do not accept your conditions, then you are free to amend, postpone, or withdraw your proposal.

Making proposals without prefacing them with 'If you . . .' generally exposes you to either a 'Yes, but' response ('yes, we'll take it but it's not enough') or to a straight 'No', which leaves you facing a series of additional concessions (and 'Yes, buts', or, 'Nos') until you have nothing more to give.

'I'm only a simple grocer'. Disarming tactic to relax negotiators into indiscretions about their objectives, tactics and hidden intentions.

You think you are dealing with a novice in the matter under discussion because he claims he is 'only a simple grocer', but in reality you are dealing with the owner of the world's largest grocery chain.

Watch out for other negotiators who make extremely modest claims for themselves. On hearing such claims it is not productive of your best interests to proceed to inform them of how much you know about the business you are in. That tells them more than enough to pitch their offers close to your RESISTANCE PRICE. In general, avoid giving unpaid seminars in the art and craft or your business in the middle of your negotiations with strangers – you might end up paying for the experience.

'I'm sorry, I've made a mistake'. Seller's tactic close to the ethics border.

You agree for a service with a seller. Later, she calls you and apologises but she has made a mistake in the arithmetic. Instead of the sundry parts being priced at 4.55 each, they are listed in the supplier's catalogue at 5.45 each and she did not notice this until she was placing your order for 1,000 of them. She cannot sell them below list prices as her superior will not authorize the order. The explanation is punctured with profuse and convincing apologies. You accept that the mistake was genuine and agree that she can adjust the total price accordingly. This claws back some of the discount you thought you had negotiated on your order.

You could cancel the order, and search for another seller. Depends on how you read the motives of the seller, how important the price mistake was against the total price, and how easy it is to find another seller. Most times busy buyers agree, albeit reluctantly, to the tactic. Sellers who learn this make 'mistakes', always in their favour.

Imports. Without which we would be poorer (see EXPORTS).
   Issues to negotiate with your supplier (the exporting company) include:

* Who bears the foreign exchange risk?
(Insist on all contract prices being dominated in your currency as these are the prices at which you sell the imports in your markets.)
* Who bears the cost of credit?
(Push this cost to the seller and pay as close to your sales activity as possible, or in arrears even.)
* Which price prevails: CIF, FOB or some other?
(Depends on the costs of shipping and insurance. Comparing CIF prices with market prices discloses your distribution costs and mark-up, which could encourage the exporter to set up in your country, sell to you from his own stock and develop rival distribution. If signing an AGENCY deal as an exporter, secure an OPTION to do this with notice, as it puts pressure on their resistance to your selling prices.)
* How is the exporter paid?
(By cheque? Good for extra credit if the cheque takes time to get back to your bank (hopefully, it is lost meantime). Try 'the cheque is in the post' ploy? Using banker's drafts and transfers speeds up payment process. Alternatively, use bills of exchange. They tie you down a little, as they are usually attached to the shipping documents, which are not released until payment is made, and have specific dates on them which restricts credit to a fixed term.)

Incentive. The carrot approach to motivation. Offer an incentive for measurable performance and some people respond. Incentive 'gifts' (a loosely termed euphemism for expensive staff presents) are a thriving industry as an aid to motivating effort from a jaded sales force. The gifts include holidays, household extras, 'executive selections' (pricey 'toys'), marketing aids, restaurant meals, weekend hotel breaks for two, car accessories and such like. Buyers' gifts cover a similar range but have to be more discreet if given to buying staff and not to the company.

see BRIBERY.

Incentive pricing. Encourage a supplier to produce efficiently. Recently popular in defence procurement where fixed price contracts for specialized products are common. Against a carefully monitored fixed price per unit bid, the supplier is encouraged to reap savings in unit costs. The savings are shared at some negotiated rate with the defence agency. The bid price is closely monitored to ensure limited opportunities for padding prices to create easy targets. Once all costs are covered, using break–even analysis, the savings are shared.

Indemnity. Expensive to buy; risky to do without.

Indemnity insurance is extremely expensive. Medical practicioners, architects, accountants, lawyers, engineers, brokers, bankers, consultants and anybody whose advice puts them at risk if somebody acts upon it are in the market for indemnity insurance as a protection against malpractice claims.

The premiums are high because malpractice claims are rife; they are rife because defendants are insured; they are insured because claims are high; claims are high because awards are high; they are high because claimants exaggerate distress; they do so because their risk is minimal; it is minimal because their lawyers are paid on a 'no award, no fee' basis; they make their money by pushing as many high value claims as they can; indemnifiers charge large premiums to offset the costs of fighting claims and the risk of high awards.

Potential defendants without indemnity insurance, and therefore no means of meeting damage beyond their personal wealth, are less attractive targets for claimants (except those bent on revenge). The concept of 'unlimited liability' for professional advisers was meant to concentrate their minds on the advisability of proffering advice. Indemnity insurance was invented to cover this risk. It is extremely expensive . . .

When should you sue? When the defendant has a means of

compensating you, or when your psychic satisfaction, net of your costs, leads you to prefer that he/she be inconvenienced (jail, bankruptcy) for your distress (see EMOTION).

When should you settle? When the confirmed offer is as good as, or better than, the amount likely to be awarded by a court net of your costs, including any contingency fees paid to lawyers (see DECISION ANALYSIS).

Information. Can help or hinder your negotiation.

Imperfect information is the norm, not the exception. It can be valuable, as when you discover how badly they need your consent and cooperation. Disclosing your needs can damage your stance.

In PREPARATION consider what information you have, what you need and where, or from whom, you can get it. Asking QUESTIONS and giving answers transfers information between the parties. Intelligence gathers information and manipulating the other side's intelligence sources (see dirty tricks) by rumours, leaks, misleading but credible stories, *agents provocateurs*, agents of influence and such like can assist in structuring their perceptions of what is possible.

Inhibition. Whatever it is that is preventing your agreeing to the PROPOSAL. You are concerned about aspects of the proposal, or the reliability of the proposers, or even what is motivating them, and this consideration inhibits you from agreeing.

Not quite the opposite of an INTEREST. Your interest may lie in keeping supplies moving to customers, your inhibitions may concern the cost of doing so under current manning levels. How can you overcome your inhibitions without jeopardizing your basic interests? Identifying the real nature of your inhibitions enables you to decide whether to present them openly to the other side and require that they be addressed in their proposals, or to leave them lurking about the discussions without being fully expressed while you present proposals that take care of them (without the embarrassment of declaring your 'prejudices'?).

Looking behind what people are saying gives you an opportunity to assess the nature of their inhibitions: they don't trust you, they are worried about precedent, they need to be paid quickly, they want to be more selective than the law allows – sexism, racism, ageism, etc. – they are frightened of publicity, they don't know if it works, and so on.

Addressing inhibitions means doing something for them in your proposals. Where inhibitions are embarrassing – people do not like to be too frank about their views on you, your creditworthiness, reliability or intentions – and you can see a way of meeting them discreetly (because it is in your interest to do so), incorporate your suggestion in your proposals. There is no point in berating them for not trusting you – TRUST is earned not imposed – or for their selfishness and prejudices. Business is business.

Integrative bargaining. Contrasts with DISTRIBUTIVE BARGAINING where the issues are perceived in ZERO-SUM terms.

Integrative bargaining is about searching for common solutions to problems that are not exclusively of interest to only one of the negotiators. It emphasizes the commonality of interests in conflict situations. It tries to reformulate distributive issues into integrative issues. For example, absenteeism could be a distributive issue if the management merely proposed a set of new disciplinary measures. Most employees, however, could discover that they have a common interest with management in reducing absenteeism: those employees who have to carry the burden of the absent employees' work load for instance.

Integrative bargaining leads to PROBLEM SOLVING. It cannot be set up in a distributive bargaining environment without PREPARATION (this would lead to exploitation of the negotiator trying to 'open' his approach). Considerable TRUST is required (earned not assumed), as is MOTIVATION to resolve problems this way. A mixture of distributive and integrative bargaining is more likely to be successful than an approach based totally on one or the other.

Interests. Not always obvious in a conflict. Views differ according to time perspectives: short-run interest (eat the seed corn to survive the winter) can conflict with longer-term interest (nothing to plant in the spring, starve in the summer).

Identifying interests is part of PREPARATION. Interests can be clouded by EMOTION, stress, prejudice, misunderstandings, confusion, lack of time to think clearly, misplaced optimism/ pessimism, temptation, weaknesses, over-ambition, lack of same, and sheer greed. Identifying your interests is hard work, all the more burdensome when your interests are in conflict with your feelings.

An interest is something that motivates you to say 'yes' or 'no' depending on whether the action is in support of your interests or contrary to them. You either perceive your interests and act accordingly, or you remain ignorant of them and therefore ignorant of the consequences of your action.

Interest rates. The price of money.

Varies widely to cover for the opportunity cost of money (how much you can get in an alternative lending activity); to cover for the risk involved (the greater the risk – 'who are you, what do you want it for, what is your record?' – the greater the premium of the interest rate); and to reflect its scarcity value for you (how badly do you want the money?).

Communist countries apply a fixed interest rate policy (usually 7.5 per cent). They do not recognize inflation and they seldom allow payments above their official rates. Some countries have religious strictures against payment of interest. They make 'administrative charges' instead.

International chamber of commerce. International organization with members in one hundred countries, aiming to codify trading standards and practice and to represent the business viewpoint to international forums, such as the United Nations, the European Community and the major trading countries. Sponsor of an international ARBITRATION system for commercial disputes, various standardization systems for trade, and commonality in contract provisions.

Interpersonal orientation(IO). Interaction between you and the other party.

You bring with you a lot of baggage: your history, your perceptions of the world and your place in it, your personality, your risk disposition, your style of behaviour, your assessment of your task and your expectations. Quite a bundle, and that is only you; there is the other negotiator as well.

"Negotiate? What is there to negotiate?"

J.Z. Rubin and B.R. Brown designed a format for looking at the basic interactions between two negotiators (*The Social Psychology of Bargaining and Negotiation*, New York, Academic Press, 1975). They divide people along a continuum according to their interpersonal orientation, or how responsive they are to other people, and how involved they prefer to be in how other people react to what is happening at the negotiation.

The negotiator who is responsive to the interpersonal relationship with the other side is said to have a high interpersonal orientation (a high IO), and to be sensitive and reactive to how the other people behave; the negotiator who is non-responsive to such relationships and is concerned only with his own interests and objectives is said to have a low interpersonal orientation (low IO).

People can also be described as being either competitive or cooperative. This produces another dimension along which varying combinations of both attributes can be placed (see figure 7).

The competitive negotiator with a high interpersonal orientation exploits cooperative negotiators. He is generally untrusting. The cooperative negotiator, high on interpersonal orientation (concerned with the personalities of other negotiators) resents being pushed around. He takes it personally and may opt for MARTYRDOM.

Two negotiators both with high interpersonal orientations who engage in cooperative behaviour are likely to PROBLEM SOLVE

Figure 7

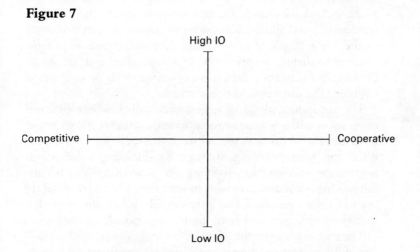

a dispute rather than see it as a ZERO-SUM negotiation. Personal relations between the negotiators are also likely to be warm.

The negotiator with a low interpersonal orientation is less concerned with the other person and aims to gain as much as he can without consideration of the other's behaviour. Such types do not take anything personally, believing that it is the balance of power pushing the other party to behave competitively or cooperatively (out of confidence or desperation). They work for their own interests and do not react to the other's behaviour. They can appear to be taking advantage of a cooperative stance and this has the effect on a person with a high interpersonal orientation described above.

Two negotiatiors with low interpersonal orientations have the same goal of maximizing their own interests. This delays settlement because moves are based on self-interest only. Finding the exact match of interests takes time, and as neither can generate bonds of TRUST (because this means involvement in the other person's behaviour), all movement is considered from a single perspective (self-interest) and not from identifying what interests the other might have and how these can be addressed. The low IO negotiator expects the other negotiator to look after his own interests and to be the best judge of them.

Obviously negotiators with a tendency towards a low

interpersonal orientation (a total absence of IO in all respects would be unusual outside a mental hospital) are not the best team members for a delicate and sensitive negotiation. They are useful in the early stages of a difficult negotiation (cease-fire, arms control, exchange of prisoners, and whenever you are under duress), but if relationships need to be warmed, or progress is required, the team should be switched.

The apparent manner of negotiators with low interpersonal orientation, offends some negotiators and causes breakdowns that have nothing to do with the substantive issues. While reserve is often the safest opening strategy for building a long-term negotiating relationship – coming on 'too strong' can be off-putting too – it is also necessary to have the ability to respond, to warm to other people as you interact with them, which is a characteristic of negotiators with high interpersonal orientations.

The choice between the COMPETITIVE and COOPERATIVE STYLE is less difficult than changing one's natural interpersonal orientation. Cooperative negotiators who meet negotiators with competitive styles soon learn to adjust appropriately. Competitive negotiators who lose business because of their attempts to exploit others, soon learn to modify their style.

Intimidation. Can be overt or covert. The overt form is close to gangsterism. It usually involves some form of COERCION. The covert form is more widespread but is less noticeable. It works almost entirely *through your own* mind. Like torture, the implied kind (running water, total silence, psychological softening-up techniques) can be as effective as the physical version. Covert intimidation is almost irresistible because of its subtlety. Most of the time you intimidate yourself because you make a snap judgement based on your deep-rooted conditioning.

You perceive a smartly dressed woman. Is she rich or poor? Rich. She orders a drink which the bar tender, after much effort, mixes correctly. Is she sophisticated or ignorant? Sophisticated. She sends it back after one sip. Is she easily pleased or fussy? Fussy. She waves away the bar tender's offer to re-mix it and sweeps out of the room. Is she rich or poor? Rich.

Yet she is none of these. She is broke and travels from bar to bar and gets a single sip of her favourite drink at each place without paying all night. (She also stole her clothes.)

Covert intimidation is possible because of the power of suggestion. It is the ultimate untested assumption. You see a rich and powerful person, dressed in a Savile Row suit, wearing Gucci shoes and a 200 dollar shirt and tie. Your expectations are confirmed. You negotiate with a bankrupt, wearing the same suit, shoes, shirt and tie and you assume he is rich and powerful. He plays on your prejudices and your associations: if the rich dress this way, then anybody dressed this way is rich. Right? Wrong!

People covertly intimidate because it works. Buyers intimidate the inexperienced because it gets them free concessions. They pretend to be busy; you perceive their hive of activity and assume that your time with them is short, too short for a long negotiation. So you jump a few steps, and start your price a lot closer to his TARGET than yours. Far from running out of time, you are running out of concessions.

Intimidation also arises from the context. Their offices are designed to intimidate: 'If they can afford such palaces they must be as sharp as shark's teeth. I'll have to go in low to get their business.' Meetings on the company yacht are fateful for the easily intimidated; being flown in by private jet can turn your PREPARATION upside down (and your stomach, which doesn't do much for your confidence does it?); and being asked if you flew first class when they know you didn't is a first class intimidator.

Counter: Examine your PERCEPTIONS; test your ASSUMPTIONS; don't fall for reverse association.

See INTIMIDATOR.

Intimidator. You may never know how you have been intimidated. Here are some well-worn intimidators:
- Uncomfortable seating, lower down than the other negotiator's.
- Poorly positioned seating, such as in a draught, facing the sun or its reflection, or in front of an open door through which other people can hear your conversation.
- You are kept waiting beyond your appointment time.
- During the negotiation the other party takes phone calls, speaks to the secretaries and colleagues and is looking at his watch.
- He tells somebody he will be free in a few minutes, and you have just started.

- He complains about your products or services, and your company.
- He praises the competition, and appears to know all your rivals by their first names (he keeps forgetting yours).
- He does not appear to be paying attention, nor is he interested in anything you say.
- He does not read your literature, won't cooperate by answering questions or stating his needs, and generally appears to be indifferent.

Intimidators are not examples of rudeness. They are aimed at forcing you to move further towards the other negotiator's target than you intended. Intimidators are applied by other negotiators because they work on the inexperienced.

K

Kidnap negotiations. May you be spared them.

The target of the kidnapper is coerced by the proposed fate of the victim, usually somebody close to the target (family, colleague), or a physical possession (painting, artefact, or revered symbol of something highly valued).

Kidnapping poses different problems to that of hostage-taking. For a start, the kidnappers' lair is not known; the forces of law enforcement are not deployed outside it. This gives the kidnappers a degree of flexibility in their choices of location, which they have had time to select and prepare. Knowing this, the security forces mount a detailed search for likely hiding places, unless they are out of reach, for example, in Beirut.

Secondly, communication between the kidnappers and the target is at the will of the kidnappers. There is no exclusive line opened between them and the authorities as there often is with an aircraft hijack.

Thirdly, the target is unable to manipulate the environment to isolate the kidnappers. The kidnappers may be stressed from their work, but they can rest at will by breaking off contact for a while. Kidnappers in constant touch with the target risk discovery by electronic means. Irregular contact (Italian style) reduces the risk of discovery (the police move on to other cases) and puts maximum pressure on the target. Lack of direct contact lets the kidnappers choose whether to continue the attempt of extortion or quit at will (which could mean killing the victim: about 20 per cent of kidnap victims are killed, whatever the outcome regarding the ransom).

The first decision for the target is whether to involve the authorities. Kidnappers, unlike terrorists, do not thrive on publicity. The most successful kidnappings are those that occur without publicity whatsoever. Where a kidnapping is for material gain (as most are), the public view appears to be hostile to a ransom being paid (if only to discourage the others). Interestingly, the media often cooperate with the police in not publicizing a kidnapping, sometimes until the victim is recovered and the kidnappers arrested. This enables the police to search for them without arousing suspicion that the target has gone to the authorities. The media seldom, if ever, cooperate to the same extent in hostage incidents that have political purposes, and where lack of publicity would deprive the terrorists of one of their main motivations.

The next decision is whether to meet the kidnappers' demands. This is a delicate problem. If the authorities are aware that a kidnapping is in progress, they must pursue the perpetrators because kidnapping is a crime; the target, aware of the vulnerability of somebody they care about, might prefer to settle with the kidnappers to secure the release of the victim. An individual can be intimidated into ignoring the legal jeopardy of the perpetrators of a crime; the state cannot.

The vulnerability of all kidnappers is acute at the point of the handover of the ransom: in order to hand over the ransom, the target has to know where and when to do so (and, by inference, so will the authorities – the kidnapper has no certain way of knowing whether they are involved or not, unless they have somebody on the 'inside'). Much ingenuity has been displayed, in the real world and in fiction, in trying to solve the handover problem.

The handover problem assumes that the target agrees, or is in a position to agree, to pay the ransom. Laws exist to prevent the paying of ransom, indeed, the entire assets of a target can be frozen to prevent it. These laws can be circumvented if the target has access to resources outside the country (owners, for example, of a multinational business with assets in many countries are likely targets for this reason), and they can give instructions to their staff without compromising the details to the authorities.

It is important to be sure you are dealing with the people who actually hold the victim, because some callers will be bogus (use agreed codewords?). If interlopers have solved the handover problem, but do not hold the victim, they could get paid by you for nothing. Evidence that the victim is alive, or the property is intact, is demanded (photographs holding today's newspaper?) in return for cooperating to pay the ransom, but most evidence is unreliable and, anyway, may be refused.

It is possible to insure against kidnapping. Multinational companies insure their key personnel from abduction if they visit, or work, in certain regions of the world. This insurance market is not always approved of by the authorities, though respectable companies can argue that they only insure their people in foreign territories where the problem is rife and where the local police are unable to help. The authorities are particularly unhappy about those organizations which insure the ransom fee and even arrange to negotiate with the kidnappers and pay it over if required. The authorities may well be involved at the target's end of the drama, but be unaware of what is happening independent of the focus of the drama.

This form of anti-kidnapping 'insurance' can go into effect without incriminating contact between the insurers and the target if there are legal complications (threats to sue the target, freezing of all domestic funds etc.). The insurer could be in a different country, or have offices abroad. Of course, knowledge of a target who has both a vulnerability to a kidnapping and 'insurance' cover of the sort mentioned is, in the eyes of the law, and surely in common sense, a temptation to potential kidnappers. The parallel pay-off arrangements solve the handover problem, assuming the 'integrity' of the insurer is accepted by the kidnappers (a record of handling kidnappings without recourse to intervention by the authorities establishes their reliability from a kidnapper's point of view).

Killer line. The killer line shakes your confidence in your proposal. High pressure killer lines that put you on the spot might include:

- 'You'll have to do better than that.'
- 'Never mind the waffle, give me your best price.'

You think to yourself, 'He would not say that unless he had a better price from somebody else', so you move. One sentence got him a major concession, so he will probably try a few more 'killers' to see just how soft you are on price. If he does it to you he is doing it to your competition (assuming you have any), and you are into a PRICE WAR or DUTCH AUCTION. In fact, you may not have any competition at all and be bidding downwards against yourself!

Counter: Seek more information. What other proposals has he received? Are they comparable or is it APPLES AND PEARS? If he has a better price or proposal, why is he bothering negotiating with you? (Do not believe it's because he 'likes' you?) Either there is something in your proposal he likes, which means your proposal is different and therefore worth its alleged price premium, or he is just prospecting with a price challenge. Before negotiating, think about your reaction to the killer line.

See INTIMIDATION.

Killer question. Like a killer line, a confidence shaker. Such questions put you on the spot. Answer 'Yes' or 'No' and you could be in trouble.

- 'Is that your final offer?'

'Yes' ends the negotiation (so if you want a negotiation to continue don't ask this question). If you state that your current proposal is final, you can hardly make another offer without destroying your credibility (he is bound to be sceptical about your FINAL OFFER if you keep making new ones). 'No' undermines the credibility of your current proposal, because this tells the other negotiator that you have other (better for him) proposals. His next question is going to be: 'Well, what is your final offer?'

- 'Is that proposal negotiable?'

'Yes' opens the negotiation on your next proposal. You have moved in response to a question. 'No' ends the negotiation (don't ask this question if you want a negotiation to continue).

Counter: 'My proposal is based on the informatioon and the circumstances as I understand them at present, but I am always willing to listen to new information or constructive suggestions that will improve the acceptability of my proposal.'

L

Last clear chance. Legal doctrine in the United States to assess who is to blame for an accident. Based on the identification of the party responsible for the *last* act that could have averted the accident. Even if both parties contribute to the accident, the one with the last clear chance to prevent it is culpable.

Applied to negotiating it is a coercive tactic. It appeals to public opinion to judge who is actually responsible for a damaging situation. To avert blame, if you are put into the position of having the last clear chance to avert the 'catastrophe' you have the unenviable choice of backing off or 'causing' it.

Examples abound: a union blames the hospital management for the closure of a ward and the discomfort of the patients; employees were sacked because they refused to work new duty rosters introduced by the management; the union calls a strike in defence of the sacked employees, not overtly against the new duty rosters and blames management for the consequences.

Possible counter: Let the men work the old rosters but announce they won't be paid until they work the new ones.

Terrorists blame a government for deaths in a hostage incident. The deaths arose because the army stormed the aircraft after the terrorists refused to surrender. In the shoot out a dozen innocent passengers were killed. The terrorists claim that the passengers were killed because the army attacked the aircraft.

Possible counter: Only use the army if the terrorists kill a hostage.

Law. Best observed. Especially when inconvenient.

The rule of law is preferred to the rule of men. For every victim of an unjust law, there are many more victims of unjust conduct. Without the rule of law contracts would be unenforceable, property rights would be meaningless, promises would not be kept, threats would be arbitrary, and lives would be in jeopardy.

While laws exist almost everywhere, they differ considerably in scope, principles and application. Common law exists in most countries of Anglo-Saxon tradition, code law in countries with European continental traditions, Islamic law in countries of the Muslim faith, and local, or tribal law in others. Alongside these law systems, there are various degrees of supranational law (European Community laws, United Nations recommended laws, and other internationally agreed legal instruments, such as the Uniform Law on the International Sale of Goods). Trading across different legal systems is perilous when things go wrong. Whose law applies? The INTERNATIONAL CHAMBER OF COMMERCE provides a useful service in trying to establish agreed principles of CONTRACT LAW for internatonal trade.

Lease. Alternative to ownership. Advantageous when:
- Acquisition costs are beyond reach.
- Tax regimes favour them.
- Political regimes are unstable.
- Partners are unreliable.
- Expropriation is likely.
- Site desired but owner won't sell.

Consider the following points when negotiating a lease agreement (whether as lessee or lessor: if the former, loosen them, if the latter tighten them)
- Who is the agreement between?

Watch for 'dummy' companies and 'nominees'; require details of registered offices; declaration of non-nominee status – if falsely declared, REVERSION applies: lease reverts with no compensation and without prejudice to money owed.
- Who is guaranteeing the lessee's obligations?

If lessee fails to meet obligations, reversion clause applies (unexpired lease is not an asset of a bankrupt company).
- What exactly is being leased?

Full description, complete with scale floor plans and location.
- How much is the rent?
- When is it paid?

Monthly, quarterly, annually; in advance or in arrears?
- Is there a premium?

On what basis? For the 'fixtures and fittings', for the 'availability' of the lease?
- How long is the lease for?

Months, years, effectively for ever (999 years)? Exact date it commences (on final completion of the legal technicalities, and when all due monies paid?). Exact date it ends. Can it be extended? On whose initiative is it extendable?
- When are rent reviews scheduled?

Every year, three years, or five years? What criteria apply: cost of living, valuation and yield of similar properties? How are disputes settled? Choice of arbitrator(s)?

- Is the direction of the rent review 'upward only'?
- Is there a 'rent free' period?

How long? Who pays other charges during this period?

- What service charges is the lessee liable for?
- Who pays the rates?
- What liability has the lessee for repairs?

Is it a Full Repairs and Insurance lease? Both internal and external repairs? What access does the lessor have for inspections? Who specifies extent of repairs and choice of contractor?

- What insurance obligations must lessee meet?

Full costs of restoring building in event of fire, explosion, accidental impact? How must lessee demonstrate insurance cover? Who decides whether insurance is sufficient, or insurer-acceptable?

- Can lessee sub-let?

With lessor's consent ('not unreasonably withheld')? Prohibited? On what terms? Within what duration of the lease (rent review period only)?

- Can lessee assign lease?

With lessor's consent only? For a share of the sale of their interest in the lease? Upside: finds a new tenant for you. Downside: prevents you from selling a new lease on the open market for gain. If right to assign given exclude right if lessee in breach of any obligations (reversion clause applies).

- On what terms can lessee surrender the lease?

Payment in full for unexpired rental period? Payment of some proportion, including insurance of building until new tenants take over? Payment of your legal and other costs acquiring new tenants? Certainly, require payment of all outstanding monies as well as above.

- Who pays legal costs of the transaction?

Tenant? Each side bears their own costs? Taxes? Common costs?

- What obligations does tenant have to planning regulations?

'Change of use' restrictions, whether imposed by the planning authorities or the lessor, are not grounds for surrendering lease without penalties. If new regulations applied during the tenancy, who pays for them?

- What obligations does tenant have to the building's fixtures and fittings and to their good care and upkeep?
- What notification must lessee give of intentions to make any alterations to the building, and who decides if the alterations may be made?
- What official regulations must the lessee meet during the tenancy?

Fire certificates, prohibitions on storing dangerous or toxic chemicals, prohibitions on certain dangerous or illegal (or disreputable?) activities, compliance with all laws regarding occupation and use of the building, official cubic space per person employed, refraining from causing a nuisance or obstruction of any kind and such like. Reversion clause to apply for serious or persistent minor breaches at lessor's discretion.

Note: When considering leasing or purchasing a property, remember that the yield on a property might be low, but the yield on paying a lease is zero.

See RENT; RENT REVIEW.

Lendability factor. Briefly, a subjective judgement (by the lender, not yourself) of:

- Your character – are you trustworthy with other people's money?
- Your record – what your recent past shows.
- Your proposition – what the money is to be used for (how it increases your NET WORTH).
- Your terms – what's in it for the lender?

Your negotiating position could be dependent on your lendability factor. To improve it you must improve the subjective assessments people are likely to make of you.

Start with your 'character'. This is an elusive concept to deal with. Your past provides inconclusive evidence of your character, as demonstrated by the number of people with unblemished records who run off with the company's money, or the country's secrets. So some past dubious behaviour need not preclude your being adjudged a good risk if you can convince the lender that it is in the past and not likely to recur.

If you have a good record, maintain it. If you prefer that your record is not examined too closely, improve on it by mending your ways immediately. The present is about to become your recent past. Build up a good record of paying back debts, no matter how trivial.

If you are running behind a repayment schedule, inform the lender immediately you realize this is likely to happen, what is causing it and what you intend to do about it. Lenders notice when payments are overdue. They worry about surprises. They worry about borrowers who neglect to keep them informed.

Regard all financial obligations as personal obligations. Don't ever hide behind legal technicalities to escape your obligations. Lenders, out of self-protection, warn each other about crooks they've dealt with and smart asses who have tried to rip them off. Data banks list honest people who are merely incompetent at managing their money. You prefer not to be in either category.

Lenders are nosey. Unless you are rich and powerful, and able to tell lenders to mind their own business, they consider the best way to mind their own business is to mind yours.

What do you want the money for? The more convincing your answers (see PREPARATION), the more likely you are to get the money. Draw up a plan showing what you intend to do with the money, including your outgoings and incomings over the period of the loan, and how the loan fits within your general business. This shows that you are serious. The lender can also spot flaws in your plan (which you ought to know about) and give advice (lenders love giving advice, free – it's their money!).

Lenders want to know what is in it for them, how secure you are for the loan, when and how you intend to pay it back and the interest you pay meantimee.

Sellable assets are security against a loan. If you default, they sell your assets. But sellable assets are not enough. Repossession is a messy business. There may be legal complications with more than one claimant in pursuit of the same sellable assets. Lenders look at how your future earnings from the use of their money generates the wherewithal for repayments.

Letter of credit. Facilities foreign trade (see EXPORTS: documentary credits).

Terms are negotiable. If exporting, require the importer to open a credit with your bank for the value of the goods plus the agreed extras (CIF or FOB). Require it to be:

- Confirmed
importer's bank guarantees payment on production of appropriate shipping documents.
- Irrevocable
to prevent importer refusing payment on any pretext.
- Transferable
to enable you to endorse it for other transactions.
- Divisible
to enable you to use it for part payments on other deals.

If importing, require the exporter to accept a letter of credit that is payable when the goods have been delivered and have passed your inspection (and, therefore, is revocable). Trade this for transferability and divisibility, which are direct benefits to the payee.

Practice varies, and reflects the balance of power. Some exporters can enforce payment of a letter of credit before the goods have been despatched (a unique concept of a 'shipping document'!); some importers can insist on payment long after documentation is supplied that clears the goods as 'inspected'.

The wording of a letter of credit is absolutely crucial, and should be scrutinized carefully. A glance at case law on disputes over letters of credit should keep you awake at night.

Level up the work, level down the price. No two BIDS are the same. If they are, suspect collusion. Each quotation includes different commitments and features. List all these commitments and features along the top row of a sheet of paper; list the suppliers in a column down the left-hand side. Now enter in the columns and rows which quotations include which commitments and features.

Select the total commitments and features that you prefer. This is your 'levelled-up specification', incorporating the majority of the commitments and features offered by all the suppliers.

Ask the suppliers to offer the levelled-up specification at or below the lowest priced quotation. This is your 'levelled-down price'. Some might drop out and not re-bid. Others might re-bid but move up on price. If anybody re-bids and meets the levelled down price, consider awarding them the contract (but beware of BLOCKING BID).

Leverage. Bargaining power. Important to know what leverage you have, even if you choose not to apply it.

Example: You own the only strip of land that gives a developer access to his site. Almost anything that you have discretion over gives you leverage. Petty officials with petty discretion slide into petty corruption by exercising their leverage. In West Africa if you need an official to stamp or sign a form, you'll hear 'Dash me, man', or its local equivalent elsewhere, which means pay them something, or wait.

Who has leverage?

• Air traffic controllers at holiday time when the skies are crowded.

• Construction workers when a project is time-critical (Olympic stadia).

• Exhibition workers when it is due to open.

• Stage hands just before the show.

• Advertisers when TV companies have spare slots.

• TV companies when prime time slots are full.

See CBP.

Counters: Not easy, otherwise it isn't leverage.

• Raise the stakes:

sack the air traffic controllers;

cancel the event;

lock out strikers for twice as long as they strike;

ban advertisers for six months;

switch channels, or media.

• Lower the stakes:

reward negotiators who do not apply leverage unfairly;

negotiate at times other than when leverage can be applied (outside holiday times, before projects commence, in between shows; do not exploit own leverage);

reward advertisers who pay full rates with prime time preference slots;

reward TV companies who give preference with off-peak bookings.

Licence agreements. See PATENTS AND LICENCES.

Lifeboat clauses. When you need a lifeboat, you need a lifeboat! Gives some protection when buying:

. . . this offer is contingent on the veracity of all statements made by the seller in respect of the proposed sale, including all statements regarding performance, quality, availability and specifications, and approval of the buyer of all matters relevant to the purchase, whether presently known or not, and any other material facts that may affect the buyer's interests.

The last phrase gives you an almost unlimited 'out'. If you find it in your interests to jump into your lifeboat.

Lifetime costs. Forget them at your peril. Remember the acquisition cost is only part of the story. How much does it cost to maintain the purchased item or service?

Serials issued over time cost a lot more than a single purchase. Publishers issue glossy serials in weekly parts ('how to cook', 'how to repair'; 'history in pictures', 'nature in all its wonders', 'space for beginners' and so on), charging a couple of dollars a part. Gross up the cost of 50 or 100 parts, and you pay a price for an unbound book that you would never pay for a perfectly bound one.

Military aircraft and major weapon systems, especially integrated command and control systems, have lifetime costs several times the original purchase. Once the costs of training, retraining, updating, operating, servicing, repairing, maintaining and supplying with spare parts are considered, the unit acquisition price can rise from ten million to 20, 30, 40 million. Indeed, competitive pressures can be so severe that aircraft companies reduce the acquisition cost per aircraft below production cost to secure the contract, and make their profit from the after-sales costs.

Motor vehicles (spare parts), computers (software, disks, paper and parts), copying machines (paper), telecommunications (extra facilities, call charges), are among other products that can be purchased on this basis.

A purchase order is also a commitment to future costs, so look for the extent of these costs. Not only might it show the purchase to be unwise (a useful test of a proposal's robustness), but it might indicate areas for negotiating better deals. For example, maintenance charges for computers are based on a percentage of the purchase price. If a computer system costs 10,000 to acquire and it has a maintenance charge of 15 per cent per year, in four years you have paid 6,000 in total to ensure that their product functions properly. In the unlikely event that they do 6,000 worth of maintenance, you are in effect paying 60 per cent more than you first paid.

Limits. The point where it is not worth your while to do business on the offered terms.

Determine your limits in PREPARATION (but see BEST ALTERNATIVE TO NEGOTIATED AGREEMENT). They help organize your choice of OBJECTIVES, because your MUST GETS represent your limits.

Your limit price for a property must be set where the prospective yield (net of management costs) from the property (rents etc.) is equal to the servicing of your acquisition costs. Even if the property is bought clear of borrowings, the alternative earnings from using your capital in some other project must not exceed your yield, otherwise you are managing your capital less efficiently than is possible, and in the extreme, perhaps, you are consuming your capital (see DEBT SWAMP).

Establishing your limits in this way improves your preparation for a LEASE negotiation. If you can raise the net yield from tenants above the market cost of capital, you can cover what you paid for the property. Determining your limit price on the basis of the likely yield and the cost of capital improves your preparation for a purchase negotiation: you know how far you must go to remain commercially viable.

Linking. Opens up bargaining possibilities.

Presented with a list of demands, or an offer with more than one element, you must decide how to handle the total proposal: do you deal with each issue separately by treating each one as a distinct mini-negotiation, or do you link them together on the basis that 'nothing is agreed until everything is agreed'?

Separating the issues has one advantage: it narrows the items in dispute as each item that is agreed is put to one side. This can block off obstructive tactics by one or more parties who hold out for concessions in one area favourable to them for agreement in other areas favourable to others. The 1980 negotiations on independence for Zimbabwe chaired by the British Foreign Secretary applied the separation tactic to stop the rival guerrilla groups, and the then Rhodesian government, using brinkmanship to force agreement to their individual ultimatums.

Narrowing the areas of disagreement has a singular disadvantage: the outstanding issues are normally highly contentious (that is why they are outstanding), and this leaves very little room for movement by the parties. In contrast, the settled issues may have been settled 'too quickly', curtailing opportunities for additional movement on them or related TRADABLES. By separating the issues, you could be restricting yourself when you come to deal with the contentious items.

By linking the issues you acknowledge areas where you can get agreement, but agreement is 'subject to agreement on all the issues'. They are set aside in reserve and are drawn into the negotiation when you are stuck elsewhere. For example, you are stuck on the size of a payment for an aspect of a total service, but you have already agreed on the level of payment for another aspect of the service. By linking the issues you could say: 'If you are prepared to raise my fee for searching for suitable investments, I am prepared to accept your offer of only 5 per cent of the value of all investment opportunities you take up.'

Linking is much more complex to conduct than single issue bargaining. Skill in SUMMARIZING all the various strands is valuable at any time, but it is at a premium in a linked negotiation.

Liquidity. Highly desirable when you need it, expensive when you don't! (See CASH.)

Assets have varying degrees of liquidity. Cash is instant liquidity in its own country, less so when held abroad (and not at all if it is mickey mouse money from a soft currency country – it's also probably illegal to possess it). It does not earn interest and holding large sums is expensive in foregone earnings. It is also risky (thieves, fire, flood, carelessness).

Money in a bank with instant access during banking hours is almost as good as cash. If your operation is large enough, the electronic money age can give you almost 24 hours' liquidity: small sums at bank cash dispensers, large sums by signal to whichever country has its banks open at that moment and in which the payee has an account.

Saleable property has a relative liquidity depending on how long it takes to complete the transaction. This does not preclude paying in kind, as long as you can transfer the title speedily (a notorized bill of sale; sometimes mere possession, if it can be enforced).

Listening. Least successful skill of the below-average negotiator. Could be the only CONCESSION the other party require: they want somebody to listen to their views, respect them and take account of them, but don't expect more than that.

Messages sent are often not received in the way they were intended (see COMMUNICATION). People are poor listeners; even if the message is heard clearly, recall deteriorates rapidly as time passes.

Listening to what a negotiator says is hard work. Experiments show how difficult it is to recall accurately even vivid messages, let alone routine ones. Take two people: ask the first to tell the second about something she feels strongly about (choose any controversial subject) for two minutes; ask the second to take the contrary view for two minutes; ask the first to report to you as observer what the second person said; ask the second to report to you what the first person said; report on how accurate were their versions of each other's statements.

How to improve listening:
- Pay attention.
- Ask questions for clarification.
- Summarize the statements to the satisfaction of the speaker.
- Don't interrupt.
- Avoid composing your rejection of what they are saying while they are saying it.
- Cease anticipating what they are about to say (you miss the surprises).
- Don't judge the message by the messenger.
- Treat their statements with respect.
- Avoid reacting emotionally to views you find distasteful or otherwise disagreeable.

How to help listening:
- Speak clearly and for short periods only.
- Summarize your points.
- Answer questions briefly.
- Avoid diluting your stronger points with weaker points that divert attention from your main message.

Loans. Against COLLATERAL, they are sensible; to friends without collateral, less so.

It makes sense to borrow other people's money for wealth-creating purposes only (see NET WORTH); it never makes sense to borrow (or, indeed, to lend) for income purposes.

In considering the making of a loan, calculate an interest charge and the rate at which the capital is paid back (see BALLOON). Ask: 'What if the borrower cannot meet these obligations?' Can you (would you) call in the loan? If you can't (ETHICS) decide whether to give the money and forget payment back, or whether to lend at all.

Why are they borrowing from you (assuming you are not a banker) when facilities exist to borrow from professional bankers? Is it the risk? If so, why can you take a risk that bankers decline? Is it the amount?

Can you cover yourself by taking an EQUITY stake?

Lock-out. Supposedly management's answer to strikes: the company locks out the employees by refusing them work until certain conditions are met (often a return to 'normal working' if disruption is being experienced, or a willingness to undertake specified duties that are being refused, such as a change in schedules, or similar working practices).

Disruptive union tactics can be countered by a lock-out, either selectively of individuals (usually provoking a strike by everybody) or collectively of the entire workforce. Unions pursue disruptive tactics either because they wish to limit the dispute for the moment, or because they are not sure of the support for an all-out strike. Those continuing in work can be levied to pay the wages of those sent home without pay for carrying out union instructions. A dispute can be prolonged for months by this tactic, causing more problems for the company than it does for union members. Where a minority of key personnel are involved the cost can be enormous (computer staff can be kept out for months, forcing the company to manage by manual systems).

Should the company increase the costs on the employees by sending the entire workforce home? Yes, if this is likely to bring a speedy end to the dispute by forcing a more realistic negotiating stance on the employees who suffer immediate income cuts. But disputes have a life of their own. They can slide into intransigence (see MARTYRDOM), even when rationally everybody has much to gain from compromise.

Alternatively, can the system cope by adapting to the loss of key staff and functions and thus isolating those whose labour has been withdrawn, while imposing levy costs on the rest?

Lose – lose. It happens. Neither party can find a compromise, either because they insist on the other moving only, or because there is no settlement range in their respective positions. (See BARGAINING CONTINUUM.) DEADLOCK ensues. Insisting on winning means they both lose.

Low balling. American term for 'come-ons'. A close relative to SWITCH SELLING tactics, with a touch of ADD-ON.

'A month in the sun from 100', says the holiday advertisement. That's for a tent, 5 miles from the beach; the hotel room is 500 a week.

'Hire a truck for 30 a day', says the advertisement. Fuel and mileage are extra; so is a usable size of truck.

The tactic is widely used in construction contracts. The tender price is low to win the BID, and then the claims department gets to work to charge extras for every single minor or major change (some companies employ more people in the claims department than they do as estimators).

Counter: Experience; a nose for phoney wordage in an advertisement that includes weasel words: 'from', 'like', 'helps', 'probably', 'feels like', 'as good as', 'virtually', 'acts like', 'as much as'; spot the SIZZLE.

M

Major sacrifice gambit. A tactic that manipulates the PERCEPTIONS of the other negotiator.

Having decided on a traded concession, you want to make the most of it. You refer to its 'significance', its 'high value', its 'emotional overtones' and so on. You build up as a major concession as credibly as you can:

'For us to give up this demand, we have had to search long and hard at our consciences. Our people will be extremely sceptical of our actions and we will have to work very hard to convince them that the sacrifice has been worthwhile.'

If they believe you, they are obligated to understand your difficulties. They might offer to help in some way (another concession on another issue?). They will certainly not push too hard in case you find the sacrifice unbearable. (See NO PROBLEM.) Suggest an area where they can compensate you for your heroic sacrifice.

Management fees. An alternative to the ownership of capital assets, which are at risk of expropriation, destruction and deterioration. You can propose a contract to manage the assets on their owner's behalf, or to provide a service which the client prefers not to supply himself.

Fee income is calculated on 'what the market will bear', consistent with a minimum level to cover actual costs. Consider a mining company operating in a foreign country. When it arrived to develop a mining concession it merely paid the titular authorities a royalty per unit extracted. In time, the authorities required more (their sons went to Western universities and learnt about monopoly rents and marginal costs). The royalty was increased. Eventually, joint ventures were set up (they put up the permission, you put up all the capital), and then expropriation followed.

Disaster was avoided because you have the technical knowledge and the marketing and distribution business outside of the country with the minerals (therefore, safe from further nationalization). Your new partnership involves your managing the extraction process for a fee (roughly equivalent to your net added value from the previous regime), and the government getting nationals trained in the processing part of the operation. Their ambitions are obvious, but their realization is not likely to be immediate.

The benefits of a management fee in these circumstances include your no longer having large capital projects at risk, nor do you have to fund them. This is down to the country that hires your services. Also, your net earnings are equivalent to your previous earnings, without the capital commitment. Your profitability looks better (and without the hassle of ownership, it feels better).

From the other side, looking at management fees is a daunting task. By definition, if you had the resources yourself (technology, trained people, access to distribution) you would do it yourself, but not having them, you are vulnerable to the management services company setting a fee structure which you cannot audit for value. If the fee exceeds the expected profit from managing the extraction process, you cannot replenish depreciated equipment (watch world prices). If the fee is squeezed down, the managers might depart, leaving you with inefficiently managed assets. Your longer-term strategy is to acquire expertise in managing through your own people (scholarships in technology to Western universities; work place training by the managers); meanwhile, your interests are met by pushing the fees down towards competitive rates by using a tender system for the BIDS for the management contract.

Management fees are not confined to overseas mineral agreements. Conglomerates charge subsidiaries a central management fee (sometimes much resented). A subsidiary that is barely breaking even within a conglomerate could become profitable under the local management freed from the burden of the management fee. This forms the basis for management buy-outs. The conglomerate frees itself from the capital charges of the subsidiary and applies the capital to a different venture, thus raising its overall rate of return. Alternatively, the conglomerate could be imposing high management fees to soak up otherwise taxable profits from its subsidiaries and to place its main tax liability where the tax regime is more favourable.

Mandate. Limits your authority.

Discretion is a heavy responsibility. If exceeded in the view of those to whom you are accountable, it can cause considerable problems, even to the point of repudiation of what you agreed.

Employees often require their representatives not to accept any proposal from the company without full reference back to them for approval. They also mandate their representatives to demand a particular item and to accept nothing less than the mandated demand. This ties the hands of the employee negotiators. It may be a tactic to enhance commitment; it may be an absolutely immovable stance taken because feelings are high, or because determination is complete.

How can you handle a mandate demand? Not by conceding it merely because the representatives have imposed a mandate, not unless you want to be on the receiving end of lots of other mandate demands (see SKINNER'S PIGEON). Is the mandate a commitment tactic? If you believe it is, treat it like any other commitment tactic (counter-commit in a reverse 'chicken'? see COMMITMENT TACTICS). Is the mandate solid evidence of the true feelings of the employees? If it is, treat it like any other expression of feeling; firmly, though gently, but with a regard to your INTERESTS.

Mandates are akin to 'chicken'. They restrict the negotiator from accepting less than the demand. But whether you accept the demand is not based on presentation format; not all mandate demands survive the first refusal.

Market. The only human creation which does not discriminate on the basis of sex, religion, status, race, religious or political belief, location, history or intention. No matter who you are, how you feel, how anybody else feels about you, or what you do, the market is neutral.

The market processes information about prices. It can be extensive in a global sense or localized. It signals discrepancies in wants and the means to meet them. It does this without central or any other kind of direction. It is robust to interference (though not indefinitely), irrepressible for long periods (though not in the short term), and everywhere it is pervasive across language, cultural and ethnic barriers.

The imperfections of markets (in terms of the economists' models of perfect competition) create the need for negotiation, for though the market signals a price, that price is the result of infinite adjustments by people to their perceptions of demand and supply. Many of these adjustments are contradictory –

people sell when they should hold on; buy when they should desist; do neither when they should do both. In fact, the constant adjustment of the market, its impermanence for more than a few seconds, its uncertainty about the future, make negotiating its ideal instrument.

Martyrdom. Never underestimate the ability of human beings to take courses of action that are clearly detrimental to their best interests. Do not assume that rationality in calculation of net benefits is a universal trait of everybody with whom you negotiate.

Negotiators can react irrationally, even suicidally, to a proposal. They know from the start that they are going to lose, but their defiance is fed by their emotions not by their intellect. Martyrdom has many comforts for the defiant, the desperate and the dedicated, which far outweigh the personal sacrifices it requires.

Threatening somebody spoiling for martyrdom plays into their hands. The underdog suddenly receives a new lease of life, and public sympathy. True, they could also be shown up to be a clown. Take care how you handle martyrs. They can be exasperating: they can also be dangerous and expensive.

Mediation. Shares a blurred boundary between ARBITRATION and negotiation.

Negotiators can get stuck in DEADLOCK, when in fact both of them want to find a settlement. Yet neither of them can move because the costs of doing so, which may be entirely psychic (loss of face etc.), exceed the immediate benefits. A mediator finds a 'safe' way for each side to make movement. Unlike an arbitrator, the mediator does not enforce movement; unlike a negotiator, the mediator does not trade movement; the mediator exposes to each negotiator the possibility of movement without being specific.

The negotiator must have private access to both negotiators for confidential discussions on the whole range of positions that the negotiators, in a variety of situations, would be prepared to adopt. In effect, the mediator is trying to establish whether there is a bargaining range. The mediator is not immediately concerned with the justice of each negotiator's position – how 'fair' or 'reasonable' it is, or how much it corresponds to the 'facts' (another distinction with the role of the arbitrator?) – though he may point out to a negotiator that their proposal contains a serious obstacle to its acceptance, because the other negotiator might perceive it to be 'unfair', 'unreasonable' or contrary to the 'facts'. It remains the responsibility of the negotiator whether to pursue a proposal.

The mediator facilitates agreement by determining whether agreement is possible, and confiding that conclusion to both sides, without revealing his views on what the settlement might contain:

'Friends, I have considered everything each of you has told me in confidence. I have looked at the situation from both points of view, and I have concluded that a negotiated agreement is possible if you try again. It is not for me to decide the content of that agreement, but what I can say is that I have held discussions with each of you in specific areas of your general positions, which if you spend some time reconsidering, you might find it possible to explore with your colleague whether there is a way out of what appears up to now to have been an impasse.'

Of course, the mediator may come to the opposite conclusion: that no matter how hard the negotiators try, given their declared confidential positions, no agreement is possible without one or both completely re-evaluating their minimal expectations. This conclusion at least has the virtue that the negotiators will not waste time seeking an impossible solution by negotiation. They can try arbitration or litigation.

Mediators achieve more by being firmly in charge of the process of dispute settlement but totally distant from the content, including neither deliberating upon nor judging the merits of the issues. The mediator should set the rules of the debate for the negotiators: non-interruption of what one person says ('your turn comes later'; non-exclusion of any option from the list of possible solutions ('any option can be put forward for discussion, no option is agreed just because it is discussed'); no negotiation until all the views of each side have been expressed.

The mediator may ask each negotiator to verify to the other the basis of their facts and claims, and to reveal the basis upon which they consider their proposed solutions should be acceptable to the other. Having demonstrated this method of assessing the accept-ability of a proposal, the parties may begin to require of each other (and themselves) a similar exposition before insisting on a decision about a proposal.

Mediators must be careful not to get involved in the fighting, not to take sides, nor appear to be doing so.

Memorandum of understanding (or agreement) (MOU). Drawn up before a legal contract is drafted, mainly to bind the parties loosely together while additional details are sorted out. It outlines the intentions of the negotiators without finally binding them into an irreversible relationship.

It ought not to be important which of you writes the MOU. If it does matter, are you sure you should be doing business with them? Whoever writes it, read it carefully before signing. It does not need to be legally watertight, and to make sure that it isn't, insert a sentence: 'This MOU is subject to final contract'. Indeed, see that this sentence appears in all correspondence referring to matters covered by the MOU.

Minimum order tactic. Enhances the value of an order for the seller. If the buyer does not accept the minimum order terms, the seller claims he cannot supply:
- 'We only sell these in packs of six.'
- 'Our minimum order value is 200.'
- 'We do not supply the connector separately; you must buy the connector with the flexihose.'
- 'We only sell forks with knives.'
- 'If you want a size 7 wrench, you must buy the set.'
- 'If we represent you in the purchase of the building, we must also act as letting agents if you acquire it.'
- 'Our telephones come with our standard features. To add or remove features is impossible without substantial re-tooling.'
- 'We supply pump spares in comprehensive sets designed to cover for most eventualities, and not individually.'
- 'You can have a mortgage on the terms agreed but only if you take out insurance with our subsidiary.'
- 'Our house sale and purchase package cannot be broken into separate services: it is all or nothing.

Counter. Test the seriousness of the seller's unwillingness to

"US and Soviet officials agreed on five adjectives to describe the meeting – interesting, useful, frank, businesslike, productive – but failed to agree on any prepositions."

supply the partial service you require when you state your certain intention of choosing the alternative of no order at all.

Minutes. The keeping of formal records of everything that is said by negotiators is unusual, except in highly structured negotiations. The need for a detailed record undermines the flexibility of the negotiators. It is a bit like a legal caution: 'say anything you like, but we are taking down everything you say and might use it against you later'. This makes negotiators nervous of saying anything that they might later regret.

Minutes that record who was present, when and where the negotiation took place, and brief notes on the agenda which summarize each negotiator's main views are a step away from a too restrictive record. Any proposals that are made could also be mentioned, and anything agreed should certainly be recorded. Commitments to look at specific topics are worth noting too.

The weakness of detailed minute-taking is the inflexibility it induces; the pitfall of taking brief summaries is the suspicion of bias it creates. Summarizing a discussion about the terms of a lease is not easy even if you are neutral; when you are one of the players it is difficult to do to the complete satisfaction of the other negotiator. Don't succumb to the temptation to 'bend' the record to suit your own interests. They may fail to notice the alteration, but they are less likely not to notice its consequences. But when they do notice the alteration, you get the benefit of the doubt once, after that they are on guard. The acid test of confusion in minute-taking is: who gains from the 'error'? It is interesting that most mistakes in minutes benefit the side who wrote the minutes (as it is with mistakes in invoices).

Money. The ultimate TRADABLE.

If they accept what you offer as money (and money can consist of many things, from recognized currency to gold, to credit instruments), it performs the functions of money: a standard unit of account, a storable asset and a means for the final settlement of an obligation.

Mother Hubbard. Price pressure tactic: 'the cupboard is bare'.

Buyers challenge sellers' prices for obvious reasons, but if you have given a BUY SIGNAL it is difficult to do so in a FRONTAL ASSAULT. Buyers thus use the Mother Hubbard:

- Establish that you desire to buy, but . . . they are in sight of a firm order, and know you are not a 'don't wanter'. They will attempt to re-sell by demolishing your OBJECTION. Remain firm.
- Convince them that your budget does not allow you to buy at the price they have quoted. This requires solid evidence, not vague suggestions. Show them tangible evidence (minutes of the budget meeting, written instructions from your people). Block off all attempts to re-structure your budget by 'running it over two periods', virement across different headings, instalments and 'creative accounting'. Your budget must stick.
- Place the onus of finding a way of reducing the price on them. Close to a sale they will search for ways of coming down in price

to your budget. Some of the changes will be cosmetic from their point of view (but nevertheless valuable to you), some will involve 'creative accounting' in their accounts not yours; some will be tangible to you (shifting the money to after sales costs; reorganizing the incidence of LIFETIME COSTS; a straight cut in price (reducing their profit; perhaps even going to a marginal cost price).

How far you place your Mother Hubbard below their quoted price is a matter of judgement – too far and they break off; too close and you pay more than you need to (though any price cut is better than none).

Counter: Difficult if the cupboard really is bare. Try to unstick their budget. Best do this by detailed questioning of their budget process, and by discovering where the authority lies to change it. Helped by not throwing everything away in the preliminaries. It is better to be over their alleged budget because you have priced the 'extras' as ADD-ONS, than over it with everything priced on an inclusive basis.

Motivation. Other people have baser motives than ourselves. This harmless delusion becomes dangerous when we act as if other negotiators respond only to the motivations we ascribe to them.

Ascribed motive	Competitive action	Cooperative action
Fear	Threaten	Assure
Pride	Mock	Flatter
Hatred	Hate	Love
Loyalty	Exploit	Reward
Money	Minimize	Maximize
Love	Withhold	Requite
Desire	Frustrate	Satisfy
Jealousy	Excite	Calm
Amtition	Block	Assist

If the other negotiators are not motivated by your ascriptions, your actions make no sense to them, unless they ascribe to you the motivation suggested by your behaviour!

Simplistic theories on what motivates people causes immense

damage to relationships. To assume that money is the only motivator of all employees ignores a whole range of other motivators, some of which, if recognized and attended to, might be cheaper than an elaborate pay reward system, or a proposal that throws money at the wrong problem. To assume that people are inevitably grateful for things you choose to do for them could be an expensive waste of your resources and frustrate your expectations (a conclusion much emphasized by Professor Herzberg from his work on 'hygiene factors').

Exploring the other negotiators' INTERESTS and INHIBITIONS is the best way to approach their real motivators.

See NEED; NEEDS THEORY; PSYCHOLOGY.

Must gets. PREPARATION tool.

In prioritizing OBJECTIVES, there is an advantage in considering what you must get if you are to do any business at all. You do not have negotiating demands that are inflexible, because negotiation implies a willingness to move; nor do you have demands that are perfectly flexible, because your needs are not infinitely small. Somewhere between your maximum demand (your TARGET) and your minimum demand (your RESISTANCE PRICE) there is a possibility of a settlement. Your must gets are the boundary between settlement and non-settlement.

Mutuality. Principle enunciated in COLLECTIVE BARGAINING. The union requires that decisions are based on mutuality, that is, that the union has a mutual right with the managment to decide on certain issues. Neither side has a greater right than the other.

Union strategy is to widen the areas of mutuality from conventional wages and working conditions to areas normally reserved as prerogatives of management (for example, new technology, new working systems, new investment, new markets, new products). Unions also seek to achieve mutuality on some older areas of managerial prerogatives, such as promotion, selection, hiring, discipline, firing and training.

N

Nash solution. An economist's model of the bargaining problem, which typically assumes away many of the inherent characteristics of real world bargaining. After John Nash, 'The Bargaining Problem', *Econometrica*, 1950, pp. 155–62.

Nash showed mathematically that if the negotiators were faced with a choice of achieving some minimum outcome (their 'security level') and incrementally improving on that minimum level by accommodating to the other negotiator, they would arrive at a solution that maximized the product of their incremental utilities. That is, faced with a choice between what they have and what they can get by negotiation, their choice would come down to sharing the incremental gains, such that the gains to one times the gains to the other would be maximized. In other words, they would share the gains equally. This solution, by assumption, abstracts from the negotiating skills and bargaining power of each individual.

Need. Negotiators have needs, otherwise there would be little point in negotiating, for they could make do with what they have instead of seeking to persuade somebody else to let them have what they want.

The negotiator's needs are not always obvious, though it is a fair bet that the other negotiator can quickly decide whether your proposal, or lack of one, or resistance to his proposal, meets his needs or not. Negotiators are the best judge of their own needs and not just in the philosophical sense of freedom of choice. Whatever they perceive to be a need is, by definition, a need, whether it is rational, realistic or otherwise.

It follows that if you meet the needs of the other negotiator, accidentally or otherwise, you are more likely to secure agreement than if you place them in jeopardy. The problem lies in discovering exactly what are the other negotiator's needs. He will not always tell you, even if he is conscious of having them, or he cannot tell you directly because disclosure would be premature, or embarrassing or to your advantage. As often as not, you may not identify the other negotiator's needs because you make no effort to do so. To you the negotiation is about the issue not the related needs of the other negotiator (you have a low INTERPERSONAL ORIENTATION).

There are two ways to discover the needs of the other

negotiator: ask QUESTIONS, and apply your experience.

See NEEDS THEORY; PSYCHOLOGY.

Need to go?. A policy well worth adopting. If something doesn't feature in the task ahead, consider leaving it behind.

Negotiators who take work with them while travelling, especially abroad, should carefully consider their motives. Is it a matter of intention or likelihood? Do they feel better because they intend to work but never get round to it, or does their experience show that they actually work on their papers on long journeys?

Travel is tiring enough; working seriously is even more tiring. Are you sure that is sensible when you face a long negotiation on arrival? Will you realistically open the file late in the evening at your hotel and set to work, or will you drop off to sleep? Should those papers, perhaps referring to other negotiations and internal data, be risked in travel? How much damage would disclosure to a rival do? (Using fax, your confidential costings can be in a rival's hands within minutes.)

Need to know. Big mouths cause costs. Security in the negotiating team is not a symptom of paranoia; it is a sensible precaution. If premature disclosure at the negotiating table worsens your prospects of a deal, disclosure away from the table (whether by accident or espionage) is just as damaging.

In some countries assume that your rooms are bugged, your mail is opened, your telexes are copied and your people are in risk of compromise. Require all personnel to report on approaches, direct or indirect, by anybody, and their involvement in compromising situations (treat these with absolute privilege and discretion: send them home with sound excuse). Watch the level of hospitality and reciprocate on a strictly comparable basis. Keep your eyes open for romantic involvements.

Negotiating teams should do their PREPARATION in secure premises (hire special offices away from the main site if necessary). Adopt a numbering system for all documents, restrict their circulation (better to brief those senior personnel in person than send them position papers in the mail or talk to them by phone). Only the most senior negotiators need to know the full picture, everybody else involved is restricted to their small patch. Shred all documents and spares once they have been superseded (and carbons, printer ribbons and disks). Collect papers in from the team. Allow no work to be taken home or on foreign trips (no exceptions, including you). It's easier to keep papers locked in the preparation suite (watch the suite!). Stress the purposes behind secuirty measures to all negotiators involved.

Only those persons who are directly involved in the negotiations should be given access to the negotiating briefs, the back-up papers, the reports and the crucial data. Many more may be genuinely interested, but it is better to disappoint them than to leak like a sieve. Screen the secretariat and the services people (cleaning company employees too). Colleagues with known temporary problems should be sympathetically relieved of involvement in a high stress negotiation.

Needs theory. Meet a negotiator's needs and you are well on your way towards agreement.

Gerard I. Nierenberg markets a negotiation method that applies a theory of needs to psychological and bargaining skills (see G.I. Nierenberg, *Fundamentals of Negotiating*, New York, Hawthorn Books Inc., 1973).

Beginning with A.H. Maslow's hierarchy of needs (1 physiological: 2 safety and security; 3 love and belonging; 4 self-esteem; 5 self-actualization; 6 knowledge and understanding; 7 aesthetic), Nierenberg categorized six varieties of application to each hierarchy of need, ranked by the degree of control which the negotiator may exercise over the outcome. These applications involve the negotiator's:

1 Working for the opposer's needs: assurance, encourage, concede.

2 Letting the opposer work for his needs: motivate, permit, challenge.

3 Working for the opposer's and his own needs: cooperate, compromise, recognize.

4 Working against his own needs: waive, relinquish, disavow.

5 Working against the opposer's needs: veto, embarrass, threaten.

6 Working against the opposer's and his own needs: thwart, renounce, withdraw.

By detailing the appropriate, or potential, negotiating tactic to each application in respect of each of Maslow's needs, Nierenberg produced a unique approach to understanding negotiating skills and to applying them to interpersonal, interorganizational and diplomatic conflicts.

See PSYCHOLOGY.

Negotiating language. Important, for although what is said is only worth 7 per cent of the message, it is still part of the message. (See NON-VERBAL BEHAVIOUR.)

Some language helps a negotiator, particularly in the bargaining phase. Assertive negotiators do better than non-assertive or aggressive negotiators.

'We require' is more assertive than 'we would like'. If it is part of a CONDITIONAL OFFER it is more likely to get full attention than a vague expression of desire.

Tell them what you want, and tell them what you are willing to trade with them to get it. A bargain is an offer to trade. Timed correctly, it does not antagonize, nor is it aggressive. There come a time in negotiation where a clear statement of what is on offer is worth stating.

Assertive language	Weak language
I require	I would like
I need	I wish
I must	I hope
I want	I fancy
I insist	I feel

Negotiating skills. What distinguishes the above-average negotiator from the rest? Veiws vary. Some go as far as to believe that negotiators are born, not made. Versions of the 'born' school ascribe the qualities of good negotiators sometimes to race, which is limiting for the rest of humankind who negotiate too, sometimes to gender, which is even more ludicrous, and sometimes to the mysticism of genetics. These explanations are non-starters. While not everybody competes in decathlons, or writes music etc., everybody negotiates, and if some are born to it, this still leaves the rest of us doing the best we can. Given that the 'born' principle can never be tested (because by definition, anybody who is any good is born to it, and the rest are not), we are left with trying to establish exactly what above-average negotiators do that is different from poorer negotiators.

"Typical Yuppie scene – renegotiating their marriage contract."

Studies of negotiators have identified some of the characteristics of above-average negotiators. If the identified differences in performance can be replicated, and negotiators can learn to imitate the best qualities of the above-average negotiators with training and practice, it follows that poor negotiators can improve their performance.

Neil Rackham of the Huthwaite Research Group (UK), and John Carlisle, studied the behaviour of negotiators and concluded that the differences in performance were sufficiently consistent as to be identified and transformed in a training programme. Broadly, above-average negotiators tended:
during PREPARATION to:

Explore more options.

Devote much more time to considering areas of potential agreement (though both spent most of their time considering their differences).

Spend twice as much time considering long-term as opposed to short-term issues (though, again both spent over 90 per cent of their time on the short-term issues).

Set objectives within a range rather than a fixed point.

Not settle on strict sequence for dealing with the issues, but leave open the order in which they are taken in the negotiation. during face-to-face contact (ARGUMENT) to:

Use far fewer irritators (self-praise for one's won proposals as 'fair', 'generous' etc.) which do not persuade and are therefore counter-productive.

Make far fewer instant counter-proposals.

Initiate far fewer defend/attack spirals.

Label their own behaviour before proceeding ('Could I ask a question?'), except when about to disagree, they give their reasons first and then state that they disagree.

Test their understanding more often.

Summarize more often.

Ask many more questions.

Give more information about personal feelings.

Refrain from diluting arguments with weaker and more vulnerable statements.

after the negotiation to:

Review the events that had occurred during it.

Negotiating styles. See CHINESE NEGOTIATING STYLE; COMMUNIST NEGOTIATING STYLE; COMPETITIVE STYLE; COOPERATIVE STYLE; CULTURE DIFFERENCES; HEADS OF AGREEMENT; INTERPERSONAL ORIENTATION.

Negotiating with yourself. Common enough activity.

You want a pay rise, but have not settled on how much you can ask for. You would like 1,000 extra a year. Your pre-negotiation thinking has led you to this figure. The problem is that the other negotiator, who can concede this rise to you, is not likely to do so in your opinion. So you reduce your opening demand to 750. On the way to the meeting you hear from colleagues that the company is in bad shape and there are rumours of redundancies. Your demand shrinks to 500. At the meeting the other negotiator is very abrupt with you, comments on your stepping out of line with this request and demands to know what makes you think you are worth a rise at all. You open at 200. You have been negotiating with yourself.

How do you know the other negotiator will not concede a rise close to 1,000? Can you read minds? Why should a company in trouble sack people like you who are assets to the profitability of the company? Surely the company prefers to sack the less competent? What has the manner of the other negotiator got to do with your demand? Perhaps her husband is rowing with her and she is in a bad mood?

Open at 1,200, with a credible case, and confine your negotiation to the person you came to see.

Net. Always smaller than GROSS, hence to be watched carefully when negotiators slip it into proposals.

The gross amount, less deductibles, equals the net amount. Deductibles are disputable. An unspecified net amount is a highly variable number, depending on who is responsible for calculating it. If negotiating for a net amount scrutinize extremely carefully what the other negotiator defines as a deductible. 'Net of costs' is not sufficiently precise to be a safe deductible; accountants can create concepts of cost deductibles of varying credibility.

The share of a net sum, be it profit, income, or interest, is of uncertain value to the receiver, and is at the uncertain mercy of the goodwill of the calculator. Insisting on a share of the gross profit, income or interest is less risky. Negotiators offer net shares, but demand gross shares.

Net worth. Roughly, deduct what you owe from what you own: the resultant figure is your net worth. If it is negative you are vulnerable, though not necessarily knocked out. Through time you prefer that your net worth is positive and rising.

Separate your personal wealth from your corporate wealth. This protects you from losing everything if a misjudgement is made. Against your corporate wealth borrow whatever you can to finance an increase in net worth. Projects that generate larger CASH FLOWS into the business than cash flows out of the business can raise your net worth when your borrowing is greater than your EQUITY, because positive cash flows add to the value of your assets, which are usually calculated on an historic cost basis – what it cost to acquire them, not what they cost or are worth today.

No come backs. The truly one-off deal.

No warranties, no promises, no returns, and no responsibility for anything once the deal is concluded. It is caveat emptor (and caveat vendor!).

You agree to buy 'as seen' (or more correctly, as perceived). If the goods are found to be damaged, or if they were not as you believed them to be, that is your problem. It's a no come backs deal, and you live with what you bought, or without it, as the case may be. Hence, be careful. Get paid in cash.

No problem. A wild concession that should be eliminated from the negotiator's vocabulary.

● 'Can you deliver overnight?'
'No problem.'
●   'We need 24 hour call-outs on this equipment.'
'No problem.'

The trouble is the 'no problem' concession is not appreciated when thrown in and it misses an opportunity to go for a trial close. They might be prepared to compensate generously for a 'no problem' concession. You don't know, if you don't try. If they need it, they value it. Conceding something on a 'no problem' basis does not get you the business: that is left to their discretion. Having conceded something of great value to them without asking for anything in return (not even asking for an agreement) you expose yourself to a DUTCH AUCTION, or a decision to 'think about it'.

Put them on the spot:
● 'Are you saying that if we do deliver overnight that you will award us the contract?'
● 'If we can offer a 24 hour service, do we get the business?'

A 'yes' permits you to decide whether the request is a 'no problem'. A 'no' tells you that your 'no problem' concession is wasted.

No sale, no fee. A version of CONTINGENCY PRICING.

Payment for services is based exclusively on results. Not always a good idea as it encourages speculative litigation. It is not always clear what it means: 'no fee' could still involve costs (advertising and other expenses) being charged even when no sale occurred, with the 'fee' being a separate item altogether. If a sale takes place, but the supplier of the services was not in any way responsible for securing the sale, can he still claim a fee? In some cases he can and does. Sellers of houses who sign several 'no sale, no fee' contracts with agents end up paying them all a fee out of the sale price when, manifestly, they could not all have been instrumental in the single sale.

Negotiators offering 'no sale, no fee' contracts are often new to the business and looking to build a client list, or are desperate for work, or are speculative agents. What fee do they charge if they succeed in selling your property? What are the exact terms of the contingency contract? Who bears the costs of an unsuccessful sale? (Watch for PADDED costs).

Noah's Ark. Buyer's pressure tactic: 'You'll have to do better than that on price because your rivals are quoting better prices than you are.'

Almost always a bluff. It's been part of buyers' repertoire of winnning moves for so long that it's said Noah must have let two of them on board.

Sometimes the buyer does have a better price for a comparable service because your package is exactly the same as your rivals in every respect. But more often the buyer does not have comparable packages from the sellers, and without this there can be no comparison of prices (see APPLES AND PEARS).

Consider the first situation: comparable package but different prices. The buyer's best line is to see if you will reduce your price below your rivals', because if you do the buyer is better off by the difference (particularly if the buyer can induce your rivals to follow suit and bid downwards against you (see DUTCH AUCTION).

Consider the second situation: non-comparable packages and therefore non-comparable prices. They buyer's best line is to see if you will reduce your prices in the belief that you are in the first situation.

Consider a third situation: rivals' prices are higher, some even though they are comparable, others though they are not (in an extreme version of this situation there are no rivals at all, only you do not know this!). Buyer's best line is to see if you will reduce your prices solely in the belief that your rivals are quoting lower than you, though they are not, or, in a total bluff, that you have rivals when you do not.

Why does Noah's Ark persistently appear in negotiations, all over the world, generation after generation? Simple: sellers invariably respond to it by cutting their prices. *Counter*: Don't. Question the buyer's comparisons; refuse to react unless you can compare the quotes directly; ask why the buyer is dealing with you if your rivals' quotes are better.

Non-tradable. See CONSTANTS.

Non-verbal behaviour. Fifty-five per cent of a negotiator's message is perceived non-verbally; only 7 per cent depends on what is said, and 38 per cent on how it is said. (A. Mehrasian: Tactics of Social Influence, Prentice Hall, Englewood Cliffs, New Jersey, 1969).

Clearly, our efforts at COMMUNICATION are often concentrated in the wrong area of what we say and not enough in the vital areas of how we say it and what the rest of our demeanour is telling the 'listener'.

It is not that a single gesture reveals all. If it was that easy we would manipulate the message. It is how our gestures, posture, expression and such like fit in with what we are trying to say. If the gestures are out of phase with the wordss, or in direct contradiction with them, then the receiver gets a different message from the one we think we are sending.

Crowding the private space of the other negotiator, bone crushing handshakes, pumping a stranger's handshake as if with a long lost friend, can set alarm bells off in the other negotiator that completely destroy the intended effect.

Touching the face, rubbing the cheek, covering the mouth and such like can mean someone is being less than candid; it can also mean that they have an itch or they were eating garlic last night. Chin stroking can mean they are coming to a decision. It's not sensible to interrupt their decision process at this point. A little silence helps, but if the other negotiator sits back, folds his arms and is about to say something, it is almost certainly going to be a 'no', so swift intervention to go over the positive points in your proposal might be helpful.

Hands folded across the chest are very defensive. This means they don't accept what you have said. There is no point bashing the same point because this only forces them to dig in. Perhaps some well chosen QUESTIONS here would help? You must find out what is wrong, from the listener's point of view, with your message if you are to continue productively. Failure to do so invites an ARGUMENT.

Non-verbal behaviour is grossly underrated by negotiators (it is also grossly overrated by some behavioural students). Much of what the non-verbal researchers demonstrate is appealing because it corresponds to how we react intuitively to what we think other people are communicating. Its importance is in the perception of the message and the messenger in the eyes of the receiver. A brilliantly manipulated message is unlikely to be successful if the content is unacceptable; the danger is that a badly sent message, that would otherwise be acceptable, is rejected because the receiver has grave doubts about the sender's true intentions.

Non-zero sum. What you gain is not at my expense.

Jargon from GAME THEORY (see ZERO SUM). The sum of the positive gains is greater than zero. Suppose you are negotiating several issues, such as a price per unit, the quantity to be delivered, when payment is to be made, the level of quality and the policy on returns of defective units. Your interests as the buyer may be best served in your view by a delayed payment to suit your cash flow, a large quantity in stock to cover surges in demand and a flexible returns policy to cover for breakages. The other negotiator may be interested in a premium price to move the product 'up market', large production runs to reduce unit costs, and a quality level that reduces inspection costs. Trading a higher unit price for delayed payment, a lower quality level for a flexible returns policy, and matching each other's needs for large production and order quantities, provides each of you with a non-zero sum settlement.

Searching for non-zero sum solutions to negotiation problems is more productive than narrowing the focus onto single zero-sum issues. This mixes the cooperative and conflict elements of negotiation to produce mutually advantageous solutions.

"I'm sorry. Mr Bartlett is busy negotiating a pay deal."

Not negotiable. Pressure tactic. Stake out a non-negotiable area and refuse to budge, and force the other negotiator to accept your exclusion tactic. The problem comes if what you are excluding from the negotiation is the central issue that the other negotiator wishes to negotiate about.

Some issues are non-negotiable, and the negotiator would prefer to resolve the dispute by other means (war, litigation) sooner than permit a negotiation on a sacred issue. But merely excluding issues does not make them non-negotiable, otherwise negotiators the world over would narrow the negotiable issues to the ones they felt strongest in, or the ones they were least concerned about (see PRINCIPLES 2).

Nothing is agreed. Nothing is agreed until it is agreed.

Listening to a proposition does not commit you to agreeing to it (don't interrupt).

Asking questions about a proposition does not signify you agree with it (ask QUESTIONS).

Listening to the other negotiator does not mean you agree with what he or she is saying (LISTEN).

Refraining from immediate comment on a proposal, or from immediately replying to a letter, a contract or a summary, does not mean that you accept what is written (think before you leap in).

Silence from the other negotiator does not mean you have a deal.

O

Objection. Defensive tactic, signalling INHIBITIONS about your proposal.

Negotiators are advised to identify and exorcise objections. Ignoring them is self-defeating, for the unanswered, undiscussed and unrecognized objection fuels the inhibitions of the other negotiator. Attacking the other negotiator for having objections is equally self-destructive. If they did not have any objections to your proposals it would hardly be a negotiation.

Experience provides you with plenty of practice in identifying objections. You have probably heard them all many times before (though never relax: a new objection is just round the corner). Don't interrupt a well-worn objection – objectors resent being cut off with well-worn answers. Listen to the objection in full (see LISTENING). Ask QUESTIONS for clarification because the objection may not be quite the same as the one you have a ready answer for.

Negotiators have a right to object. Recognize their right and you are half-way to satisfying them. Show empathy ('Yes, I see what you are getting at'), not contempt ('Yes, some less informed people do worry about that.').

Address the objection with a full and frank exposition that eliminates the other negotiator's concerns. If their worries are founded on a misconception of the features of your service, gently correct the misconception, support your exposition with a review of the benefits, and ask positively if their anxieties have been satisfied.

When the objection refers to something that no amount of exposition can satisfy – your service does not cover the situation they are worried about – avoid trying to bluff your way to an agreement. Honesty is better than fraud. Direct their attention to considering how the feature they are worried about compares with the benefits from the rest of your proposal:

'In sum, while the Opal PC does not provide a graphic colour networker, you might consider how often your people will actually use that feature against the real savings you achieve from their daily use of its high quality desk-top printing and on-line fax capabilities.'

An objection answered is a step towards agreement.

Objective. What do you want? What do they want? Best to answer these questions before you meet the other negotiators.

Quantified objectives are meaningful; non-quantifiable objectives are suspect. If your first look at your objectives produces some intangibles or vague aims ('a better deal"; 'a happier employee'; 'a wage increase'; 'a price cut'), transform these into quantifiable objectives by considering the steps needed to bring about the unquantified objective. What constitutes a better deal? What would make this employee happier? How large a wage increase? How small a price cut?

Above-average negotiators quantify their objectives by setting a range of acceptable quantities rather than choosing a fixed number: 'between 100 and 150 at between 7 and 11 per cent', is a better objective than '130 at 7 per cent.' Why? Because what is your position if they offer 129 at 8 per cent? A range enables you to choose your responses according to how the negotiation develops and it forces you to consider alternative trade-offs (your nascent negotiating strategy) before it starts.

Objectives should be ranked in order of priority. Some objectives are more important than others – if not, you are saying that every objective is of equal importance, which contradicts common sense. If everything is equally valued, how do you conduct a negotiation which requires you to move from your FIRST OFFER? Ranking objectives means prioritizing them according to their value to you. Your opening, or first offer, assembles your target objectives; your FINAL OFFER regroups around the remnants of your first offer which are most important to you. In between there are a number of positions bringing together various combinations of your ranked objectives; you could be at your BOTTOM LINE limit on some TRADABLES, and hardly off your first offer on others, with the rest spread across the settlement range (see BARGAINING CONTINUUM).

Set out your quantified objectives in a list, commencing with your targets and thereafter the various values within each objective's settlement range down to your RESERVATION PRICES (using 'price' as a surrogate for value). This gives you your negotiating plan. The more thoroughly this is prepared, across the maximum number of tradables, the more confident you will be in the actual negotiation. (See figure 8).

Off the record. Many negotiators find the way out of DEADLOCK in an off the record discussion. An ADJOURNMENT in a difficult negotiation in which, for example, the principals 'meet' in the washroom and in private discussion, out of earshot of their colleagues, agree to settle, is more common than observers of their conduct at the negotiating table would credit. If using a 'washroom' type settlement, check the stalls first in case an outraged colleague puts the 'off the record' settlement on the record.

Negotiators also meet informally for coffee. Two negotiators in a crowded room can casually signal over a coffee a private trade-off which they could not do in public without risking unhelpful reactions from colleagues ('Harry, if you drop to 10 per cent, I'll argue for a while about early payment, but settle for 90 days. OK?').

Off the record meetings are risky. They can backfire. Your conciliatory moves can be made public to embarrass you (denials might placate your troops or confirm their suspicions). Use them only with negotiators you know well, and trust.

Developing TRUST relationships based on mutual respect is a long-term investment that might one day lead to a major pay-off. Diplomats learn this in their early careers and deliberately cultivate junior opposite numbers who might one day be foreign minister in their country. Employers and trade union officials do likewise: young aggressive go-getting managers become directors and young firebrand union officials become presidents. An ability in mature years to cross the divide on an off the record basis is a worthwhile asset.

Off-set. Increasingly common in major international business transactions. A UK customer buys American if the US firm places orders in the UK to off-set the purchase price. Suitable for major manufacturing deals, such as in aerospace, defence, or civil engineering.

It is not the same as a BARTER arrangement, as no direct transfer takes place between the supply of goods and the off-set activity. The aerospace company might place orders for parts in the client country, for instance.

The attraction of off-set is largely political, not commercial. Domestic manufacturers lobby the government to persuade/force other companies not to buy from foreign suppliers. This can be very compelling with a government under fire for high domestic unemployment. The off-set counters this type of lobbying by showing that the foreign contract also brings work to the domestic economy. Offering an off-set element in your package could overcome domestic political resistance.

The question is complicated because it is not always clear whether the off-set element is new additional work or whether it is merely a collection of existing or proposed work that would be placed in the country anyway. Too much emphasis on the conditional nature of the off-set element (it comes with the order or not at all) sets off alarm bells about restrictions in trade. But there is no doubt that offering an off-set package could swing the order your way if your rival is unable to match you on off-set. Of course, this could be an expensive way to 'buy' business.

Offers. An offer should always be conditional: *If you* do such and such, *then I* will do so and so.

Unilateral generosity seldom has any other effect than to invite the other negotiator to take advantage of you.

Experimental research and experience show that unconditional offers rarely solve the problem – the other negotiator almost always asserts that your unconditional offer is not good enough, and uses it as a base to press for more. And why not? It you are throwing concessions away for nothing, why should the other side not press to see if you have yet more to offer. They can always make a conditional offer in return on the basis of what you have already given away.

When making tentative proposals, frame your conditional offer along the following lines:
- Be specific about what they must do.
- Be vague about what you might do in return.

Example:

'If you undertake to cover all the inspection costs of this shipment, and do so throughout Ramadan, then we will consider ameliorating the visa requirements for domestic visitors.'

A tentative proposal that is too specific in all aspects is more likely to be taken as a bargaining offer. There are many reasons why you do not want to be too specific about your end of the offer, not the least that they might have higher expectations about where they need to settle than you have so far estimated. Being too specific tips your hand into view, causing them to revise their expectations to your disadvantage. The non-specific offer is suitable for the ADD-ON; it gives you room to manoeuvre at a time when you might need it.

Bargaining offers are always conditional (there are never any exceptions where they are not) and they are always specific (if they are not specific they are tentative and therefore merely a proposal).

See BARGAINING LANGUAGE.

Offer they must refuse. Offer deliberately set to be rejected.

Contractors overloaded with work make a 'high' BID to avoid winning a contract when not bidding at all would antagonize the buyer and endanger future contracts.

Such offers are used when negotiators wish to avoid low profit contracts, or contracts below a minimum value, or in places where they do not want to do business, or with people they prefer not to deal. They are also useful when negotiators want an excuse to get out from a deal. They introduce unacceptable demands, or demands they know are outside the other negotiator's limits (such as deliberately declaring something to be 'non-negotiable' that is vital to the other negotiator).

Problem: Sometimes the 'offer they must refuse' is accepted and you are left to get on with it!

On taking it personally. Negotiators are human: they get upset very easily. In my clinics I occasionally find seasoned negotiators getting extremely emotional during some of the artificial cases they are asked to negotiate. They know it is a game before they start and they have no personal interest in the outcome. They know it does not matter whether they reach agreement or not; or what agreement they come to. Yet they fight. Yes, fight. They get angry, make threats, raise their voices, shout, curse and remonstrate. Sometimes, though rarely, they walk out and protest at the other negotiator's behaviour.

If some seasoned negotiators get emotional when none of their business interests is at stake, how many more get emotionally involved when their interests are threatened or thwarted by other negotiators? From observation, most negotiators slip into unprofessional involvement some of the time. They get emotional, angry and competitive on issues that cooler consideration would steer them away from. They take things too personally.

Counter: Consider the story I end all my clinics with. A lieutenant-colonel I met some years ago told me of his first experience of combat. He was sent to Korea as a second-lieutenant within three months of graduating from officer training. His platoon sergeant was a veteran of the Second World War, with combat experience from D-Day to the Rhine. Most of the other men had seen combat and all of them had been in the army for several years. He, however, had never heard a shot fired in anger. One morning his platoon was on patrol and suddenly they came under fire. He dived for the nearest cover, as did everybody else. He rolled over on his side and shouted to his sergeant: 'Some bastard over there is trying to kill me.' The sergeant ran over and patted him on the shoulder, saying: 'Now, now, son, don't take it personally, or we'll all get killed.'

In negotiating, don't take it personally, or we'll all be worse off.

One-offer-only. Procedure whereby the supplier gets one chance to offer his best price in competition with others. Knowing this, suppliers shave their prices.

It is best used for the regular purchase of standard products that are well specified. It can also be used occasionally for expensive mandatory non-specified services, such as audits, banking services, legal representation, pension fund management and insurance cover. Test the market by calling for tenders for your business for fixed periods of say two or three years.

If the specification is unambiguous, there is nothing to negotiate about, other than price. If you are solely price conscious, and there is no legal collusion between sellers, you can be sure of a competitive price (somebody is almost always willing to discount a price for business).

If the specification is complex, or the purchase is so separated in time as to be unusual, you should purchase by negotiation. Not being too sure about what you want could lead you to specify something that a negotiation could improve upon.

Behaving inconsistently as a buyer, sometimes calling for

one-offer-only bids and sometimes opening up the bids to negoti-ation, undermines your negotiating credibility. Suppliers, unsure on what basis they are bidding, always PAD their offers, and camouflage their padding with all kinds of plausible excuses. Prices will move up against you.

One price, one package. Seller's defensive tactic.

Having quoted a price for a detailed package, you can expect the other negotiator to push you either on the price, or on the package. If he looks for ways of extending what he gets for what he pays, he is signalling that he accepts your price but not your package. To clinch the deal he 'needs' this or that extra, or demands them as ADD-ONS inclusive of your quoted price (see YES, BUT).

Apply the principle 'for this package, there is this price; for another package there is another price'. First, bring out all the extras or changes that the buyer wants to your proposed package. This blocks off a 'yes, but' approach. Then price these extras or changes as another package. You can trade-off changes in the package against the change in the price; or turn it into a straight price negotiation.

If you accept changes without charge you are doing more for your price than you planned. Even where you planned for mar-ginal adjustments in the package, failing to price them to the other negotiator either undermines their value (free gifts are seldom appreciated as much as the things we pay for), and misses an opportunity to educate the buyer that you negotiate by trading not by unilaterally conceding. Precedents are promises for the future.

One truck contracts. A risky way to do business by which you undertake a transaction with a minimum of discussion about the contingencies that might arise. If these contingencies are expen-sive, there is a risk of a liability claim.

Hiring a truck with a minimum of fuss has its advantages: 'one truck, 150 a day rental'. But trucks are not just hired, they are used for some purpose, and in using a truck all kinds of possibilities emerge. Who pays for repairs while on hire? Who recovers the vehicle if it breaks down? Who pays for fuel? Is it replaced if it is stolen, or breaks down? Who is legally liable for its mechanical condition? Is it warranted for the use to which it is to be put?

It is not necessary to draw up a complex legally watertight rental agreement (though most rental companies have pre-printed contracts with every imaginable contingency covered either in detail or through LIFEBOAT CLAUSES). You are advised to consider the possible contingencies and negotiate for some of the major ones to be covered.

Option. Protection against gazumping.

A lot of grief is caused to potential buyers who agree to purchase say a property by a certain date, subject to normal safeguards such as a detailed structural survey. Before the selling date materializes, the buyer is GAZUMPED. Somebody else offers the seller more money, or a quicker sale. The original buyer is left in tears (of woe or rage!) and the so-called 'deposit' is returned.

When buying offer the seller an option instead of a deposit. This 'locks in' the seller to the transaction and protects the buyer from gazumping. It works like this: you offer the seller a cash consideration for the purchase of an option to buy the property at a given date for an agreed price. The option is legally binding, and being so, courts will award against a seller who defaults (the mere threat of which is a deterrent against gazumpers). If for any reason you fail to buy the property, the seller keeps your option money; when you buy, you apply the option money against the purchase price.

Will a seller accept an option to purchase agreement? That depends on the terms of the option (how long before purchase?) and the size of the option payment (how much?). Payment of 1,000 for an option to purchase within three months could look a very interesting proposition to a seller. If you fold before the option must be exercised, the seller keeps your 1,000; if you exercise your option, he or she sells the property for the price you agreed.

Manipulate the option money downwards and you can buy options on high value properties for small cash outlays. If the option period is long enough, and subject to extension, you can put the property on the market and seek a buyer willing to pay you more for the property than you offered to pay in your option. If the two transactions coincide (you take title the same day as you sell it on), you make a profit on the difference in prices. If you cannot find a purchaser at a price that produces a profit, you can forego your option money, which is cheaper than buying a property on speculation and finding it won't sell.

Sellers have an interest in raising the amount of the option money; the higher it is the more determined the buyer will be to exercise his option. You sell your property. Moreover, if the option price is acceptable to you, it does not matter if the buyer sells on the same property at a higher price. Indeed, this can be particularly helpful: selling an option to a buyer who wants to sell the property on is like having a selling agent pay you for selling your property, which is the reverse of what happens when you hire an agent to do this for you at a charge of anything from 1 to 5 per cent.

Sellers can be gazumped in reverse. Buyers drop out of an agreement to purchase, sometimes for valid reason (they cannot raise the money, their circumstances suddenly change) and sometimes not. The result is the same. The seller has to go to the expense of selling the property again. Yet buyers who default for any reason lose their option money, which is an incentive for sellers to sell options to buyers.

Or else. Ultimatum tactic.

'Either you meet our demands, or else we call a strike.'

Such tactics can provoke the very resistance they are trying to overcome. Have you thought through all the consequences of implementing the 'or else' threat? If they believe that your threat is empty, or can be ridden out, they might choose to take the threat rather than give in. They might still take the threat option even though you have overwhelming power (see MARTYRDOM).

See THREAT.

Order taking. A sign of a jaded salesforce.

Sellers who merely meet customers to take their regular orders are missing opportunities to negotiate better orders. It is also cheaper for a company selling from a regular low value list to use a telephone sales operation. Not only are all outlets covered this way, but with on-line direct input into a computer ordering system, stock can be dispatched to customers more quickly.

Conversely, merely calling a supplier to give an order is a sign of a jaded buying operation. What special offers are available? You won't know if you don't ask, unless they volunteer to tell you.

Over-and-under tactic. The impossible response to the impossible demand.

The other negotiator sometimes springs an 'impossible demand' upon you:

'Give me 5 per cent early settlement discount.'

Spring back an over-and-under:

'If you agree to a 5 per cent premium for late payment.'

'I require a 30 per cent deposit.'
'If you agree to pay interest at four points over base while you hold my deposit.'

'The men want Saturday shifts cancelled this week to watch the Rose Bowl.'
'If they meet this week's production targets, I'll pay them for the day off.'

P

Packaging. Unwrapping and re-wrapping proposals to make them mutually acceptable.

You seldom have only one proposal on the table. Both of you put various proposals forward, some parts of which are mutually contradictory, some parts of which overlap. By packaging those parts of the other's proposals that you can accept with the re-wrapped parts of your own, you automatically move towards BARGAINING.

Packages address the expressed INTERESTS and INHIBITIONS of the other party; they appeal to the interests and accommodate inhibitions. If the other party is keen on the money (interest) but worried about getting paid (inhibition), devise a conditional package that copes with his needs but is consistent with your own.

Consider the TRADABLES. Can you invent new ones? Every variable generates options, and the more options the less likely is DEADLOCK. Can you re-package them in a different way? What are the shared interests in particular options? Can you trade movement on a preferred option for movement on a less important option?

Consider what they are asking for. Consider what each element in their proposal is worth to them, not what it costs you. If they ask for something, they value it, and so should you if you are offering to trade what they want for what you want.

Pad/padding. A negotiating margin.

Prices are padded when sellers expect a negotiation. The padded price gives them negotiating room. To present your 'best price' first is a mistake when the buyer believes that the price is negotiable and expects some movement from you. If you have no room to move on your price you could end up losing the business, or buying it at the expense of your profits.

Hence, pad your prices when you expect a negotiation. Also, pad them when dealing with negotiators who make last minute demands (see COMMUNIST NEGOTIATING STYLES), when dealing with negotiators who do not have final AUTHORITY, when you expect a multiple re-BID situation, when dealing with PRICE BLIND clients, when you can avoid COST BREAKDOWNS, when you are going to have to wait for your money, when a COUNTER-TRADE proposition is likely, and generally whenever you can get away with it.

Partners. Partners share your problems and the profits. If they generate more problems than they ease, consider their cost in foregone profits.

Disputes between partners generally originate from differing perceptions of their mutual contributions and how each continues to fit into the future direction of the business. When partnerships break up it is more complicated than a divorce. As with divorce, it is better to negotiate the terms (how the assets and liabilities are shared) of a dissolution of the partnership before it is formed, rather than when a break-up is imminent. Likewise with the rules for removing somebody from the partnership who is incompetent or otherwise no longer suitable, and what they get for going 'quietly'.

To avoid smouldering distrust of your partners it helps to know where the money is at any time, what is happening to it and how much is yours.

Partnership law is a rich seam for lawyers (most of them in partnerships). Partnership is the goal of many professional people (accountants, architects, surveyors, solicitors, actuaries, brokers and consultants of all kinds). Some partnerships are bound by strict professional rules (being 'professionally qualified' can be one of them); most maintain strict secrecy about their financial affairs (assets, income, salary scales, shares of profits and perks of various kinds), and all carry unlimited liability by law. There can be gradations of partners, from senior partners and partners to salaried partners. Below these wait the candidate partners or senior managers. Some operate an informal 'up or out' policy: either you make partner by your 40th birthday, or you quit.

Advice about forming partnerships: If you don't have to do so, don't.

Partners can be golden aids to mutual profit. They can also be leaden weights to mutual disaster. It is tempting to look for a partner when you are entering a new field. If you can do it on your own, getting somebody to hold your hand is comforting but risky. People fall out because their interests do not coincide. Best to limit hand holding to courtship (itself a rich field of mutual disasters).

One-deal-at-a-time partnerships are safer than permanent ones. The obligation and the possibility of mutual damage is limited to the one deal. Keep strict accounts showing costs and profits and what has happened to the money each of you put up. Do not run on one deal to another one, even if convenient. Close the accounts on each deal before opening another. This way you can quit if you discover you don't like, trust, or feel happy with your erstwhile partner, or vice versa, without there being an implied partnership in law between you.

It is difficult to accumulate capital in the business this way (which is one of the motivations for forming a permanent partnership or incorporating your interests in some way). If things work out well between you, fine. You can extend the times you work together. Lasting partnerships grow out of a fusion of interests over a period, rather than a declaration of intentions in the flush of a first deal.

You feel the need for a partner most when you need access to something the other negotiator has plenty of, such as capital, or contacts. Consider your interests: why give away things you will value later for things you value now, if the consequence is that you have to share everything (the worth of the business, plus its profits) long after your initial needs have been met? Offer a high return on the capital invested (10–20 per cent, or a fixed mark-up above market interest rates) rather than a partnership. Once you pay the lender off, everything the money has helped you to create remains yours.

Patents and licences. Products and services can be licensed. This enables the licensor to receive monetary rewards for creating the product or service which the licensee exploits in a defined territory. The licensor's interests are protected and the licensee earns profits from marketing or supplying the product or service.

There are pitfalls in allowing somebody else to exploit a product or service, but there is also a considerable body of experience available that should protect the main interests of the licensor who prefers not to exploit his property directly.

Patent law is a complex subject and consultation with a specialist lawyer is advised. Different laws apply in different regions of the world. European Community law is different (mainly to the detriment of the licensor) from elsewhere and careful attention to the details of what is proposed in a licence agreement is necessary to insure that you do not breach Community rules.

In negotiating licence agreements consider the following as a minimal list of points to bear in mind:

- Who are the parties to the agreement?
- What is the licensor granting to the licensee?
- For which specific territory is the licence granted?
- What is the licensee entitled to market or sell?
- Which specific patents, trade marks and know-how is the licensor licensing?
- How exclusive is the licence? Is it to cover the sale but not the manufacture of the licensor's products or services, or to do both?
- Is the licensee allowed to sell outside the specific territory?
- Can the licensor also supply, independently of the licensee, the products or services in the licensee's territory? If so, on what basis? Are specific clients reserved to the licensor who might have premises in the licensee's territory?
- Are other licensees of the licensor permitted to sell or supply in the licensee's territory?
- If the licensee fails to meet market targets, or to supply known demands for the licensor's products or services, can the licensor supply direct, or contract with another licensee to do the same?
- How much does the licensee pay for the licence: on signature of contracts; on delivery of the product or materials or know how for service; on commencing production or supply?
- Is the licence fee a royalty on gross or net turnover?
- If net, how is this defined?
- How regular are the payments to be: monthly, quarterly or annually?
- What separate accounts should the licensee keep? How regularly may they be inspected? Who shall audit them?
- How long should the agreement last?
- What notice is required for the licensee to terminate the agreement? What notice can the licensor give?
- Under what conditions can premature termination occur (breach of contract, *force majeure*, bankruptcy of licensee, merger or take-over by another company)?
- What must the licensee undertake when the licence is revoked for any reason? What must be returned? What restrictions on the

licensee are imposed? What happens to all current stocks or client services?

● What obligations are there on the licensee to preserve confidentiality both in and out of contract?

● What protections are required by the licensor? Unconditional acknowledgement of the licensor's exclusive copyrights and patents? Full support to protect infringements within the territory? Agreement to mark all products or literature describing services as supplied under licence from the licensor? Reporting of all suspected infringements of the licensor's rights by third parties? Imposition of strict confidentiality on all employees of the licensee and all relevant restrictions on their activities during and after employment with the licensee? All employees to sign appropriate and legally binding agreements to this effect?

● What guarantee of quality must the licensee give in respect of the production or supply of the licensor's goods or services?

● What restrictions are to be imposed on the licensee for supplying similar goods or services to the licensor's?

● What training and support is the licensor to supply to the licensee, how regularly is such support to be available, and how are its costs to be met?

● How are improvements in the product or service to be transferred to the licensee and on what basis?

● What general obligations will the licensor undertake in respect of the licensee's interests? What general obligations is the licensee under in respect of the licensor?

● How are disputes between the licensor and the licensee to be resolved? Which law is to apply in the case of contractual interpretation?

See REVERSION.

Patience. More than a virtue – a tactic.

One of the most expensive costs of negotiating is not the costs of concessions or precedents made to get a settlement, it is the time they take. Senior staff are tied down in long negotiations, sometimes away from their home base, and meanwhile their other work comes to a complete stop. This induces the CONCORDE FALLACY: the project must continue to save wasting what we have spent on it already. So you stay with the negotiations, ever keener to come to agreement and less reluctant to concede. Costs mount, both in time lost and in concessions made.

Patience reduces time pressures. If the negotiation is likely to be a long one, you settle in for the long haul. You arrange coverage of senior staff so that other work does not suffer. You rotate staff to reduce isolation and fatigue. You reduce your reliance on the outcome of the negotiation by organizing other work.

If you desperately need the business from a long haul negotiation, reconsider your ALTERNATIVES (BATNA). Dependence increases with time and puts your profitability at risk. Should you be so dependent on this one negotiation? Consider cutting your losses quickly when it looks like narrowing your options by dragging on.

The time factor tactic is chosen to bind you into the other negotiator's demands for concessions. Sit it out by all means, but send patient people to negotiate, not those who prefer, or have reasons, to be doing something else, somewhere else.

In your favour, patience gives you second and third looks at the other negotiator's proposals, and a chance to review your own. A few months later things might not look so hot as they did in the early flush of excitement about the prospects of a deal. You can change your views and your proposals. Time takes a toll of people. You can change your team. Slowing down to the pace of the other negotiator takes pressure off you, and might put it on him. Whoever is in the biggest hurry concedes the faster.

Penalty clause. Assurance against failure to comply with promises. Include such clauses in a contract if you doubt the ability of the supplier to meet delivery dates or performance standards (see PERFORMANCE BONDS). They can be a fixed sum for late delivery, or an escalating sum for each week or month. Insist on an option to cancel the contract at your discretion if delivery is unduly late.

When pressing for penalty clauses you can argue that if they have confidence in their performance they have nothing to fear from such a clause.

Resist penalties if the nature of the work creates unique uncertainties: unforseeable geological conditions, very narrow weather windows, special safety hazards, political instabilities that threaten access and egress, unresolved legal complications, dependence on suppliers outwith your control, technological frontiers, untested designs, reliance on client's data, subjection to client's changeable specifications and managerial directions.

Your performance guarantees only operate if spares, inputs and materials meet your own specifications (which they must guarantee); that operators and anybody connected with the process are properly trained (to standards set by you); and that the working environment is suitable for the process (which they must disclose and demonstrate to you). Insist on the right to on-site inspection, to replace or repair, and to decide if any working practice is in violation of your warranties.

Insist on a 'stop-the-clock' procedure in the contract. If delays are caused by the client's failure to meet obligations (drawings, formal orders to change specifications, inspection, formal notices to proceed etc.) the penalty clock stops at your notice and is re-started (at your confirmation) only when the client complies (which means when these papers, or their people, actually arrive at your premises, not when they leave theirs). Make sure that this moves *all* consequential critical dates back to new dates, and not just the dates of the immediately affected segment.

Penalty clauses are sometimes used for an entirely different purpose. Suppose a supplier is in tough price competition with others and cannot get down any more without offending 'unfair trading' rules. One desperate competitive but credible way to do so is to quote a price (beating a 'dumping' or 'illegal subsidy' rap), and take on substantial delivery penalties. As delivery could not possibly be met inside the promised dates, the penalties come into force. This is the same as a price reduction to the customer. You get a bad reputation for delivery, but you get the business (best confined to state-owned industries).

Pendulum arbitration. Arbitration whereby the arbitrator must choose one or other negotiator's FINAL OFFER and not seek a compromise between them.

Negotiators are influenced by the format of the arbitration. A negotiator refuses to settle on the grounds that if the arbitrator's decision is a compromise between the two final offers, an improvement in the other negotiator's 'final offer' is bound to result. This could encourage obstinacy and the manipulation of the arbitrator system.

When the arbitrator must choose one or other of the 'final offers', the negotiator has an interest in the character of his offer. If it is too extreme, the arbitrator is likely to choose the other negotiator's less extreme position. Adjusting one's final pre-pendulum arbitration offer to make it attractive to the arbitrator also makes it more attractive to the other negotiator. When both negotiators do this, they move to more conciliatory offers, which improves their chances of finding a negotiated solution.

Pendulum arbitration punishes extreme positions and outright obstinancy. The least accommodating of the negotiators risks having the other negotiator's offer imposed.

Perception. Seeing ourselves as nobody else does.

Your perception of something can be illusory, in the sense that it does not correspond to what is actually happening, or likely to happen. You are the best judge of your own interests, but your perception of the best way to develop those interests is at variance with what is possible, given the perception the other negotiator has of his interests and opportunities.

Other people's behaviour influences your perceptions. What you perceive confirms, or amends, your aspirations. Confirming them does not mean they are achievable, nor does amending them make them more realistic. The other party works on your perceptions in order to re-structure them in his favour, by shaking your faith in the viability of your current offer, and/or by increasing the sense of inevitability of settling at his current offer.

Structure your opponent's perceptions by your apparent:
- Willingness to deadlock.
- Indifference to settling quickly.
- Confidence that you have options.
- Resolve not to compromise.
- Professional success.
- Confidence in your current proposal.
- Willingness to listen.
- Reasonableness.

Use tactics that:
- Weaken your opponent's confidence.

Ask for the criteria, method of calculation, statement of the 'facts', and references to precedent or convention which support

the other negotiator's case; then closely question the answers, looking for inconsistencies, alternative 'facts', dubious assumptions, omissions and unwarranted conclusions. A single damaging rebuttal is worth a dozen point-scoring irrelevances.
- Deter resort to COERCION.

Assert your desires for a negotiated settlement to save unnecessary costs to both sides: 'ultimately, this matter will be resolved by negotiation, and it behoves us both to seek that solution without recourse to the expense and stress of outright conflict'. Propose an adjournment to 'cool off' and think through the consequences of not coming to an agreement by negotiation. Show willingness to continue negotiations for 'as long as it takes'.
- Enhance the viability of your own proposals.

Show confidence in your presentation, your grasp of detail, your willingness to understand their needs and to consider options that bridge your differences, and your intention of coming to an agreement as soon as possible (though you are more than willing to wait, if needs be).

Performance bonds. Varying degrees of onerous burdens imposed by buyers on sellers.

It comes down to power: if the other party have it, they use it, and if one of their demands is for a performance bond you have not got a lot of choice.

Originally the performance bond protected the client from buying a lemon: the dam leaks; the power station has not got any; the bridge is unsafe for bicycles; the hospital is more dangerous than the surgery; the air conditioning doesn't; and the consultants you send are unemployable, etc. Being liable for a performance bond concentrates your efforts to ensure that your promised performance meets agreed standards. If it does not, the client cashes the bond and captures a large predetermined amount of your money. If he is dishonest your money disappears into an untraceable Swiss bank account; if he is honest, you lose the interest it could have earned.

It is not necessary for the client to prove that you failed to meet agreed performance levels in order to cash the bond and take your money. The performance bond could be unconditional. Some clients insist upon an unconditional bond that gives them a right to present it, as the fancy takes them, to a bank or insurance company for payment. Some sellers agree to this arrangement in an act of reckless desperation for the business, or because they believe they have nothing to fear in the quality of their performance.

The trap is easily sprung. Refusal to agree to a performance bond disqualifies you from the business – on the grounds that you have something to fear from agreeing to one – so you agree. You want the bond to be conditional on sound evidence that you have failed in some material respect, and if agreement cannot be reached that you have failed, you want independent ARBITRATION invoked to decide fairly. But the logic of demonstrating confidence leads them to demand that the bond is unconditional: 'If you are really confident you would agree. What are you hiding?'

Performance bonds shift the risk from the buyer to the seller (if buying, demand one). And the risk is transformed from one of performance to one of whether the client invokes payment. The power balance determines whether you agree to their terms. Government purchasing departments, especially in developing countries, demand them. Beware: unscrupulous officials who control the process of invocation of performance bonds sometimes press for a side-payment (see BRIBERY) from you as an inducement for the bonds not to be invoked.

Perry Mason tactic. Behaving like legal counsel and interrogating a hapless victim, who happens to be the party you are trying to negotiate an agreement with.

The tactic consists of asking a string of questions, the answers to which are at first apparently innocuous. As you receive the answer 'yes', you move in for the killer question:

'You agree that the delivery was made?'
'Yes.'
'You accept that your people signed for the quantity as per the invoice?'
'Yes.'
'Your people are aware that the driver only unloads if instructed by the client to do so?'
'Yes.'
'Then why are you persisting in your claim that our delivery was unauthorized?'
('Because, nobody authorized the order in the first place.')

Often the Perry Mason is quite illegitimate. There is no connection between the lead-in questions and the ultimate questions. Your opponent senses this, and tries to evade even the most obvious of questions ('You agree that today is Tuesday?' 'Er, well . . .'). They are wary of what is coming. If they agree to one question you pronounce them 'guilty'. Hence, best not to answer any questions at all.

Counter: Ask 'what exactly are you getting at?'

See QUESTIONS.

Personal relationships. Never underestimate their value. Only trespass on them once. Do not rely on them. Business is business.

While you seek to cultivate sound personal relationships based on demonstrated trust and reliability, you must recognize that other people's commitment to your interests, when the bullet slides into the breach, is fragile.

Commercial negotiators, diplomats and bargaining agents inevitably form relationships, if only from getting to know each other. These relationships are important, however tentative they may be, for negotiating with somebody you do not know is more difficult than negotiating with somebody you do (ask sellers whether they prefer cold canvassing to hot leads).

The basic principle of establishing a personal negotiating relationship is not to push the other negotiator into the ground by COERCION; it is not even to push them to your TARGET PRICE; it is to assist them to achieve their OBJECTIVES within the boundaries of your own. In short: don't take undue advantage of their predicament.

Sounds soft? Not really. In those cases where a personal relationship is possible, and desirable (yes, you have a motive!), there is a pay-off, both in regular business, to your mutual profit, and in occasional special favours, without which you could be in trouble.

Consider the apocryphal story of David Frost calling his friend and business associate Kerry Packer by telephone and asking him to buy for an exclusive Australian showing the first Richard Nixon TV interview after his resignation as President. Frost asked for $360,000. Packer said it was too much. Frost said: 'Kerry, I need $360,000.' Packer could have squeezed Frost at this point, for Frost had disclosed a VULNERABILITY. But business is business, and there is no business like long-term business, so Packer offered to toss a coin. If Frost called it right, he got $360,000. Packer tossed (or did he?), and Frost called 'heads' down the telephone. Packer told him he was right, and agreed to pay $360,000. If Frost had no relationship at all with Packer, if he had been overstretched on his first deal as an unknown and Packer did not care to exercise his discretion, how would the coin have landed?

Persuasion. Most common form of discourse when you face a problem. Also the least effective.

People whose interests are different from yours are not easily persuaded if the stakes are important to them. They are unwilling to accept your mere persuasion. The irony is, when they are not persuaded by your reasonable, logical, sensible statements, you are frustrated, you become annoyed, you perceive a wickedness in their inability to see your point of view. The result: an ARGUMENT, a breakdown in the discussions, a time for plotting their downfall.

You limit the likelihood of failure by:

● Attempting to persuade them of simple, easy to agree points, rather than complex, controversial issues.

● Emphasizing your eagerness for reaching an agreement, not complying (i.e. do not mix persuasion with THREATS).

● Restricting yourself to a few robust arguments in favour of your position that stand up to scrutiny rather than diluting them with an encyclopaedia of spurious arguments that collapse as soon as the weakest is challenged.

● Offering to trade movement on things they desire for movement on things you desire (i.e. BARGAINING is the most powerful persuader in the business).

Positional bargaining. Build yourself a position, fortify it.

You want the highest price? Fine. Determine what that price is (your TARGET), add a bit for negotiating room (your SHAM OFFER), and set to work defending your position against all-comers (even people who want to do business with you within your settlement range). Pity you miss out on a deal!

This is partly a caricature, but it is how positional bargaining is

"Aha! Trying to buy us off with huge salaries and great working conditions, huh?"

seen by critics. Negotiators, it is argued, get stuck into defending positions instead of seeking a reconciliation of interests between the parties. The process of defending a position automatically involves attacking the other party's position, and this leads to destructive ARGUMENT, ultimatums, impossible 'either, or' choices and DEADLOCK. Adjusting your behaviour from 'hard' to 'soft' is not a solution.

An alternative approach is through principled bargaining (PRINCIPLES 2). Briefly, concentrate on the problem not the people involved; focus on INTERESTS not positions; search for options (see TRADABLES); agree to objective criteria for choosing the solution.

The criticism is worth noting, but it is not enough if it involves dramatically changing the way negotiators behave. Applying objective criteria to impasse and deadlock is a useful device, if the other party agrees to do so, and if you can find mutually acceptable objective criteria (see FORMULA BARGAINING). But your criteria may produce results inimical to me, and therefore we remain deadlocked.

We can learn to avoid destructive argument. We can focus our attention on our interests, and we can broaden our options to create trade-offs that resolve the problem). Bargaining along a single continuum (ZERO-SUM) or between two disjointed variables (you gain nothing by trading one for the other as they are both detrimental to your interests) is weaker than opening up numerous variables for trading, some of which are beneficial for you.

Some criticism of so-called positional bargaining, like the caricature above, is a trifle sanctimonious: 'You may lose because they use brute strength and ignorance, but you are morally in the right.' But being 'in the right' is not enough, if insisting on 'being right' is an obstacle to an agreement.

Power. Like the wind, felt rather than seen. You have power over the other negotiator to the extent that you can induce him to do something he would otherwise not do. And vice versa.

But why should he do your bidding? Is the reward (positive inducement) sufficient to alter his preferred behaviour? Against what alternatives does he measure the reward? Is the threat of some sanction (negative inducement) sufficient to alter his preferred behaviour? Against what alternative costs does he measure your threat?

Much could be said, and has been said exhaustively elsewhere, by many people, about the nature and the 'mystery' of power. But here we need little more than a simple cut at the meaning of power in a negotiating context. Chamberlain's model of bargaining power is adequate for this purpose (after N. W. Chamberlain, *Collective Bargaining*, New York, McGraw-Hill, 1951; see also H. M. Levinson, *Determining Forces in Collective Wage Bargaining*, New York, John Wiley, 1966). Your bargaining power, as is your opponent's, is a function of the relative costs of disagreement to each of you. Specifically:

$$\text{your bargaining power} = \frac{\text{(cost to them of rejecting your terms)}}{\text{(cost to them of accepting your terms)}}$$

$$\text{their bargaining power} = \frac{\text{(cost to you of rejecting their terms)}}{\text{(cost to you of accepting their terms)}}$$

In general, if your calculated ratio (ignoring the question of whether the ratios can be calculated accurately) is greater than unity (the costs of rejection are larger than the costs of acceptance), then you have bargaining power over the other side, and vice versa.

Operational content can be put into the ratios by calculating the actual costs of rejecting their offer. These costs must be probabalistic: there is no certainty that their last offer is their FINAL OFFER, nor that the threatened, or implied, consequence (strike, lock-out, cancelled contract, divorce, war etc.) will materialize. Moreover, your estimates of the costs of accepting their last offer may be pessimistic (in labour and international negotiations it is easy to believe your own rhetoric of 'mayhem' and 'disaster'; perhaps this is because they are conducted in a semi-public manner?).

Power is a subjective concept. You perceive their power according to many influences flowing into your mind, some of them unconsciously, some of them mistaken.

See NEGOTIATING WITH YOURSELF.

Praising the product. Don't. It only encourages them to charge more for supplying it.

Pre-emptive bid. Tactic to jump a queue before an AUCTION. You bid an amount chosen to induce the owner to accept it in preference to waiting for the auction.

If the bid is 'high' enough, the inducement is plain. Can the owner do better by waiting? If the owner is pessimistic about reaching his RESISTANCE PRICE – you are the only person to show any interest for example – even an 'ordinary' or 'low' price might be enough. What does he gain by waiting, if, meanwhile, you look elsewhere? He could ask to see your bid, and then reject it in the belief that you will re-bid at the auction and might offer more, or at least re-present it as it stands.

Apply extra pressure: make your pre-emptive bid conditional on its almost immediate acceptance. State that if the bid is rejected you will not re-bid subsequently at any price whatsoever. Mean it.

Premium pricing. Another term for SKIMMING. Premium brands are marketed at higher prices than regular or economy brands. The price mark-up may not reflect anything substantial in terms of product differences. If the other negotiator perceives your product to be superior to substitutes, he might be persuaded to pay a premium (i.e. higher) price for it.

Preparation. Jewel in the crown of negotiation. Get this right (and merely doing it is not enough) and your performance in the negotiation dramatically improves.

The best preparation is knowing your business better than anybody else. If you don't know your business well enough, you can rely on your rivals to teach you. (See TRADABLES).

● What are my INTERESTS? Remind yourself what business you are in and why.
● What are the issues? Itemize the details for negotiation.
● What are my TARGETS? Quantify them.
● What are my priorities? Prioritize them.
● What are my RESISTANCE POINTS?
● What probability of success is there for varying offers between my resistance point and my targets? (See DECISION ANALYSIS.)
● What don't I want, and how badly? (See INHIBITIONS.)
● What does the other party want?
● What might be their targets?
● How might they prioritize their targets? (See PRIORITIES.)
● What information have I got that helps me?
● What information could hinder me if disclosed? (See DEADLINES.)
● What information do I need to verify my assumptions?
● What is my STRATEGY? Select offers with acceptable possibilities of success. Keep it simple.
● What happens if it isn't working? Select a fall-back strategy.

Write everything down. A preparation planner is a useful tool for developing your ideas during preparation. This can be set out on a single sheet of paper in a notebook, or, for complex negotiations, a chalk board or several sheets of flip chart paper can be utilized (and displayed along the walls).

Essentially, your objectives are listed in a column down the lefthand side of the paper (see figure). Starting at the top, set out your MUST GETS, followed by your Should Gets (of intermediate priority) and Could Gets (of marginal priority) (see PRIORITIES). In a relatively simple negotiation covering only a few issues, a single sheet of paper can accommodate all your objectives (see OBJECTIVES).

EFFECTIVE NEGOTIATORS prepare by establishing a range rather than a fixed number as their target for each objective. Across the page, you should enter in the range of values for each objective that you consider to be achievable in the negotiation, beginning on the left with the worst acceptable terms and ending on the right with the best (credible) terms (see figure 8).

Figure 8

PREPARATION PLANNER OBJECTIVES

	RANGE		
PRIORITIES	Minimum	Maximum	FIRST OFFER
Must Gets			
Should Gets			
Could Gets			

In the final column on the righthand side of the paper, enter the details of your FIRST OFFER. This might be your maximum target value for that objective, or you might decide in the circumstances to PAD it to give you additional negotiating room. The activity associated with systematically preparing using a planner in this way has the advantage that it makes you (and your team) think about and discuss each of your negotiating objectives, and, in doing so, ensures a greater familiarity with the details of the negotiation than a casual run over the issues just before you meet the other negotiators. The original preparation planner also forms the basis for your post-negotiation REVIEW.

Price. First unassailable law of the market: the selling price of a single item is not what it cost its owner, but what it is worth to the keenest person to acquire it.

The total revenue from sales of volume items equals price per item times quantity sold, and total cost from producing the volume items equals cost per item times quantity produced, giving the second unassailable law of the market: if total revenue minus total cost is greater than zero you make a PROFIT and stay in business; if it isn't, you go bust eventually, unless you can borrow or subsidize the difference permanently. To stay in business, find enough buyers keen to acquire your output at a price which raises total revenue above total costs.

Problem: Your costs are your affair; your selling price is set by the market.

All problems of companies usually boil down to how they handle the cost/price problem. You cope with the second law (see above) by driving down costs per unit (search for efficiency), finding the price that captures the most profitable total revenue (net of marketing costs), or some combination of both. Troubles begin when companies kid themselves that they are 'driving down costs' when all they are doing is ignoring them – 'write offs', altering attributions across cost headings, changing depreciation practice etc. Alternatively, they kid themselves that they are 'capturing the most profitable total revenue', when in fact they are simply indulging in creative number juggling – 'marginal cost pricing', 'pricing for contribution to overheads'; 'pricing to fill unused capacity' or to 'clear the shelves'.

Price blind. Being utterly indifferent to price.

Such buyers are not always a joy to sell to as sometimes they are obsessed with quality, both in what they buy and how they are served during and after the sale. But most price-blind people are indifferent because they cannot count or cannot be bothered to do so. Naturally, mostly they are rich but the poor too can be price-blind. Sometimes their indifference to price arises from their concern with the product or service, confirming that negotiations do not always, or even often, turn on the price alone. People buy for all kinds of reasons, some of them more the private concern of their analysts than their suppliers.

Price negotiations. Prices are determined by the market, but what is the market? It is not a list of prices available to everyone (that is a fiction from Economics 1). In fact, most people have very hazy ideas about 'the market price'. If you researched hard enough, checked out every supplier and customer and considered every conceivable influence on your price, you might discover 'the' market price, but by the time you do, the market moves on (and so will your customers). You do not sell to markets, you sell to people, and these people do not have perfect information (another fiction from Economics 1).

It is the inevitable lack of information in a complex society that makes markets more efficient than non-markets as the ultimate allocator of resources, but the lag in the dissemination of information is such that it takes time for buyers and sellers to correct their behaviour after they receive new information about prices different from the ones they are trading at, or about different versions of products or services from the one they are trading in.

Imperfect information is both your edge and your torment: am I selling/buying too low/high; could I do better with somebody else's offerings; is this the best price I can get, or should I try for a better one? The uneven landscape of the market enables you to differentiate your offerings from the competition.

Against this background, you negotiate the price of what is on offer. If buyers are queuing six deep to buy your stock, your price will be higher than if you are in a six deep queue of sellers waiting to sell it. But if it is 'down to price' and price alone, consider getting out of that line of business (see PRICE WAR).

A pure price negotiation is a ZERO-SUM game. But you don't want to get into pure price negotiations. (Note: If the buyers are six deep, why are you negotiating?). Your most profitable strategy is to widen the negotiation from price alone to other TRADABLES. Separate yourself from the competition. Form a queue with only one person in it: yourself! Go for the big numbers (test the quantity discounts available from sellers; test the total revenue available from buyers). Go for the ADD-ONS (test the buyer's price sensitivity; test the seller's mark-up). Go for the cooperative relationship (test the buyer's INTERESTS; test the seller's reliability). Go for the mutual WIN-WIN (test the buyer's room for manoeuvre; test the seller's room for manoeuvre).

Where should you open a price negotiation? Certainly not too close to your RESISTANCE PRICE. Negotiations, however, fill the time available for them, and if your FIRST OFFER is at the top of the SHAM range you are either going to have to move quickly (losing credibility) or going to have to extend the time available for negotiation, which won't happen if the buyer gives you 'ten minutes only' (INTIMIDATION by DEADLINE). See also USED CAR SALE.)

Price versus cost. Tactic to protect a price from a buyer's challenge. Example:

'Do you want low price or low cost?'
'I don't follow you.'
'Low priced products cost more when you use them. They break down more often and have a short life.'
'You just want me to pay your high price?'
'Sure I want you to pay my price, but I also want you to benefit from a longer lasting product with lower costs over its longer life than a cheapie.'
'So?'
'Well, you pay my price only once, but how many times will you pay for the cheapie?'

Price wars. Avoid one. Move into some other business. Move up market or move down market or move sideways, but don't join in. If forced in, restrict the conflict to a narrow front.

Price wars are won by the big batallions. If your market share is one per cent, you won't drive a Fortune 500 competitor, with 20 per cent, out of the market by slashing your prices. They could give your one per cent volume free to your customers and wait until you ran out of breath.

Prudent counter: Position yourself in the market outside of their reach.

If the big batallions go to war – to eliminate overcapacity, to reorganize the market, to drive out intruders – act prudently. To protect your market segment from collateral damage, don't provoke the contestants by a high profile attack on their flanks; consider their strengths, find the niche in their strengths where you can do better, and attack that niche, but quietly.

Example: A leading sales training company opened a price war on the per head cost of a one-day seminar. They slashed the going rate by 70 per cent in one jump. To cover costs they had to attract volume attendances; to do this they had to book large venues, advertise massively and hire expensive visual aids. This shoved up their costs (wars are expensive) and increased their VULNERABILITY (fighters of price wars do not take prisoners). Another market leader, perceiving the razzamatazz, and not wishing to be driven out of business, joined in, and slashed its prices by 40 per cent. Expensive advertising from both companies hit the sales training market, putting pressure on everybody's margins ('Why should I pay your 115 a head for a one-day training seminar when I can go to the 'road show' for 30?').

Marginal training companies went out of business, or slashed staff as much as they slashed prices to compete with the leaders. We didn't. We re-positioned ourselves as consultant negotiators' not sales trainers, maintained our fees for one-day seminars at 115 per head and narrowed the focus of the war by running more two-day seminars. By raising our fees on all programmes over one day, we rode out the war. If we had slashed our one-day rates, and widened the war by slashing our prices across all courses, we would not have survived, nor deserved to. The market leader who started the war went bust.

In a price war if you cannot keep out of it the objective is to survive, not to win (for there are no winners). If you can stop one starting, do so. When Robert Maxwell (*Daily Mirror*) and Rupert Murdoch (*Sun*) were on the brink of a price war, Maxwell threatened to cut two pence for every penny Murdoch cut. Murdoch did not get where he is today by throwing good money after bad.

Principal. The organ grinder.

Advantages of dealing with principals:
- They make the final decision
- They can authorize changes.
- They can accept unusual offers.
- They are closest to the money.
- They can come to a decision quickly.
- You have equal status.
- You eliminate wallys.

Disadvantages of dealing with principals:
- No appeal against their final decision.
- They are not always on top of the detail.
- They are too busy for slow-moving negotiations.
- They do not believe in equal status.
- They are emotionally involved with their properties.
- Some of them are wallys.

Principles (1). Sometimes it is necessary to rise above them.

Negotiators who affirm to having principles generally mean the beliefs that sanctify their prejudices. These people are extremely difficult to negotiate with, for their 'principles' are a barrier to movement. Examples are: 'I never negotiate under duress' (irre-spective of the continuing misery caused by this principle?) or 'I will never negotiate with Communists/Jews/terrorists/South Africans/blacks/whites/muslims/non-muslims/infidels/traitors/Palestinians/fascists/Catholics/Ulster Protestants/feminists/males/Indians/Chinese' (enter any other category).

COERCION to get negotiations started is duress and reinforces the self-fulfilling prejudices of the party with the principle; it is also bad news for those demaged collaterally. 'Every inch of our territory is sacred' (including the uninhabited crown of a glacier 15,000 feet above sea level?).

Principles (2). 'Never yield to pressure, only to principle', after R. Fisher and W. Ury, *Getting to Yes: Negotiating agreement without giving in*, London, Hutchinson, 1983, Houghton Mifflin, Boston, 1981.

Objective principles are not obstacles to agreement. They assist the process. Instead of battling over conflicting demands, the negotiators search for objective criteria to judge the merits of alternative solutions.

If objective criteria are agreed (and this is not certain: see FORMULA BARGAINING), these become the principles that determine the joint solution. You appeal to 'fair standards', to 'fairness' generally and to criteria independent of both of you (market valuation, scientific measurement, legal precedent, actual costs, agreed objectives and so on). You may have to modify your demands in the light of the mutually chosen criteria and you must be willing to do so.

If pressure is applied, resist it. Insist on determining the issue by principles. Who wins? As usual it depends. If they have the POWER, it is decided their way, not yours. And this is the weakness of this excellent approach to negotiation: there is seldom a unique set of objective criteria for each dispute. Indeed, the parties can DEADLOCK over the choice of criteria, with each backing a selection that enhances its own position, taking us back to the problem of POSITIONAL BARGAINING.

Priorities. Best sorted out in PREPARATION, not while negotiating face to face.

Objectives in negotiation are not all weighted with the same degree of priority, otherwise there would be room for movement. Some issues are more important than others and their ranking should be decided beforehand. The most important issues are MUST GETS – you genuinely prefer no agreement at all to not securing your must gets. Other issues can be graded into should gets and could gets. These are issues that you can TRADE to get agreement.

Events in the negotiation could prompt you to revise your priorities and you might wish to ADJOURN to consider the changing circumstances. Establishing your priorities is meant to be an organizing not a stultifying activity. The act of prioritizing objectives or issues ensures a firmer grasp of the detail of the negotiated issues than opening with a hazy notion of what is important to you.

Prisoner's dilemma. There is no solution to a dilemma – that is why it is a dilemma. You face many dilemmas in negotiating: where to open, when to move, whether to agree or deadlock? Whatever you choose in a particular negotiation becomes part of history – you do not get a second shot to play it differently. True, you can try something different the next time, but it is a different time, and what works, or does not work, that time, in those circumstances, with those people, over those issues, has no bearing on the outcome of any previous or subsequent negotiation.

The nature of dilemma is illustrated in a game known as the prisoner's dilemma. Two suspects are questioned separately by the District Attorney about a major robbery which they committed (though the DA does not have enough evidence to convict them yet). He does have enough evidence to convict them both of a lesser offence. The prisoners are interviewed in separate rooms with no possibility of communication. They are each given a choice between confessing and not confessing to the serious crime. The DA's proposition is: if you confess, but your partner does not, you turn state's evidence and go free, and your partner gets twenty years; if you both confess you each get ten years; if neither confesses, you get five years each for the lesser offence. The pay-offs are shown in figure 9, with prisoner B's pay-off first in each box.

Figure 9

	Prisoner A	
	Confess	Not confess
Confess	10, 10	0, 20
Prisoner B		
Not confess	20, 0	5, 5

If you were prisoner B, what would you do? You could reason thus: 'If I can rely on my partner not to confess, we both get a short sentence (five years each) if I do not confess too (bottom right-hand box), but can I rely on him? Suppose I can rely on him out of loyalty not to confess, why not turn state's evidence and confess? That way I get off and he gets twenty years (top right-hand box). But if he is thinking of turning state's evidence, and relying on me not to confess, I take a twenty-year rap (bottom left-hand box). On the other hand, if we both confess, believing that the other is turning state's evidence, we end up doing ten years each (top left-hand box). I wonder what he is thinking about what I am thinking about what he is thinking?'

Applying the prisoner's dilemma to a commercial problem consider the following scenario. You are approached by a stranger in a foreign country which has a ridiculous notion of what its currency is worth in exchange for yours. The stranger offers you a deal in which he purchases your spare currency at 200:1 instead of the official rate of 4:1. His proviso is that because the transaction is illegal and carries heavy penalties he cannot be seen handing over the money to you in public. Therefore, he suggests that you leave your dollars behind a shed in the park, and he will leave his quonks in exchange under the bed in your hotel room. You agree to the transaction and the arrangements for the exchange, and set off to complete your side.

What goes through your mind? If you leave your money in the park, and he leaves nothing in your room, you lose your money (pay-off: minus your money); if you leave nothing behind the shed, and he leaves money in your room, you gain his money (pay-off: plus his money); if neither of you leave anything behind the shed or in the room, you gain nothing (pay-off; zero); if you both leave money as arranged, you profit on the transaction by the difference between the official and illegal exchange rate for your money (pay-off: Q196 = $1). This is set out in figure 10. Think through what you would do.

Figure 10

		Stranger	
		Cheat	Don't cheat
You	Cheat	0, 0	Q,–Q
	Don't cheat	–$, $	Q, $

Note that cheating is a result of total lack of TRUST, and this drives you into mutual losses. One-sided cheating aims to take advantage of the other party in pursuit of unilateral gains; if you both try for these you both lose. Alternatively, if you cooperate (don't cheat) you can make mutual gains.

These dilemmas have valid applications to the negotiating situation. They help spell out the implications of COMPETITIVE and COOPERATIVE STYLES of strategy and behaviour. Going for shot-term gains (the 'cheating' choice) can severely damage your long-term gains (a cheated stranger is unlikely to become a cooperative friend). Going for long-term gains (not exploiting your bargaining position) could be beneficial in the long run, but it is also risky in the short run if you are modifying your gains with someone who regards you as a one-off temporary partner.

See TIT-FOR-TAT.

Probability. The future is uncertain. Some events are more likely than others. Estimating the likelihood of a future event is one means of planning for the future.

Something absolutely certain to happen is assigned the number 1; something absolutely certain not to happen is assigned the number zero; all other likelihoods of events occurring are assigned numbers between 1 and 0. For example, something with an even chance of occurring has a probability of 0.5 (or 50 per cent); an event with a higher probability of occurring is assigned a number such as 0.7, and an event with a lower probability of occurring is assigned a number such as 0.3.

The value to you now of a future uncertain event is its value (or pay-off) times the probability of its occurring. This is its expected value. Which would you rather have: a 0.5 chance of a 1,000 profit, or a 0.8 chance of a 600 profit, or a 0.2 chance of 10,000 profit?

See DECISION ANALYSIS.

Problem solving. Requires TRUST between the parties and confidence in each other's motives. Unilateral attempts to problem solve a dispute expose you to STRATEGIC INTERACTION by the other party if they continue to use a COMPETITIVE STYLE.

Problem solvers aim to maximize joint gains; focus on common interests, not differences; are non-confrontational, non-argumentive and apply standards of 'fairness', 'common sense' and 'reasonableness' (see PRINCIPLES 2). They believe the other party can be motivated to replace egoistic with enlightened self-interest.

Procedure. Formal negotiating procedures are common in COLLECTIVE BARGAINING. These usually involve formal rules for initiating grievances and claims. They cover the varying levels at which negotiations are conducted, from the workshop floor to the company president, and what arrangements there are for ARBITRATION if FAILURE TO AGREE continues.

For example, a procedure agreement between a trade union and an employer would set out formal recognition of each side's rights and interests. The union will be named in the agreement (and this is of great value to the union). Individual union members are required to take up any grievances they have with their immediate manager in the first instance. If they fail to agree, the next level of management can be contacted, usually through, or accompanied by, an officially recognized representative of the union (who might be another employee of the company or a full-time official of the union). Accreditation of the union representatives is another important issue for the union, and procedures lay down how accreditation is to be secured.

If the local officials cannot settle the grievance, they can invoke higher levels of representation within the union who will be accorded higher level access with the company. Where the company has more than one plant, the higher level management will deal with the national officials of the union. A grievance that survives the early opportunities for resolving it is clearly likely to be of significance to both sides. The union will take a view on the significance of the member's grievance and how it relates to union policy. This acts, in theory, to filter out trivial grievances before they reach senior management levels. In practice, the union can loosen the filter when it wishes to impose pressure on the management – it lets grievance cases through to clog up the negotiation procedure, and use up management time, which normally it would block.

Companies considering formal procedures with a union should be wary of conceding 'closed shops' or '100 per cent union membership agreements'. Membership of a union should remain a voluntary decision of the employees and those employees who do not wish to join a union should not be discriminated against in any respect. Companies should consider requiring the agreement to be of fixed, rather than the more normal, indefinite, duration. They should be sure to include a statement that 'no accredited representative of the union will be accorded special privileges as an employee and at all times will be subject to the normal disciplinary rules that apply to all employees'. They should reserve their right to communicate directly with all employees on any matters, and at no time concede this as an exclusive right of the union. In their own long-term interests they should also exercise this right on a regular basis, as communicating with employees only in crises with the union can be counter-productive.

Progress payment. Reduces exposure on long leadtime projects.

Paying for materials for major construction projects imposes costs on the supplier (the capital tied up, perhaps for months or even years, has a cost in its alternative profitable uses). There is also a risk of financial failure by the client, of a change of government policy or a change of government (some regions are renowned for political instability) and of a cash crisis in your own operation.

Progress payments are made for identifiable progress in the project. They can be triggered off by completion of specific stages, from the arrival of the materials for processing, through to delivery on site and fabrication.

Alternative systems include paying up to one-third of the cost of signing the contract, one-third at specified stages during construction and one-third (less 5 per cent) on completion. The 5 per cent balance is paid after the project has experienced a running-in period as a security against unforeseen, or hidden, failings in the structure and an unwillingness on the supplier's part to rectify the problem. When ordering major works, including domestic improvements, insert in the contract a right to retain 5 per cent (or more) for this purpose. When forced to comply with such a request, counter with a demand for interest on the outstanding balance.

Promises. Best kept.

Proposal. The only thing that can be negotiated.

You cannot negotiate an argument, a belief, an opinion, a prejudice, a principle, a hope, a grievance, a fancy or a fact. Confine your debate to such as these, and you won't do much negotiating.

A proposal is a tentative suggestion for resolving the issue, contrasted to a bargain which is a specific offer to resolve the issue. Like bargains, proposals are best made conditionally, using a format that puts the condition first: 'If you will do the following, then I am prepared to consider doing such and such.' The condition protects you if it is rejected: you need not fear that your offer to do something in return will be ambushed and left on the table. If they do not accept your conditions, they cannot have the benefits of your offer.

True, making a proposal discloses information about your SETTLEMENT RANGE (see BARGAINING CONTINUUM), but that is inescapable (it being impossible to propose and simultaneously hide your offer). That is why your proposal is specific about what you want them to do, and vague about what you would do in return. The vagueness loosens your attachment to a specific number or a specific course of action: 'consider', 'look at', 'do something on the penalty issues', and 'see what I can do about', are typical vague offers associated with proposals.

Some negotiations require (by statute, custom, necessity, convenience or tactical advantage) that initial proposals be made in writing. These should follow a FIRST OFFER format – SHAM if open to informal negotiation (answering a request for broad details of charges); close to TARGET if open to formal negotiation (approaching an imminent decision or TWO OFFERS ONLY); close to RESISTANCE if a competitive bid (ONE-OFFER-ONLY).

Verbal proposals have the advantage that you avoid the necessity of outlining your settlement range before you have had an opportunity to assess their expectations through constructive ARGUMENT. They have the disadvantage that you can fumble the presentation, disclose too much about your priorities and true aspirations (see NON-VERBAL BEHAVIOUR) and make premature concession exchanges. To obviate these disadvantages, proposals should be:

- stated briefly
- without long explanations
- SUMMARIZED.

Handling proposals (written or verbal):
- Avoid:
instant rejection
instant response
instant agreement
instant counters
instant argument
emotional outbursts
inputing motives
making threats.
- Seek:
clarification and understanding
details of criteria used
the thinking behind suggestions.
- Do:
listen to the answers
treat each item neutrally
summarize your understanding
look for bridges between your respective opening positions
consider possibilities for PACKAGING

consider your response(s) and how you should present them: alternative proposal or package?

Psychology. The psychology of negotiating is a complex subject. People are different. Smart asses believe they know what's going on, the rest of us are left wondering.

The two great drives of human endeavour are our motivations and whatever we perceive the world outside to be (our cognitive perceptions). These do not always match.

Taking motivations, these are best summed up by Maslow's hierarchy of needs (after A. H. Maslow, 'A theory of human motivation', *Psychological Review*, 50 (1943), pp. 370–96, and *Motivation and Personality*, New York, Harper & Row, 1954) (see also NEEDS THEORY.)

Human needs are expressed in an ascending order of importance as each level of need is satisfied:

1 Phsyiological needs (hunger, thirst).
2 Safety and security needs.
3 Love and belonging needs (acceptance).
4 Esteem needs.
5 Self-actualization needs.
6 Needs to know.
7 Aesthetic needs. Experimental and empirical evidence for this order of needs, particularly for the higher level needs, is mixed. But as a working hypothesis it appears to fit the facts. The starving are hardly likely to be concerned about status (unless it is related to access to food). But satisfy the basic needs and the other needs come into play. For negotiators these needs are important.

For example, a new buyer in the market, unused yet to the hustle and bustle, will choose products that meet his security needs (well-known brands, not new ones that might be risky; this is why corporate advertising to position your product as safe and secure pays off with new buyers entering the market). If you are an unknown quantity, you have an uphill struggle to convince him to buy your product. When executives decide to purchase equipment (for example, computers) they often go to the biggest name in the business because they perceive that the biggest name is safer than the newest name.

Negotiators with a need to be loved (i.e. respected) are VULNER-

ABLE. They behave according to what they think is pleasing to the other party, but are not sure whether they should behave to please their own masters instead. In short, they dither. Unable to decide whom to please, they try to please everybody. They are no pleasure to deal with. Either experience improves their performance or they quit the business.

Self-esteem is a powerful motivator, whether it is the knowledge that we are worthy of respect because of our professionalism (negotiating a good deal for our side, or making the other side work hard for their gains), or whether we are proud of our achievements when set against recognized perceptions of the difficulties involved in achieving what we managed. This last creates opportunities to manipulate other peoples' perceptions of the difficulties we faced in a negotiation, or to present our negotiating goals in a modest way such that when we exceed them we reap yet higher esteem than our strict entitlement in the circumstances.

Actually achieving first class results in a negotiation which stretch us to the limits of our powers conforms to our self-actualization needs. The appeal of the search for excellence, currently fashionable in the almost evangelical school of management personified by Tom Peters – *A Passion for Excellence: the leadership difference*, Collins, London, 1985 – finds a direct response among managers susceptible to this motivator given their position or aspirations in the hierarchy of needs.

Our cognitive perceptions of the world have a complex source. The set of beliefs that we work to have roots that go deep into our psychology, our past, the past of the society we grew up in and our perceptions of the world as adults. This makes international negotiations particularly fraught as the cognitive structures of the collective entity known as the nation are not easily or quickly changed. Which explains why commentators on a country's negotiating stances on international issues (such as Roger Fisher of Harvard University) who have not sought nor been elected to public office – and thereby have never had to face absorption into the 'public' consciousness of these issues – can often see 'solutions' to these problems which in the circumstances are impractical, in the sense that no party articulating those solutions could get elected (even though the solutions may be eminently rational in themselves).

Our cognitive disposition includes our prejudices, folk myths, and taboos. Negotiating with union representatives also involves negotiating with people imbued with a sense of the history of their union. There is not always a common language accepted by the negotiators. 'Profit' to a manager may mean 'exploitation' and 'theft' to a union member; 'efficiency' could mean 'slave driving'; a 'good deal' could mean a 'rip off' and so on. Internationally, the paucity of common meanings separates the negotiators of more than one country and political system: consider the different interpretations of the words democracy, justice, rights, welfare, equality and defence found in representatives of states as diverse as the United States, the Soviet Union, Iran, Nicaragua and New Zealand.

There is a wilderness of scope for finding contradictions in the cognitive disposition of other negotiators. People are capable of holding passionately to totally contradictory beliefs. These intrude into the negotiation as naturally as people blow their noses when they have a cold. Frontally attacking somebody's belief system is rarely successful. If a negotiated peace requires the other side to suspend its entire belief system as a first step, there is little hope of success. Hence, negotiators preparing a strategy should consider how to advance their proposals without setting off psychological resistance through antagonizing or irritating the other negotiator's belief systems, or undermining their personal motivations.

In effect, recognizing the legitimacy of the other negotiator's personal motivations, and refraining from disrespect towards their system of beliefs (no matter how alien you consider their 'weird' views to be) are healthy first steps towards effective negotiation with them. This probably explains why powerful opposites – the fiercely anti-capitalist Maoist Chinese and the as fiercely anti-communist President Nixon in the 1970s for example – are able to find common ground more easily than 'softer' leaders who are ostensibly more liberal towards each other. Those leaders who are furthest apart in their cognitive perceptions often find themselves in mutual respect of each other, and this appears to be conducive to reaching a settlement on the practical issues of their relationship when circumstances dictate that such a negotiation is necessary.

Public stance. A COMMITMENT TACTIC.

By taking a public stance, the negotiator signals commitment to the declared outcome, ostensibly putting pressure on the other negotiator. It sometimes works. The other negotiator knows that you cannot back off a public statement without considerable loss of face. This induces him to believe that you intend to fight might and main for your publicly declared objective. In consequence, he gives more than he intended.

Alternatively, your public stance imprisons your negotiating flexibility. A reasonable compromise is excluded because of its threat to your public credibility. News editors are not given to explanations in public interest stories – either you won or you gave in, that is how it appears in the media. Your heroic 'statesmanship', your finesse, your brilliantly executed manoeuvre etc. is lost in the public attention to the newspaper headline ('Big Mouth Gives In').

Moreover, public stances complicate already complicated disputes. Neither side can move because it has publicly declared that it would not do so. Agreement is inhibited by public stances; think carefully before going public on a negotiating objective, especially in response to reports of the other negotiator's public statements.

Q

Questions. Important advice to all negotiators: Ask questions and listen to the answers (see LISTENING).

Open questions are better than closed ones. Examples of open questions include:

- 'How did you calculate the rental charge?'
- 'What do you think we should do about office security?'
- 'Where do we draw the line on these debts?'
- 'What suggestions do you have for settling this compensation claim?'

Open questions invite the answerer to respond with extended statements rather than single word 'yes' or 'no' (closed answers).

Examples of closed questions include:

- 'Do you think this policy is fair?'
- 'Are you in favour of an options clause?'
- 'Can you redraw this boundary?'
- 'Will you withdraw that threat?'

Closed questions are easy to formulate – they are the most common form of questions – and yet they are the least effective in securing information. There is not a lot you can do with a 'yes' or 'no' answer. The room for signalling is restricted, and even if the answer is clear – they do not want it – you are not told anything about how badly they do not want it, or whether some adjustments in the proposal would be sufficient to satisfy them.

To unblock DEADLOCK, ask open questions. Get into the habit of reformulating your questions by pausing and considering what type of question it is. It is your responsibility as the questioner to get the most detailed and helpful answers that you can, so make it easier to achieve this goal by asking the right questions (content) the right way (open, not closed).

Question no–nos. Avoid questions that:

- Expose you to mockery.
- Expose your ignorance.
- Are sarcastic.
- Are embarrassing.
- Cause trouble.
- Are point-scoring.
- Imply they are dishonest.

And those where you do not wish to hear the answer.

Question the criteria. Tactic to undermine the other negotiator's
PROPOSAL.

Proposals that are based on facts, rules, formulas, assumptions,
precedents and interpretations of 'fairness' are vulnerable to
requests for a clear identification of how they have been
formulated.

Ask the other negotiator to explain how they arrived at their
proposal. What did they take into account to calculate the figures
they have used? What statement of principle has formed the basis
of their claim? How did they do their arithmetic?

Watch out for references to 'normal' assessments of the market,
'standard practice', 'straightforward' yields, 'present values' and
such like. These could hide a mountain of phoney assumptions
not applicable in your case. (See 'I'M ONLY A SIMPLE GROCER').

Compelling the other negotiator to justify in detail his proposal
and its derivation gives you a chance to look inside his method.
You can choose to quibble with his assumptions, his facts, his
arithmetic; you can also learn something about a market with
which you are unfamiliar (do not assume you always negotiate
over issues completely familiar to you). There is plenty of scope
to decide on the relevance of his criteria, on their proper application, on the reliability of his sources, on the accuracy of his
arithmetic and on the valuation of the inevitable intangibles that
support a proposal. Exposing criteria to daylight creates
negotiating opportunities that were previously hidden in the
plausibility of jargon or assumed expertise.

If you disagree with the criteria the other negotiator has used
you have a more defensible negotiating position than if you
merely accept the criteria but disagree with the conclusions.

Quick deal. Often regretted.

Quivering quill. Buyer's pressure tactic.

Negotiators close to agreement experience euphoria. It is
almost over, the tension is falling, the shape of the deal is known
and cooperative feelings are running high. In addition, the seller is
feeling pleased at the prospect of earning the value of the deal,
perhaps with some of it as a commission.

The buyer is believed to be about to sign the contract, but his
pen hovers over it. The seller's anxiety levels leap upwards. 'What

is this? You need 2 per cent off the price? But we agreed that yesterday.' The buyer puts his pen down and sits back. Panic in the seller. 'Look, if I give you 1 per cent, will you sign now?' Buyer picks up pen and leans forward over the contract. The quivering quill having quivered, quivers on. 'Make it 1.5 and we have a deal?' Desperation in the seller: 'OK, OK, just sign it.'

Counter: Same as for 'YES, BUT'. Don't spend the profits until they are earned, control your euphoria (or at least recognize it for what it is).

R

Raiffa, Howard. Leading US negotiating theorist and consultant. Formerly a mathematician working on management decision theory, he switched to the study and teaching of negotiating via GAME THEORY. Co-author with R. D. Luce of *Games and Decisions*, New York, John Wiley, 1957; and author of *The Art and Science of Negotiation*, Cambridge, Mass., Harvard University Press, 1982. Raiffa teaches at Harvard University.

Rapport. Helpful, but not sufficient to secure a negotiated agreement. It is helpful because the relationship is positive between the negotiators. Lack of rapport certainly can inhibit agreement, or slow down progress towards it.

You can help establish rapport by matching your pace to the other negotiator's (particularly when negotiating across a cultural divide), by taking a genuine interest in his contribution to the discussion, by asking questions that indicate your interest and by steering gently rather than aggressively towards the settlement you are looking for.

Realistic offer. An offer that can be defended credibly, rather than one that is fanciful. An offer's credibility is decided by the other negotiator, not by you, nor by some independent sages sitting in judgement and removed from the context of the negotiation. If the other negotiator believes your offer is realistic, then it is realistic.

Unrealistic offers tend to cause vigorous dissent. The other negotiator reacts strongly and could call the whole negotiation off. This is not an excuse to NEGOTIATE WITH YOURSELF and back off from what you consider to be realistic in the circumstances, but bear in mind that the further apart you are, the longer it will take to negotiate an acceptable solution. If you do not have that time available, consider whether to pitch your offer within reach of the settlement area or way outside it. The other negotiator may be shocked at your offer, and might accept your explanation as a good enough reason to adjust his own prior expectations of the settlement price. Alternatively, he might break off discussions on the grounds that you are too far apart.

Rent. Rentability determines property values, not the reverse. It is a question of what the asset can earn in the market.

If negotiating for the landlord, maximize the net lettable space; if for the tenant, minimize it. The net lettable space is the square footage (or metres) that is usable by the tenant. This is not an exact science. I have seen three chartered surveyors calculate three different usable spaces for the same property, with a standard deviation of 15 per cent.

Watch for measurements running from inside the window alcove to the wall not the skirting board. Watch for deductions for central heating apparatus by the walls (when letting, fix a wooden shelf over them and count the space back in). How are columns in the floor area treated? If leasing, check that the space they occupy is excluded. These are not inconsiderable spaces; in downtown centres your wastepaper basket occupies as much space as a typist's chair and adds to the rent, and including them in or out can adjust the rent by 10 or even 20 per cent a year. How should stairs, landings and lifts be calculated? What about common toilets? Don't forget the storerooms, corridors (go right into the door when letting; doors set 3 inches into the wall add a square foot to the rent.

Rent review. Rent reviews are designed to adjust rents more quickly to market conditions. The price per square unit of lettable space is determined by one factor: what somebody is willing to pay for it. Be guided by the rents realized in adjacent or similar buildings. Rents move upwards when space is relatively scarce and downwards otherwise. But the change in rents is not immediate. Most rents are for fixed terms which do not coincide with market movements in supply and demand.

The LEASE will include a provision for a rent review at some specified date in the future. If you are a landlord in a tightening market, impose an 'upward only' rent review. This restricts changes in rents to those that work in your favour. If you are a tenant in a slackening market, force deletion of the 'upward only' term when the rent review arrives on pain of moving elsewhere in a more favourable market.

Landlords who impose regular inspections of the property pick up evidence of actual as opposed to chargeable use (they also protect their interests and can spot misuse that lowers the value of the property). A cabinet in a corridor that is not presently included in the net lettable space should be mentioned at the rent review because of the tenant's usage. Tenants should require notice of an inspection and use the time to remove all evidence of usage of uncharged space.

Tenants facing a rent review should research the market for evidence of going rates for lettable space. It is worth checking the measurements of the property (see RENT) just in case some structural change has occurred (a room knocked through by the tenant, a space now occupied by a boiler) and its rentable implications have been overlooked. If forced to accept increased rents, tenants should list the defects in the property that are a proper charge on the landlord and require him to trade rent for repairs. Landlords can avoid this by imposing full repair and insurance terms in the lease, preferably on both an external and internal basis (but certainly the latter as a minimum).

Landlords face costs in finding new tenants; tenants face costs in finding new premises. These costs are avoided by negotiating a new agreement, but they are willingly faced if the offered terms are too onerous. Changes in circumstances are reasons for changing rents. A property let at a premium because it had outstanding views, was close to a public railway, had easy car parking, was air conditioned and was newly painted and decorated is worth less if a new building blocks the view, the railway closes, car parking becomes restricted, the air conditioning is faulty and the property needs redecoration (hence, keep the landlord's brochures on file and re-read them before a rent review).

Reputation. Lose it and you reduce your opportunities. As your reputation depends on the PERCEPTION of other negotiators and not upon your own, it is easily lost or damaged (in fact, you could lose it without noticing and without good cause).

What reputation do you want? And with whom? Your colleagues or the other negotiators? Or both?

In Britain a millionaire entrepreneur has established a reputation as a very tough negotiator with the unions. He has invested heavily in this reputation. He has been known to sack and reinstate a workforce four times in as many weeks in pursuit of a settlement. He throws his considerable weight around, but always settles somewhere short of his first, very tough, demands. He 'allows' the unions to persuade him to be 'reasonable'. His public image is such that only the very toughest and determined stand up to him. Most can't stand the stress of deciding whether he is bluffing or serious. Many potential business partners avoid getting involved with him for the same reason. Still, by most standards, he is a successful businessman.

Investing in establishing a negotiating reputation is commonplace: 'This company must establish that it says what it means and means what it says, even if in the short run it costs more than its worth.' Sometimes, a reputation for consistency is earned, other times a reputation for inconsistency and wildness achieves the same effects (TERRORISTS increase the value of their threats by having a mentally disturbed gunman among them). A reputation, once undermined, is less easily put right: it only takes one dispute, where the balance of power is reversed, for a 'tough' reputation to crumble in a single retreat.

Moral reputations are more vulnerable. Interpretation of motives is not an exact science (as any court demonstrates daily), and the same action is judged differently by different negotiators. Being openly untrustworthy or dishonest damages a reputation, perhaps beyond repair. Even taking a short-term view being manifestly 'unfair' in a negotiation with somebody you never see again (an insolvency case for example) can come back to haunt you in the business community's judgement of how your firm behaves when it has the upper hand. Other 'one-off' deals bypass you, because the negotiatiors know of your reputation.

Resistance price. The point where you prefer 'no deal' to a deal on worse terms.

PREPARATION involves thinking about your resistance price. At what price does it become unprofitable to do business? You should consider this question without necessarily getting into too firm a decision about its precise location on the BARGAINING CONTINUUM. Do not confuse a desirable BOTTOM LINE with a truthful one. You do not know the full facts before you enter a negotiation and circumstances may evolve that suggest your original resistance point is unobtainable. Of course, beware that you are not rationalizing a surrender under pressure.

Your resistance price may be established arbitrarily by your seniors – beyond this point you get sacked. If it is unrealistic, the time to discuss that is during preparation and not in a post mortem of what went 'wrong' in the negotiation. Experience shows that there is almost no bottom line which desperate sellers will not cross in hot pursuit of an order. To prevent this happening, think through the implications of and the criteria used to determine your resistance price.

Restrictive covenant. Buyer's protective device.

Buyers of business can protect themselves from future competion if they negotiate a restrictive covenant on ex-owners. The ex-owner agrees to a legally binding contract that prevents him opening a similar business close to their original business. How close is 'close to' is negotiable. For small businesses trading in a local area the restrictive covenant bars them from trading within that area; for national businesses, the restriction may apply to the entire country, or even the world as a whole.

The geographic extent of the restriction, its scope and its duration is negotiable. The ex-owner may be barred from trading in that business, or one closely related to it, for a fixed term of years (2 to 5 is common), or even indefinitely (though a total ban would need to be reflected in the price paid for their business). The restriction may be confined only to the current clients of the business but permit the ex-owner to generate new business (as is common in advertizing agency and similar acquisitions).

The scope may be narrowly defined (brewing but not barring distribution of beer) or widely defined (design, manufacture, distribution and finance of the product). A narrow scope permits the ex-owner to move into a different segment of the same market, for example, out of the manufacture of clothing and into retail distribution of clothes across the country.

Publishers sometimes impose restrictive covenants on authors which prevent them producing similar works for other publishers that 'materially effect the sales of the book'. Film producers also impose restrictions on writers, and not so long ago studios imposed extremely restrictive covenants on actors (since made ineffective by the negotiating power of 'stars', and a few court cases).

Some employers impose covenants on employees to protect proprietary information. If the employee leaves a business he or she agrees not to use information and know-how gained during their employment. This protection is often sought by high technology companies, particularly from their research and development personnel. Licensors also impose similar conditions on the employees of licensee firms and require the licensee to guarantee protection of the licensor's know-how.

Whether you sign a restrictive covenant or not depends on your perception of your negotiating power. A minimum strategy would be to limit the extent and scope of the restriction and its duration. One entrepreneur who sold up in the United States and was restricted from conducting business in North America, promptly moved to New Zealand, set up the same business there and eventually expanded into Australia and then Europe (where he now competes with the owners of his former business in the USA). Failing to consider the potential need for a restrictive covenant could cost you dearly a few years down the track.

Reversion Useful clause in a contract to cover your interests in case of default or some failure to meet the contractual obligations by the other negotiator. Insist that failure to meet obligations, or circumstances such as his bankruptcy, triggers reversion to you of all your rights, property and monies, irrespective of his obligations to others.

This is particularly important in LICENCE AGREEMENTS. Liquidators sometimes take very legalistic views on what property is forfeit in a bankruptcy. Make sure that yours unambiguously passes back to you. Give notice of reversion immediately you discover failure on the licensee's part to meet the agreed obligations and insert in the agreement that your notice is unconditionally sufficient for reversion to take effect.

Review. Post-negotiation exercise essential to long term success. Both successful and unsuccessful negotiations should be reviewed.

Reviewing the outcome of a negotiation is as important as preparing for one. The lessons for all those involved can also be shared with those likely to be involved in future negotiations on similar issues.

Like preparation, the review should be structured. Use the original preparation plan (see PREPARATION) as the basis for evaluating performance. How does the content of the negotiated outcome compare with the intentions set out in your plan? Compare each agreed issue with your original objectives. Where did you do better or worse than you intended?

Next, consider the process of the negotiations. How did this unfold? What events were unexpected? Where do you think you (and your team) did better/worse than you expected? What were the main mistakes? What can you learn from these mistakes? What were the successes? Ask yourself (and the team) what was the single most important lesson of the negotiation? Discuss all suggestions.

On the basis of the lessons you identify in the review, draw up a list of actions to be undertaken by all concerned to transform these lessons into improvements in future performance.

Risk. Never eliminated, but it can be reduced or priced.

To reduce risk:
- Seek COLLATERAL.
- Avoid dodgy deals.
- Restrict their discretion.
- Seek GUARANTEES.
- Require a PERFORMANCE BOND.
- Insist on a deposit.
- Sell or buy forward.
- Help them count the money.
- Help them collect it.
- FACTOR your invoices.
- Sell/take an OPTION.
- Insist on regular payments.
- Find out for yourself what the trouble is and what will put it right.
- Spread the risk across more than one basket (if you can't: watch the basket!).
- Calculate everything on a conservative basis.
- Cut your losses.

To price risk:
- Charge more for the risk.
- Judge worth by expected value (see DECISION ANALYSIS).

Royalties. Authors get them, but few live like royals. Royalties are a percentage share in the retail price of the book, play, video script, poem etc. Ordinarily about 10 per cent for hardcover books and 7.5 per cent for paperbacks, and then escalating moderately as sales reach targets.

Publishers prefer fixed percentage royalties that do not escalate with quantites sold. As an author you should require that they do escalate and cut the qualifying quantities they propose. Watch for the 'new edition' ploy, i.e. the royalty clock re-starts with each new edition. Challenge their estimates of re-setting costs. If the money at stake is large, check a printer for a quote for your book. Show them you have done some PREPARATION (see COPYRIGHT).

Have you got the courage for 'Samuelson's gambit'? According to legend, Paul Samuelson, Nobel Prize winning author of *Economics*, did not ask for immediate royalties for his book when it was first published in 1947. He told the publisher that he wanted no royalties until many thousands of copies had been sold. He required instead a very high royalty rate on all copies sold from then on. His publisher agreed (unlike authors, most publishers are pessimists about sales), assuming that, like most books, it would sell enough to wash its face and no more. It became the world's number one textbook and Samuelson's gambit paid off. They had to buy him out at the tenth edition.

Rules. There are none. What is proper is decided by the negotiators involved, and even they have no right of 'appeal'. Courts decide on legal merits not standards of fairness.

Informal 'rules' have emerged for different usages. They have no status other than what the negotiators concerned accord them. For every 'rule' there is an exception, and for every negotiator there is a time and circumstance where the 'rule' is abandoned.

Some so-called 'rules' include:

- Agreements should be honoured.
- Sanctions are permissible as complements to the negotiation but not as substitutes.
- Neither negotiator should revert to an opening position because a current (improved) position is not (yet) acceptable.
- Solutions should not be imposed on a take-it-or-leave-it basis.
- Neither negotiator should interfere in the internal affairs of the other to disrupt his negotiating position or cohesion.

- Negotiators should act in 'good faith' and not behave in a reprehensible and destructive manner.

All these 'rules', and many others, are breachable, and have so been many times by negotiators. Often one negotiator abides by one interpretation of a rule and the other by another. The alleged 'dishonouring' of an agreement is the subject of many negotiations. At what point a sanction is unacceptable as a negotiating tactic is a matter of great contention between negotiators. Sometimes 'take-it-or-leave-it' is all that is left when faced with an obstinate opponent. Negotiators do interfere in each other's affairs – that is what propaganda, leaks and rumours are all about, let alone threats – with a view to weakening the opposing coalition. Disputes about 'good faith' fill the courts and arbitration sittings every week.

Russian front. A tactic to make you accept an unpalatable option by forcing you to choose between two unpalatable options, with one of them so unpalatable that you opt for the lesser one.

It is an allusion to the effect on German soldiers of threats of being sent to the 'Russian front' in the Second World War. If the officer making the threat was perceived to have a credible power to send the object of his attentions to the Russian front, he could exact compliance with his wishes. The unfortunate victim of the threat was so terrified of the prospect that he cringed: 'No, no, *anything* but the Russian front.'

Examples:
- 'At these prices we will have to make this a barter deal by offering Nanking sand in exchange.'

'Forget the sand, I'll take another 10 per cent off.'
- 'Seems to me we have two choices. Either you send me a list of the ten least efficient people to be made redundant in your operation, or I will assume that it doesn't matter who is made redundant (including yourself) and I will sack ten people at random.'

'Do you want the list typed or can I use a pencil?'

S

Salami. Close relative of the BAGATELLE tactic. They don't go for the whole sausage in one, they take a slice at a time. 'A slice of a cut loaf won't be missed'. And it isn't.

Can you PACKAGE your proposition using a salami?

'Give me the Albany run for six weeks as a trial, which is only two per cent of your transport usage, and I will hold your invoices to the last week of the trial. If you want to quit using our transport there and then, that's fine. You pay the invoices and we quit. If you want to try us on other runs, I can offer you the same trial terms.'

Children use salami. You tell them not to go out of your sight at the park. They move away but stay in sight. Then they sit on the ground and you have to strain your neck to see them. Then they lie down, so you have to get up to see them. They they slide down the slope out of sight, but return every few minutes in case you are checking on them. Sometimes you see them, sometimes you don't, but they return enough times to stop you worrying too much, and anyway, you are getting tired jumping up and down to look for them. Then they go off for longer spells. You fret. They are off for an adventure but come back, eventually. They salamied you.

Sanctions. Any measure aimed to coerce the other party (see COERCION).

Sanctions include:
- Employee relations:

go-slows, overtime bans, strikes, working to rule, discriminating against identifiable groups, worktime meetings, refusing duty, withholding necessary consents, documents, formal requirements, occupying places of work to prevent others working, picketing, banning specified inputs, refusing to work 'blacked' materials, imposing bans of any kind, ignoring safety rules, mislaying materials, papers, information, sabotage, withdrawing special cover (safety, security), SECONDARY BOYCOTTS, sympathetic actions of any kind in support of other disputes, clogging up the disputes procedures with spurious cases, prolonging meetings to waste time, refusing to meet, making public statements of a confidential nature etc.

- Commercial relations:

cancelling contracts, returning work unfinished, holding on to drawings, ordering litigation, calling in loans, changing suppliers, withholding consents, mislaying necessary documents, returning work on trivial technical grounds, refusing to pay invoices, holding up payments on one contract while there is a dispute on another contract, refusing to maintain equipment, withdrawing supplies except on onerous or cash terms, calling a creditors meeting, appointing a receiver, reporting alleged offences to an official agency, professional body or the general public, withdrawing financial support, liquidating the business, selling shares, placing votes in a shareholders' meeting, not electing directors, sacking employees, including directors.

- Trade relations:

discriminatory trade practices, quotas, tariffs, non-tariff burdens, selective import controls, withholding export guarantees, restricting or banning investment, selective sanctions, general sanctions, closing loopholes, dumping, using vetoes in international organizations, administrative delays, embargoes.

- International relations:

withholding support in public, working behind the scenes to withhold support, making public condemnations, joining in coalitions to oppose specific interests, applying trade sanctions of any kind, blockade, using military force at any level, including war, taking hostages, taking punitive action against specific citizens, terrorism.

Schelling, Thomas C. Probably the most cited scholar in the literature on conflict analysis. His book *The Strategy of Conflict*, Cambridge, Mass., Harvard University Press, 1960, carved out an entirely new territory in the study of the nature of conflict, whether applied to bargaining, diplomacy or limited war. In chapter 2, 'An Essay on Bargaining', he developed the concepts of COMMITMENT and THREAT much as they remain today. Schelling took GAME THEORY from the abstract to the concrete and demonstrated the logic of conflict handling policies for practitioners. This rich seam of seminal ideas is still being mined by students of negotiating.

Secondary boycotts. Heavy coercive tactic by unions (see COERCION). Illegal in the United States and the United Kingdom.

Sympathy strikes in unrelated businesses are used to put pressure on an employer: e.g. bakers in a strike find the flour mills are on strike too, or blacking supplies, and shop unions won't handle their produce.

As an enforcement tactic it is total war. The union organizes strikes or boycotts of suppliers and customers. To strengthen a coal strike, the union demands solidarity action by electricity power workers and the dockers; airport baggage handlers demand support from refuelers, check-in staff, engineers, firemen and pilots; printworkers demand support from transport drivers, rail staffs, shop and distribution workers.

Seeking clarification. Proposals are not always clearly stated. Clarification is essential if you are unclear, and bridge-building even if you are. People like to be treated seriously. Asking clarification questions helps to build rapport.
- 'Could you go over the second clause. I am not sure how you intend it to operate.'
- 'Am I right in thinking that your liability clause would cover us in the event of a failure of the piping up to two years from installation?'

Questions sometimes finesse explanations that provide additional information about their OBJECTIVES and PRIORITIES. They can lead on to criteria questions.

See QUESTIONS; QUESTION THE CRITERIA.

Sell and lease back. A way to raise capital on your assets.

Lenders supply funds against first class assets, such as prime site properties. You receive the capital for other purposes and lease the properties you formerly owned. Sometimes there are tax regimes that are favourable to these deals. Could be attractive to a take-over bidder who wants to release funds from the acquired company to pay back money borrowed to finance the take-over without damaging the income-earning capacity of the business. In the short term this is a cheap way to acquire businesses – the target for the take-over pays for you taking it over.

The disadvantage is that you lose control of your properties, and can face rising rents at subsequent RENT REVIEWS. One way round this is to separate out a company's properties from its main business by placing all the company's property into a separate property company. This new company then borrows against its property from lenders and pays off the borrowings out of rents it charges the main company for use of the properties. The loan is secured against the property company's assets, which remain within the control and ownership of the main company, and cash is released for other purposes.

Sell cheap, get famous. Buyer's con tactic.

Anybody new to a business has at least one drawback: they have no track record. Newcomers cannot attract the premiums that go with experience. Buyers exploit this opportunity.

The tactic aims to persuade the newcomer to accept a lower fee or price for their services. The buyer asks:

- 'How many plants of this type have you designed?' ('This is my first contract.')
- 'How many times have you acted the lead in a TV show?' ('I haven't yet.')
- 'How many times have you been consulted about this type of business problem?' ('I did something similar in my MBA course.')

The buyer often asks these types of question when he knows the answer. He is softening you up for a low fee pitch. But there is an upside: he doesn't just push you down on price, he makes out he is doing you a favour.

- 'Design this plant for the fee I have suggested, and you will establish your reputation and earn big fees on all subsequent work.'
- 'Don't think about the fee; think what the lead role in this show will do for your career.'
- 'Invest in solving this problem and you will soon be quoting with the big league consultants.'

You are encouraged to sell your service cheap with a view to recouping the situation in future business. Some negotiators, finding it hard to get started in business, are known to offer their services free to clients just to get a track record, or, in another version, charge on a CONTINGENCY basis – 'no results, no fee'.

Counter: With difficulty, if your track record is a blank sheet of paper. If forced to accept a lower opening fee (don't fall for the 'get famous' bit), go for a version of the contingency ADD-ON: 'If the design is accepted, then you pay me a second fee of 30 per cent'; 'Sure, but if the show grosses your projections, then I get 10 per cent of the gross'; 'If my solution is adopted, you pay me another 5,000'.

Settlement range. See BARGAINING CONTINUUM.

Sham offer. Using a FIRST OFFER to disguise your TARGET and protect your RESISTANCE PRICE. You open with a sham offer of 400, leaving room to trade back to your target price of 380. Your resistance price is 360. Opening at your target, forces you to trade below it, which mocks your concept of a target.

If they accept your sham offer, apply the ADD-ON.

Shock opening tactic. Abrasive pressure tactic.

The other negotiator opens with a price or a proposition that is wildly outside your expectations. You are shocked into stunned surprise. If they follow through with a credible reason for their proposal, they persuade you to review your expectations.

The key requirement for a shock opening is to be credible. A defendable proposal has a lot going for it. The other negotiator, hearing a shock opening, is forced to reconsider the basis of his own position. 'Perhaps my price is too high'; 'I never thought of it that way, perhaps I should move to a more realistic position'.

Even if the shock opening only moves the other negotiator part of the way from his expectations towards yours, your opening shock has been effective.

Shut up. Silence. There's not a lot of it about. Add to what there is by LISTENING more than you talk. Why? Because you know what is in your mind but you don't know what is in his. You won't find out by talking.

Shut up immediately after you
- make a proposal
- summarize
- ask a question
- reach agreement.

And wait until they speak before you do again.

Shut up when you have nothing to say. Get used to silence. You do not have to fill every silence with your words. Let the power of silence put pressure on them.

Another good time to shut up is after they have made a proposal. Hold back your reaction. Why? Because many people making a proposal can't cope with silence, and chip in an extra concession to break it.

Always shut up when the other party is talking: do not interrupt. It irritates the speaker and irritated negotiators move less often than the other kind.

Signal. Subtle change in negotiator's language, indicating a willingness to move.

What is 'impossible' becomes 'difficult'; what was 'never done' becomes 'not normally done'; what was 'contrary to company policy' becomes 'without precedent or prejudice'; and what was 'no way' becomes 'not under current circumstances'.

Without signals negotiators would have considerable difficulty in moving from an opening offer without giving the impression to the other negotiator that they were about to surrender. Everybody has a facility for making signals – most people do not realize that they are signalling – but many negotiators miss the signals because they are not LISTENING.

Some negotiators punish the signaller: 'I see, so you are no longer holding to your ludicrous opening offer?' This drives them both back to ARGUMENT, and delays a settlement. Don't punish a signal. QUESTION it for CLARIFICATION, encourage the other negotiator to elaborate:

● 'You say you have a difficulty with my request. Is there any way that I could make it easier for you to meet my needs?'

● 'Under what conditions would your company be willing to make an ex gratia payment in circumstances like mine?'

Signals are normally preludes to PROPOSALS, and no negotiation can get very far without the presentation of proposals.

See also BUYING SIGNAL.

Sizzle. 'Don't sell the steak, sell the sizzle.' World's most successful selling technique, developed by Elmer Wheeler, who believed that 'the heart is closer to the pocket book than is the brain' (from *Sizzlemanship: New tested selling sentences*, Englewood Cliffs, NJ, Prentice-hall, 1940, p. 21).

Find the sizzle in a proposition and put that to them. It goes down better than dry facts. It breaks through their INHIBITIONS.

*"God has also chosen me to
speak to you about insurance"*

In a competitive market why should an exporter ship with you rather than anybody else? Give him a reason: don't sell cargo space (all your competitors have space), sell guaranteed delivery. Why should a bank choose your firm to liquidate a business? Don't sell accountancy knowledge (competing accountants have that too), sell a hassle-free liquidation.

Counter: When buying, 'buy the steak, not the sizzle'.

Skimmer. Somebody who gets between you and the deal, and insists on being 'taken care of' (see BRIBERY) before the deal progresses much further. In some countries they pop out of the woodwork at short notice and unexpectedly. They wait until the contractor is chosen and then get between the contractor and the client. That way they get paid off, no matter which of you wins the contract (see GO BETWEEN). Their position (perhaps a connection with the ruling family, perhaps a crucial role in the final decision) guarantees their ability to frustrate the deal. You pay up, or get nowhere.

Sometimes you can block the skimmer by making a fuss with the ruler, though more than likely the skimmer is working for the ruler, who prefers not to sully his reputation with an open statement of his needs. Try padding the price with the skimmer's pay-off if the approach is made before you get to price; more realistically, the price will be set – that is why you got the contract – and his (large) fee comes out of your profit. From the client's point of view, the skimmer keeps some of the money within the domestic economy, instead of its being repatriated to you, the foreigner.

Beware of phoney skimmers: people who claim to be able to block your deal but who are in fact only charming chancers. Pay them and you cut your profits, and if the real skimmers turn up, demanding their share of the cake, you're going to be working for nothing.

Skimming. A pricing strategy. Some people are price blind when it comes to new products. They want the very best and expect to pay for it (if you don't go in high they think your product is a cheapo).

Luxury cars, yachts, electronic gadgets, new products of all kinds (even the original Biro pen) are ripe possibilities for a price skimming strategy. The market is limited, deliberately so, but it is lucrative until the competition starts up (they see your pricey products and the people with money wanting to buy them).

Markets for the same product can be segmented by price: one price for the 'de luxe' version, another for the 'economy' or 'regular' version. Skim the 'cream' with the high price strategy, then expand output and lower prices gradually, as you work your way into the next segment of customers who want the product but are more price sensitive than the people at the 'top end'.

Skinner's pigeon. An allusion to the work of Professor B. F. Skinner of Harvard University who claimed that human beings could be conditioned into behaviour patterns given the right stimulus and reward system.

An apocryphal version of this view, known as 'Skinner's Pigeon' relates how the professor demonstrated his theory by training a pigeon to pick out the ace of spades from a deck of cards, no matter how they were shuffled. The lesson for negotiators is to consider the relative size of the brains of a pigeon and a human negotiator (roughly a pea to a cabbage). If a pigeon can learn to choose the ace of spades, how much cleverer is a human being learning from the behaviour of another negotiator? Moral: Beware of underestimating the intelligence of the other negotiator.

Negotiators learn to say 'no' if they find they get concessions when they do so, hence don't stimulate their resistance by rewarding it.

Soft/softness. Soft negotiators are characterized by their willingness to move in large steps from any position they adopt. Their basic fear is that of not securing an agreement. For them, any agreement is preferable to DEADLOCK.

They often fall into the trap of NEGOTIATING WITH YOURSELF, crumble under threats and have an extensive repertoire for rationalizing acceptance of any agreement offered. They tend, also, to talk too much, qualifying any offer they make with SIGNALS of how far they are prepared to move if it is not acceptable.

Split the difference. Settlement tactic. Negotiators stuck on two numbers can move to a settlement by 'splitting the difference'. You offer 80, they offer 40, split the difference gives you 60.

It sounds fair and equitable and sometimes it is. Other times it's not. It can also be expensive – perhaps you cannot afford to split the difference?

To avoid its being sprung on you, stick to numbers that do not have an obvious split point. If your offer is 83.5 and theirs is 40 it is not obvious what the split the difference number should be, and that which is not obvious is not so 'fair' as that which is.

An offer to split the difference is risky. You disclose immediately a willingness to move 50 per cent of the difference between you. The other negotiator could spring on that SIGNAL and refuse to move, leaving you with a more difficult task in defence of your original number. He could also offer a different split: 'I can't go 50–50, but I will consider 30–70.'

When an obvious split point emerges – you have proposed 10 per cent and they have replied with 8 per cent – move to bury the obvious split point by offering 9.85 per cent (conditionally).

If the difference is trivial, there are bigger issues at stake and your relationship with the other negotiator justifies it, agree to split the difference as part of a larger package and not in isolation
See LINKING.

Standard terms. Alibi for loading the contract terms against you.

Publishers' contracts include an option to publish your next work. Score it out. You might be given good reason to change publishers.

Sellers often print their terms and conditions on the reverse of their official letters confirming an order or they are printed on their order forms which they expect you to sign. These standard terms always restrict their liabilities and are onerous to you, not to them, which is why they are printed. Read these carefully. If you cannot accept them all, acknowledge their order in writing with a minor reference that it is accepted subject to your terms (enclosed), or to the exclusion of their specific term (reference number only). They may be so desperate to receive your goods that they waive their own terms. Later, they could change their minds but they are unable to enforce them once waived.

Printed terms are intimidating. They imply that they cannot be changed (which is why they are often printed close together, so that changes are near impossible). To avoid signing an official order form with its specific terms, send them an order in writing with your terms on it.

Standard terms, like any other, are negotiable, but only if you take the trouble to query them.

Strategic interaction. Jargon from GAME THEORY. Useful for describing how negotiators manipulate the information they pass to each other.

You do not know what is going on in the head of the other negotiator. He has an incentive in being less than candid about his predicament – you might exploit this information. He thinks how you are likely to react to his behaviour; how you are likely to react to his behaviour knowing that this is a reaction to your behaviour; how you think he thinks you think he thinks you think . . . Taken too far, concern with strategic interaction could paralyse the negotiators in infinite regresses.

Strategy. Best kept simple. Complicated strategies fail within a few moves because the other negotiator has not read your script – he has a different plan.

The strategy is dependent on the circumstances and the issues in the negotiation. Not mentioning money, for example, might be a strategic objective when the value of what is for sale is not obvious (neither negotiator knows for certain the other negotiator's valuation). By keeping money in the background until they have ascertained enough information to set the 'price' the negotiators prevent an early 'over' or 'under' price being established.

Strategy should also be flexible: if it isn't working don't persist (THE SOMME fallacy). It should also be linked to your marketing and pricing plans. Consideration should also be given to the AGENDA, the order of business, whether to link or separate the issues (see LINKING), to the use of TRADABLES and when to deploy them to break out of DEADLOCK.

But, above all, remember what Robert Burns said about the 'best laid plans of mice and men . . .'.

Stress. Negotiating is a stressful activity. You are anxious about the outcome, emotional about their behaviour, unsure of the implications of offers, worried about their intentions, concerned about not doing as well as you, or your peers, expect, and generally tense as well as tired.

Stress cannot be eliminated; it can be reduced. The professional negotiator tries not to take things personally, tries to separate the issues from the personalities and tries to concentrate on interests rather than issues. Basically, you should slow down the pace (ask more QUESTIONS), relax before and after sessions, and set REALISTIC rather than fanciful targets.

Strikes. Withdrawing labour is a legal right of employees. In democracies it is a right that is exercised.

Strikes are called to influence negotiation. Normally, the strike is a prelude to a negotiated settlement. Sometimes it is a substitute for a negotiation. These latter strikes are bitterly fought because they are usually over highly contentious issues (new technology), or they raise important principles (should decisions be made by coercion or negotiation?).

The strategy of the strikers is to prevent normal business being conducted; the strategy of the employer is to ensure that normal, or near normal, business continues. If the strikers are successful in stopping normal business, it is a matter of resource attrition – which side runs out of resources first? If the company is successful in continuing with normal business, it is a matter of time pressure – how long before the strikers give up? Of course, if the employers have to use abnormal methods, or incur abnormal costs, to achieve 'normality' in their business affairs, they face resource attrition and time pressure (how long will the government or public put up with the abnormality and the costs?). If the strike is 'bloody', it could cause great offence to the law abiding public; but sympathy is fickle, it could swing towards the 'underdog'.

Public relations are important in strikes. Denouncing strikers as 'extremists' when they manifestly are not is counter-productive; exposing 'underdogs' when they are manifestly extremists is helpful. Negotiators who call strikes before exhausting the opportunities for negotiation are in a weaker position than those who are driven to strike by the outright intransigence of the other negotiators. Being careful to avoid being provoked into a strike is sound advice, as is avoiding arrogance when considering the other negotiator's options (you might not be as indispensable as you think – as air traffic controllers, coal miners and printworkers have discovered in recent disputes).

Managements who make public statements about the 'damage' done by, or the costs of, the strike strengthen the strikers (they feel they are achieving something). Other companies who rush into the media with horror tales of the effects of the strike merely prolong it. Strikes that appear to be going to last a long time are over quicker than those that appear to be short term (hence, do not talk about how long you can last; if asked, answer: 'indefinitely').

Handling 'peace' talks is difficult. A total media blackout is preferable to public stances and reports of what is happening. If talks break down, avoid shrill denunciations of the other negotiators – the calm acceptance of failure, in sorrow not anger, wins more votes in the public relations war. It also makes it easier for talks to recommence when the other negotiators are willing to have another go.

Employers should seriously consider opening the plants to employees who want to work if the issue is important and the strike is being used as a substitute for negotiation. Cooperate in closing down your operation with the strikers and you seriously undermine your future leverage. You also enhance the power of the strike leaders over your employees, which is contrary to your interests. A back-to-work movement forces the strike leaders back to the negotiating table, hence their hostility to 'scabs'.

Paying strikers their wages for time lost in a strike is absolutely senseless. It is practised in Australia, which, in consequence, has a strike-prone workforce nobody else envies. Labour mediators justify it for cases where the employer was at 'fault' and the employees struck in defence of 'justice'. The fact is, 'cost free' strikes expose an economy to more damage by strikes, and create the illusion among strikers, but nobody else, that the economy is a 'safe' place to have a strike in.

'Subject to board approval'. You have been negotiating with the monkeys, not the organ grinders. There is always an organ grinder on the board who thinks he could do better than the monkeys, and he demonstrates his superiority by sending the agreement back with his amendments.

Counter: PAD offers that are subject to board approval.

See AUTHORITY.

Summarize/summarizing. Simple but effective negotiating behaviour.

Negotiations are not like a game of tennis: I hit the ball, you hit it back, I hit the ball, you hit it back. They are far more chaotic. The verbal interaction tends to wander. People join the flow of conversation and set it off at a tangent (or back to something already covered). Interruptions occur, both planned and unplanned. A summary re-focuses attention on to the issues, what has been said about them, what each side is proposing, what the differences are, what remains to be agreed and what has been agreed.

Summaries should be short (they are a summary not a blow by blow account), and neutral (cover each side's point of view and what they have proposed). Neutral summaries are more constructive than biased summaries. The biased summary inflames the argument by starting a new one. The neutral summary placed in the midst of a long lost bout of verbiage, or at the moment when the debate is wandering off into unhelpful territory, can work wonders on even the most jaded or hot tempered of negotiators.

- 'It seems to me that we are in danger of drifting round in circles. George, can you briefly summarize our respective views as you see them?'
- 'Before we begin after our adjournment, I would like to summarize where we had got to before we took a break to consider what had been said.'
- 'Let me summarize the proposals on the table.'

Summarize during all phases of the negotiation, particularly when:

- Argument is dominating the exchanges.
- Immediately after you have made a proposal.
- When calling for an agreement.
- After agreement has been reached, to check that what you think you have agreed corresponds to what others believe.

See LINKING.

Switch selling. Seller's ADD-ON tactic. You think you are negotiating to buy a deluxe model widget, but before you know what is happening you find yourself in discussion about acquiring the super deluxe mode. The seller has 'switch sold' you up the range.

Sometimes this is to your benefit – the super deluxe is really more suited to your needs – but often this is to the advantage of the seller. They might have enticed you into the initial negotiations by advertizing what appears to be a fantastic bargain. When you get there you find they have sold out of the 'bargain' but they do have a few 'slightly more expensive' versions available, 'would you like to see them?'.

Switch selling is a LOW BALLING tactic.

Counter: Insist on the original deal and walk away from the 'up grades' that just happen to be available.

T

Table. Like the VENUE, if it matters to one of you, it matters, to both of you.

Negotiators like to sit behind a table. And not just to lay their papers or elbow on it. A table between you and the other negotiators 'protects' you in the same way that you place your arms in front of you when walking in the dark. Partly instinctive, you use your legs and arms to cover parts of your body when you feel threatened or unsure (see NON-VERBAL BEHAVIOUR).

Negotiators are in a quasi-threatening conflict situation. Putting something between you and them reassures your subconscious anxieties. If you did not feel comfortable at this level you would perform less well, even display overt antagonism.

Some 'experts' think you should reform the structure of the negotiation by forcing the parties to sit next to each other in an 'open' formation. They believe that the table intrudes and exacerbates the conflict. Evidence suggests they are confusing cause for consequence. Open seating relaxes people until they start negotiating, so it could be useful before the sessions begin, during lunch breaks and informal adjournments, including photo-calls.

The table itself is a negotiable item. American and Vietnamese negotiators had a lot of trouble agreeing on the shape of the table at the start of the Paris peace talks to end the Vietnam War. The US suggested a four-sided table, two sides for the North Vietnamese and the Vietcong, and two sides for the South Vietnamese and the Americans. The North Vietnamese countered with a demand that they could not contemplate a negotiation that implicitly recognized the 'government' of South Vietnam. The issue was eventually resolved by settling for a round table, with each side choosing who sat at it.

Tacit bargaining. Where communication is not possible, or extremely circumscribed, and the parties make their moves on how they expect the other party to behave, or in reaction to how they perceive them to be behaving (see PRISONER'S DILEMMA). Example: In a telephone conversation, you are cut off suddenly. Do you ring back, or wait for them to do so?

In competition with a rival firm, you have a choice of increasing your prices or maintaining them (perhaps costs are rising and squeezing profits for both of you). If the price elasticity of demand is high (the proportionate change in quantity sold resulting from a change in price is much greater than the proportionate change in price), brand loyalty is low and the market is saturated, an increase in your prices, which your rival does not copy, reduces your total revenue (customers switch to the rival's cheaper products).

Collusion between suppliers is illegal. You respond to his behaviour. You announce a price rise, he announces a marketing campaign to emphasize his lower prices. A PRICE WAR follows. Losing total revenue forces you to regain volume, so you cut your prices below his and, the market being fickle, you win back your lost customers and more still. Instead of you both moving towards profit restoration, by simultaneously raising your prices, you now face a ruinous price war.

How can this be averted? Faced with a common need to raise prices to maintain profitability, if your rival raises his prices, you copy the rise; he should do likewise. If he reduces prices, you copy. A tacit collusion develops, and ruinous price wars are avoided (see TIT-FOR-TAT). Tacit bargainers shift their competitive efforts from price wars to advertizing campaigns, which have the same aim as a price change (capture more customers), but do not provoke the same reaction (they could also be 'ruinous' in profit terms).

Applying this conclusion to other tacit bargains, consider warfare. Gas was not used in the Second World War, though both sides had supplies. One side making a localized gain through its use had to weigh up the consequences of all-out gas warfare. The combatants developed equally awesome, and in some cases worse, weapons to inflict casualties, but did not resort to gas, nor to an explicit bargain to refrain from doing so.

Take-off. Reverse of the ADD-ON. Tactic to raise your prices safely, or when a buyer challenges your price and you have PADDED it.

Asked to quote your price you do so. Your price covers your costs plus add-ons. Suppose you supply a service which you normally price at 600. In addition you have expenses of 90. These are priced separately. You want to move up your prices but are not sure how the market will react if your new price is way above the competition. Consolidate your price and expenses to a price of 700. Test reaction:

'My normal price for this service is 700.'
'That's far too high, and way outside our budget.'

Take off a little:

'You realize I have included my travel in the price.'
'A bit better, but still. . .'

Take off some more:

'Plus my hotel subsistence.'
'I see.'

You have entered his budget area. No need to take off any more, though you had your documentation expenses ready, leaving you with the extra 10 you slipped in to round up the price.

The take-off gives you room to raise your prices safely. If challenged, you retreat a little. If unchallenged apply the add-on: add your expenses on top of the 700.

Target/target price. The negotiating objective you aim to reach if you can. It is your desired, best terms, objective, what you would like to settle on.

Whether you open with your target price, or another price somewhere slightly above or below it (your SHAM OFFER) depends on how you perceive your prospects. If you open at your target you are likely to be forced to move away from it by the other negotiator (unless he surrenders to your FIRST OFFER).

See FINAL OFFER, PREPARATION.

Taxation. An avoidable, but not evadable cost.

When negotiating your percentage of an income stream, ensure that it is the gross income and not one that is net of taxes. Deducting taxes (which one(s) – corporation, income, excise, valued added, property, state, payroll and disguised ones like 'state health insurance'?) reduces an income stream remarkably, and with it your percentage share (10 per cent of a hundred is larger than 10 per cent of 45).

Who pays the taxes? Shift as much of that burden on to the other negotiator as possible. If leasing property, assign property taxes to the lessee; if selling equipment shift the value added or sales tax to the buyer; if quoting a fee, give its tax inclusive price, or state the price, plus taxes (see BLACK ECONOMY).

Can you negotiate with the taxman? Yes, to a limited extent. If the Revenue believe that unambiguously you owe them money in a clear-cut case, where legal precedent and legislation is beyond doubt, and they believe you can pay it, there is not a lot of negotiation involved: they issue an instruction to pay and you pay up, subject to your rights of appeal. You can arrange payment terms with their consent, but depending on circumstance you cannot demand them if you have been caught evading payment, and have obstructed their investigation with prevarication and outright deceit (the 'vengeance' factor).

The tax authority's interest is in collecting as much taxation revenue as the law prescribes. Thus, where the legal issues are complicated (nobody has devised an unambiguous tax system yet) and the outcome of an appeal to the courts uncertain, your opportunities to negotiate are stronger. In these circumstances, the tax authorities are willing to negotiate how much you pay and when you pay it, in order to collect something for certain as opposed to an uncertain amount later, and to avoid the risk of losing the case and letting others know of the loophole (tax cases are widely publicized).

Taxes collected by the customs authorities are less open to negotiation. The customs have vast experience of collecting excise and other duties and their personnel are notorious for their unwillingness to consider a compromise, even where the issue is doubtful. This may arise from their daily dealings with smugglers – perhaps they see every tax supplicant as a potential drug smuggler?

Teaching wolves to chase sledges. Often futile concession to generate goodwill.

You are under pressure. The other negotiator is challenging you hard on price; you think the best way to relieve the pressure is to concede something small. You do so. Nothing happens. The pressure continues so you concede something more. Same result. You are perplexed.

You ought not to be perplexed. Your behaviour is inducing the pressure not relieving it. If you concede in the face of pressure, you teach other negotiators to pile on the pressure. Like trying to discourage wolves from chasing your sledge by throwing food to them. This does not stop them chasing the sledge; they are learning that if they want to be fed, they should chase a sledge.

Teamwork. It has advantages and disadvantages. Both can be optimized by PREPARATION and discipline.

The leader carries the bulk of the burden of conducting the negotiation. He must make the decisions and call the shots. Unfortunately, the people not directly involved in the actual exchanges can slip into the role of spectators, which, as any player will tell you, leads to them assuming they can do better than the players. They are tempted into interventions, not always well timed, and, in the extreme, they attempt military coups (never well timed).

Teams must be disciplined. The leader takes responsibility for the negotiation and the only appropriate time and place for criticism and dissent is in private adjournments, not in front of the other negotiators.

Who should be the leader? On many occasions this is resolved by the inclusion of a senior manager in the team, who by virtue of that position assumes the leadership. For some circumstances it is more appropriate for somebody else to conduct the negotiations, such as when the degree of expertise required, or immersion in detail, suggest that the natural leader is the person best qualified to do so.

There are also occasions when deliberately not involving the most senior person is the best policy, as this leaves a 'long stop' in case progress comes to a halt and only the 'top' decision-maker can get things moving again. If the most senior person is not conducting the negotiations, but is present at some of the meetings, or present at functions associated with the meetings (social, diplomatic and other receptions), it is important that no unintentional 'put downs' of the leader occur. Transforming a leader from an organ grinder into a monkey by asides and remarks is likely to prove unprofitable (let alone unforgiveable).

What do the other members of the team contribute? If there is no obvious answer, why are they there? A lot of time is taken up with meetings, of which negotiation is one element, and people who are not needed should be sent to do something more productive. Forming teams on the basis of matching the other team's numbers is not very sensible. A well-briefed team need not be the same size as the other side's. There is no 'safety in numbers', only expense.

A team needs a summarizer. A facility for SUMMARIZING at critical stages in the negotiation, especially when the discussion is wandering or getting heated, is a great help to the leader. It provides a well-needed break, reduces tension and demonstrates how well your side is listening to what the other negotiators are saying. It also re-focuses the negotiations on the issues.

Some teams require the presence of experts and specialists, who can be consulted readily, or invited to contribute on narrowly defined lines to the discussions. If technical issues are central to the negotiation, have people present who can contribute sensibly; do not have them present if their talents lie in total immersion in technology and not at all in commercial judgement. Once technical people start drifting into *affaires de technique* with their opposite numbers, they can destroy a negotiating position without even being aware of what they are doing. It's too late afterwards, so choose your experts clearly and brief them well, including in matters relating to the conduct of the negotiations. Interactions between them and the technical specialists on the other side are best kept restricted (otherwise your negotiating position is likely to be compromised, or your company's role transformed into an adjunct of a cosy technical seminar between the experts). The leader leads, and does not always take advice (technical or tactical).

An extremely useful role for a team member is that of observing and recording. It is always 'easier' to analyze a negotiation (or any other interaction) from the observer's position than it is if you are caught up in the debate and are contributing to what is going on. Adjournments are opportunities for the skilled observer to contribute to the team's assessment of the state of play and to make recommendations for future actions.

Teams should, ideally, consist of negotiators experienced in the style and conventions of the particular type of negotiations they are called upon to service. The basic advice to anybody joining a team for negotiations with which he or she is not too familiar is to confine your interventions to things you are familiar with and meanwhile observe and learn about the unique features of the negotiations at hand until you know what you are doing.

Tender. See BID.

Termination. Useful clause in a contract. A specified date for the termination of the current contract covers you against a perpetual contract that contains, or might be seen to contain as circumstances change, some onerous consequences.

Of course, this works both ways: it might end for you some beneficial consequences before you are ready to give them up.

Contracts can be reviewed, but it may not be enough for this to be implied. A specific termination date is a legitimate opportunity to review the mutual rewards arising from the contractual relationship. What looks good today may look awful in a few years when the income projections are greater/smaller than those expected when you signed the deal. In the absence of an ESCALATOR schedule, a termination clause might be a useful safeguard.

The Somme fallacy. Fallacy of negotiators welded to a STRATEGY that is not working. They keep trying it out, no matter what the other negotiator is doing. They believe their strategy will eventually prove its worth, if they keep at it long enough, so they keep going. Much like the strategy for the battle of the Somme in the First World War: to keep assaulting the enemy positions until they surrendered. But the generals ran out of troops before the enemy ran out of bullets. In negotiating, you run out of steam before the other negotiator runs out of defences. If your strategy is not working, change it!

Thousand exceptions. A tactic to weaken the implementation of a policy.

Attacking a policy head-on is not always fruitful. The momentum behind it is so great that it sweeps all before it. The thousand exceptions is a reverse SALAMI: instead of helping to introduce a policy by restricting its immediate application, you help discard a policy by limiting its application.

The opportunity to apply the tactic is found in the negotiations to turn policy into a practical proposal. Any policy is vulnerable when its practical details are considered. A general implementation could be limited by the sheer administrative cost of applying it everywhere at once. Discover exceptions, create exceptions, list exceptions, and do this in a way that does not indicate your total opposition to the theme of the policy (which its supporters would latch on to and isolate immediately). In fact, the more committed you appear to be to the policy, the more convincing your 'regret' that 'unfortunately, for the moment, and with current resources, it would be wiser to confine it to this significant, though limited application'.

Civil servants are experts at this tactic against policies given to them to implement by 'radical' ministers. Two examples: whereas Germany in the 1930s built hundreds of miles of autobahns between the cities in a 'Keynesian' type injection of demand into the economy, Britain managed to emasculate a similar programme of public works down to a single road, 32 miles long, from London to Southend; whereas some European Community members developed thriving 'free ports' bereft of bureaucratic red tape, Britain's free port creations ended up with as much red tape as before and no trade. In both cases, and many others, the policy was killed by dedicated application of the thousand exceptions tactic.

Threat. Unlike a promise, something that you preferably do not implement.

Threats are part of the repertoire of COERCION. They can be of two kinds:
• Compliance
unless you do the following specific things, we will do the following to you.
• Deterrence
if you do the following things, we will do the following to you.

The consequences of a compliance threat can be avoided by doing what the threatener requires. Examples of compliance threats include threats to strike unless the company pays higher wages; threats to attack unless a country withdraws its forces; threats to leave unless your partner stops drinking.

The consequences of a deterrence threat can be avoided by refraining from doing what the threatener objects to. Examples of deterrence threats include threats to use force if you attack them; threats to strike if you sack employees; threats to leave if your partner starts drinking.

Threats are judged on the capacity of the threatener to carry out the threat, and on the likelihood of them doing so if thwarted in their other intentions. They must also be judged by their likely effects if they are implemented. The threat may be credible because the threatener has the capacity and the will to implement the threat, but it may be disregarded because its effect may be judged to be minimal on the person threatened. A threat from a Gaddafy-type leader to 'destroy' the United States may have less impact than a similar threat from the Soviet Union.

Note that the 'minimal' effect consideration is not confined to those where massive damage is likely to result: a lonely individual on hunger strike against a powerful corporation may have no physical effect on the corporation as a result of his threatened suicide, but the publicity effect may outweigh the one-sided result of his dying of hunger.

Threats visibly raise the tension of a negotiation. Once started, a threat cycle – escalating threat exchanges between the negotiators – is difficult to stop. People do not like to be threatened, because, apart from the disagreeable consequences to them of the threats being implemented, they do not like to have their choices circumscribed. If they comply/desist it appears they did so because of the threat, thus encouraging more threats, when they may, for other reasons, wish to adopt a course of action, or inaction, which corresponds to the threatener's preferences.

Threats are inevitable. A prescribed time limit on a negotiation is an implied threat (you propose to search for business elsewhere); a revealed RESISTANCE PRICE is also a threat (you propose not to do business on worse terms).

Threats may be believed and achieve their aims without being implemented, or they may not be believed and have to be implemented or withdrawn. A threat that achieves its ends without being implemented could be the result of a tactical adjustment by the other negotiator temporarily unable under existing conditions to resist the threat. But as soon as those conditions change, the negotiator who was forced to crumble under duress, seeks and finds alternatives, or even revenge.

Making specific threats is more convincing than being vague, but it is also more restrictive for the threatener (see SALAMI). If the threat is ignored, the threatener has little choice but to implement the threat or lose credibility. A war or strike could start because the threatener's loss of face exceeds the cost of implementing the threat, unless the threatened helps to get the threatener off the hook.

Similar situations could arise if those threatened so resented the use of a threat, or felt the loss of face in succumbing to the threat was too great, that they refused to budge and forced the threat to be implemented. This is more likely with public threats than private ones, but the threat alone is enough sometimes to force it to be played.

Making vague threats leaves initiative to the threatener as to whether, or how, the threats are implemented, but the vaguer they are the less troubled the threatened may be about them. Threatening to 'seriously consider taking our business elsewhere' is hardly likely to be taken as seriously as threatening to 'award the contract to Smith's if agreement is not reached by 5 pm'. The threatened could test that deadline by running on to 5.30 pm, or calling for an adjournment at 4 pm to consult the board. In diplomatic negotiations the parties often agree literally to stop the clock just before the deadline to enable negotiations to continue, providing agreement appears to be possible.

Bluffing threats are risky because they might be called (loss of credibility). They could be called because the threatened knows (intelligence, own assessments of the situation) that you are bluffing. They could be called because the threatened believes you intend to implement the threat and reacts by taking pre-emptive measures to resist you. And could end up in a war or a strike even though you were bluffing. If you must bluff, be vague in your intentions, as this gives room for doubt about what triggers the threat's implementation.

Time. The great pressurizer.

Negotiations fill the time available, and if that is less than planned for, the negotiator either quickens the pace (moves faster more frequently) or blows it. Time pressure is uncomfortable. It adds stress to an already stressful situation. It forces hard choices and can split a negotiating team apart, because their perceptions of what is now possible do not adjust at the same rate. A command decision is needed to prevent disarray.

Faced with a competitive situation, negotiators are under pressure and the buyer/seller knows this. Add a time problem, and the pressure mounts. Time can either be compressed ('we decide by 5 pm'), or extended ('we will call you when we have considered all the proposals'). In the former, the negotiators are racing the clock, in the latter they are watching it. Negotiators working against time prefer to postpone the other negotiators' making a decision until they have had a full chance to influence that decision; negotiators kicking their heels waiting for a decision rapidly reach the point where they don't care what decision it is as long as it is a decision.

Counters: Have more than one time plan for a negotiation (a long one and a short one, and be ready to work whichever plan suits the time that becomes available).

Maintain strong communication links between the negotiators and the home base, including regular briefings if possible, or long phone calls if not.

Adapt the negotiators to the time climate by sending in support if the negotiation is compressed (don't leave it to stressful meetings of pressurized team members), or by pulling out people if they can be used elsewhere while fully supporting those who are left.

Tit-for-tat. A winning strategy.

Suppose you were faced not with just one PRISONER'S DILEMMA type of game but a whole series of them with a single opponent. What would be your best strategy over the long haul?

For a single play of this type of game, given a choice between cooperating or defecting, you are likely to choose defection (or putting it another way, if you don't defect it is fairly certain the other negotiator will – which is why you choose to defect etc.). Now consider playing five games in sequence. Whatever you do in the first game is known to the other player, and this affects his behaviour towards you in the next four games. Your best play (the one that maximizes your total 'profit' from the five plays) is to cooperate on each of the first four plays, and defect on the fifth. If he defects on the first, you are likely to defect on the second, or certainly by the third play (unless you are a glutton for punishment).

Professor Robert Axelrod in *The Evolution of Cooperation*, New York, Basic Books, 1984, showed how the best strategy for an indefinite run of the plays is for the players to adopt a tit-for-tat strategy. Using this strategy, the player cooperates on the first move and from then on does whatever the other player did on the previous move. This result has important implications for negotiators. The strategy 'teaches' the other player that the benefits from cooperation are available if they choose a cooperative option, but that if they choose to defect, so will their opponent. As the rewards to each from cooperation over the long run are greater than the rewards for mutual defection, they have a strong incentive to cooperate.

But signalling cooperation without being exploited (see INTERPERSONAL ORIENTATION) is the most difficult task facing a negotiator. Tit-for-tat is a workable strategy partly because it is so obvious what you are up to (see SKINNER'S PIGEON). It is simple. It works best when the negotiators take a long-term view of the relationship (a useful starting point for arms control negotiators?). Short-term gains can overwhelm a negotiating stance, even though the negotiator knows they are irrational in the long run.

Playing tit-for-tat you never defect first, which makes you 'nicer' than the guy who does. But if the other negotiator defects you immediately react – you have a low threshold to provocation. Waiting to deal with a defection actually weakens your position. You let them know immediately, or as close to immediately as you can, that their actions are unacceptable to you. This ensures clarity in the SIGNAL you are sending; delay, and they do not relate your reaction to their action. Shouting your disapproval to the neighbours about an all-night party they held last week might connect in their minds with what they did, but they could as easily conclude that you have had a domestic row and that you are taking it out on them. If they defect, you defect immediately on the next play.

Suppose they get the message, or decide to cooperate again. Forgive them for their defection and immediately cooperate again. Do not exact a punishment of another defection 'just to show them'. You dilute your main message if you do. They could fall into a long chain of defect–defect plays, missing the significance of your response to cooperate plays because you bury it in a lot of punitive responses. Remember your objective is to educate them into cooperation, not punish them for not realizing this sooner. But also remember, your forgiveness is in response to their cooperative play not a quest for goodwill divorced from their actions.

Tough guy/nice guy. A low ball tactic (see LOW BALLING). It works best on sensitive negotiators (see INTERPERSONAL ORIENTATION). Essentially it is an act, or more accurately a duet. The negotiators alternate between a tough uncompromising stance, highly COMPETITIVE and aggressive, and a softer more COOPERATIVE stance, willing to listen to you and understanding of your problems.

Naturally you prefer to deal with the softer guy, but his 'hands are tied' by his colleague, and the guys back at home base who are even less helpful. He wants to help you, you want to help him – he's the closest you have been to a decent guy in weeks. To help you, he needs you to help him. You can see what he is up against, so you are willing to move considerably further down the road towards his position than you intended, but you are comforted by the illusion that this is a lot less far than you would have had to go to satisfy the 'gorilla' who did all the shouting and made all those impossible demands.

You have been had, of course. The duet was a set up to make you concede. The two of them work as a team, neither is nicer or nastier than the other. They compare notes afterwards, and laugh all the way to the next negotiation.

Toughness. Has little to do with Rambo.

Tough negotiators aim for the TARGET, having made proper PREPARATIONS beforehand. They are not afraid of DEADLOCK and do not give up easily. They open with a REALISTIC OFFER and move modestly. They LISTEN carefully to what the other negotiators say and closely scrutinize all the details of what they want and upon what basis they have decided they wanted them.

Results of EXPERIMENTAL NEGOTIATIONS indicate how toughness influences outcomes in negotiation. Equating toughness with the level of ASPIRATION of the negotiator, some experiments (in highly artificial contexts) showed that negotiators who open with high levels of aspiration (which could be a high price if selling, or a low price if buying) are likely to produce concessions from the other negotiator (SOFTNESS), which meant higher levels of profit for the tougher negotiator. But be warned: tough negotiators are also likely to have a low probability of reaching agreement. This suggests that they succeed if they happen to be paired against someone who wants to do business, but are less successful when they either meet another tough negotiator or someone less keen on settling.

Tradables. The currency of the bargaining process.

Movement is secured by offering to TRADE something that you have for something that they have. Anything that you can trade is a tradable.

Common tradables include:

• Money

price, wages, finance, currency, credit profits, income, taxes, bonds.

• Time

when it happens, who to, who from.

• Goods

quantities, quality, features, substitutes.

• Specification

marginal changes, peformance standards.

• Services

standards, personnel, performance.

• Guarantees

guarantor, liability.

• Warranties

duration, extent, coverage.

• Risk

extent, who carries it, shares.

Practical exercise: Ask all your colleagues to list the tradables in your business. If the headings are too general, call for breakdowns of each heading. Set about the exercise as if you were briefing somebody completely new to the business as to what you could negotiate about if you had to do so. Compile a common list from all the lists your colleagues provide. Go through it in detail. If new tradables are suggested, add them to the list. It does not matter how long the list gets, as it is to be filed as a 'Negotiator's Tradables Manual' for your organization.

The act of considering the tradables available to you as a negotiator gives you ideas for PREPARATION, for new strategies, new proposals, new ways to get out of deadlock.

Trade. Never give an inch. Trade it!

The offer to trade or the act of trading constitute the singular difference of negotiation compared to other forms of decision-making. What is traded may be tangible or intangible, it may be something in the present or a promise of something in the future, it may have value to both or only to one of the negotiators. Trade involves exchange: one negotiator gives up something he has, or controls, or can promise for the future, in exchange for something the other negotiator has, controls or can promise. Negotiation is about the terms of the trade: how much is given in exchange for how much of what is received.

If one party can impose its will on the other there is no negotiation involved. If one party requires the consent of the other party in order to do or not do something, then a negotiation is possible on the terms for that consent. Some decisions involve a mixture of COERCION and negotiation. The extent to which the terms are decided without THREATS and coercion defines the boundaries of decision by negotiation.

Trade unions. Employees' bargaining agents (see COLLECTIVE BARGAINING). Some are ideologically motivated, some have connections with enforcement gangs. Most are professional negotiators, well aware of the limitations of what can be achieved in open societies.

In theory, most are run by their members; in practice, they are run by small minorities of 'active' members. The quality of elections and decision-making processes varies widely. Some members are fiercely loyal to the union, while most blow hot and cold depending on circumstance. It rarely pays to make the union an issue, unless it has gone over the top with serious misbehaviour (intimidation?).

Individuals in free societies have a right to be represented collectively by an agent. Unions based on product industries are in decline because their industries are in decline. Membership is holding up because of the unionization of the state bureaucracies. If you work in the service sector, in new high technology, or in marginal employment, you are unlikely to be in an old style union, or have to negotiate with one.

Trade-in. Used machinery, motor vehicles, yachts, aircraft and such like can be traded-in and the price they raise set against the purchase price of a new model.

Trade-in prices vary enormously. Dealers subscribe to lists of recent trade-in values. These show a range of prices applicable to specific used models, depending on their condition and age. These are only 'guides' not mandatory offers. There is no guarantee that the dealer will even quote you a price within the range in his guide. He might go below it if he thinks you will accept a lower price.

Ask questions about the recommended price range. If he declines to show you the published guide prices, it suggests he is being less than candid with you. Tell him that is how you interpret his reticence. If he is quoting a price at the lower end of the range, ask for justification. He will point to perceived defects in your model. The repair of these defects could cost much less than the difference in prices within the range. In short, negotiate with him on the trade-in price. The more you can push this up, the lower the cash cost of acquiring the new model. If he can push you down, the higher his profit, both in the re-sale value of the trade-in (dealers use the guide for inter-dealer transactions), and in the sale price of the new model.

Trust. Earned not deserved.

Trust is unlikely to flourish when the negotiators are:
● Suspicious of motives, intentions, capabilities or past behaviour.

- Hostile for any reason.
- Highly competitive.
- Contesting vital issues.
- Having a lot at stake.
- Feel threatened.
- Ignorant of each other.
- Have recently been tricked, or trounced.

Trust flourishes when the negotiators have:
- Demonstrated their reliability, trustworthiness and credibility.
- Experience of each other in a variety of circumstances.
- Invested in confidence building measures.
- Reciprocated in helpful ways and not taken unfair advantage when they could have.

Does trust pay off? Not if its consequences are assumed without being tested. To trust someone recklessly is as risky as dealing with someone who is totally untrustworthy. If trust is earned by being of proved quality, it pays off handsomely for the negotiators concerned. Win–win outcomes are easier to arrive at if the negotiators are able to be open about their needs without fear of compromising their TARGET aspirations. Trust does not push the negotiators to their RESISTANCE PRICES (if it did gains would be possible from STRATEGIC INTERACTION). Rather, mutual trust enables the negotiators to increase the size of the cake by exploring, in a safe atmosphere, TRADABLES not included in the original problem.

Two-offers-only. Method of bidding useful for complex products which are not always suitable for ONE-OFFER-ONLY.

Several different designs may be viable for a major project. Tightly specifying such projects does not solve the problem, and anyway it is expensive to design everything yourself. Other people's engineers can create design solutions that your own people have not thought of. So divide the bidding into two rounds: the pre-qualifying round that eliminates the unacceptable designs and prices, and the final round that sets the contract price.

Hire a consultant engineer to examine submitted designs from bidders in the pre-qualification round, and then invite the surviving bidders, whose designs qualify them for the work, to re-bid on price.

Invite the pre-qualifyers to amend their bids in the light of technical data provided by other bidders (e.g. what would they charge for including the marina in their breakwater design?).

U

Ultimatum. See FINAL OFFER: OR ELSE

Unblocking strategems. Finding creative ways to conclude a deal that is blocked for some reason.

People who want to sell in a hurry usually want to GET OUT FROM UNDER. Their creditors are closing in, they can't make the business work, they have been hit with an unexpected tax bill, they are hassled by the paperwork, they have inherited a mess and so on. Their main interest in life is in selling to pay off their pressing obligations. Can you take over their obligations? At one stroke you relieve the pressure. This is reflected in the price you offer. The other negotiator does not have to deal with the, often unpleasant, collectors knocking on their door. You do that for them. They reduce their price to you. (Downside: watch out for blanket assumptions of their debts – some hidden nasty ones might emerge after you have paid. Specify the debts you are assuming.)

Example: The owner of an office block wants to sell. He intends to move out and find another office for lease. You cannot meet his price. Can you offer him a rent-free period? A rent-free year could be worth an eighth of the selling price. Make him responsible for taxes and insurance. He benefits by not having to move immediately, you benefit by reducing your outlays. As he is likely to have padded the price of the net lettable space (to maximize your buying price) (see RENT), you can legitimately use his calculations to arrive at the annual rent he is nominally paying, in order to take that off his asking price (he can hardly admit to padding can he?).

The owner wants to dispose of her business to help finance another venture. Can you offer her high monthly payments that cover her borrowings from a bank for her other venture? When your payments cover the selling price of the business, you own it; she achieves her own goal of acquiring the other business.

You want to buy a business from an owner who intends to start up again. Can you offer them a two, three or five year management services contract with a high salary to entice them to stay on working the business? This might induce them to accept a lower cash price for the business, keeps them working for your own goals and prevents early competition emerging.

Unconditional offer. Music to the ears of the other negotiator. Hence, refrain from making one.

An unconditional offer is a wasted offer. It is seldom refused and ever more rarely does it satisfy the other negotiator. They accept the offer with a 'but', and usually come back for more. One-way conceding is no way to conduct a negotiation. If you are giving things away for nothing they might as well hang out for more, to see just how much you will give away before you require anything back from them. If all you require is for them to say 'yes', they might as well hang on to their consent until you stop throwing concessions at them. The only way they will negotiate is for you to make CONDITIONAL OFFERS.

Unilateral final offer. See BOULWARISM.

Used car sale. Classic example of DISTRIBUTIVE BARGAINING.

A used car is on sale at 5,400. The seller's minimum acceptable price is made up of the acquisition costs (4,000), overheads and expenses (200) and minimal profit (200), totalling 4,400. This is his RESISTANCE PRICE. If offered less than this, he prefers to wait and sell the car to somebody else. He places it on the market at 5,400 (his SHAM OFFER) and he is willing to come down if necessary to a price of 5,000 (his TARGET PRICE).

You are in the showroom looking for a bargain. Suppose your target price is 4,600 and you decide on a sham offer of 4,400. If necessary you can go up to 5,000 but you will (and must!) walk away at any price over that.

Figure 11 is a model of the BARGAINING CONTINUUM.

Figure 11

```
BS
SR        BT              ST              SS
├─────────┬───────────────┬───────────────┤
4,400    4,600           5,000           5,400
```

Neither the used car seller nor you knows the other's resistance price, nor whether the first price mentioned is a sham offer or a target price.

You do better as a negotiator by treating all FIRST OFFERS as sham offers. Whatever they open with – no matter how good it looks alongside your target and resistance prices – HAGGLE.

Your tactics as a buyer include:

● Convincing the seller that he prefers a sale on terms more favourable to you than he originally expects to get (he should move his target and resistance prices downwards).

● Convincing the seller that your terms for buying the car at all are less favourable to him than he expects (your target and resistance prices are lower than he thought they were).

In practice, your assault on his perceptions requires you to demonstrate that a quick certain sale to you *now* at a lower price than he anticipates he can get from somebody else is better for him than waiting for an uncertain future customer.

Emphasize your ability to settle immediately if the price is right; undermine the value of the car to you by reference to 'high mileage', 'old style', 'body defects', 'tears in the trim', and 'loose switches, handles, doors, etc.'. All positive comments on the vehicle's characteristics, or the maker's reputation, or your need for it, undermine your tactics.

Make no reference at all to your available budget. The seller asks early on 'what price range are you interested in?' He is assessing your resistance price, not saving you time looking through his range. So don't tell him. Ask to see his cars. Once the seller has invested time in trying to sell you a car, he is even keener to come to a deal. So take his time up. Ask questions. Keep him waiting while you go over every inch of the vehicle. On no account appear either to weary with, or show keenness for a particular vehicle. Let him do the selling, which generally means he is revising downwards his likely profit from the transaction in order to close the deal. Open your offers at 4,400. He has opened his at 5,400. The rest is a haggle. As your prices approach each other, move into BARGAINING LANGUAGE.

Happy motoring!

V

Valuing concessions. It is not what it is worth to you that counts, it is what it is worth to the other negotiator.

The temptation to give things away that are of little value to ourselves is universal (see NO PROBLEM). Value everything in the other negotiator's terms. Ask yourself: 'What is it worth to them?' If they want it, then they value it, and if they value it, what can I get back from them that I value?

Negotiating is decision-making by trading, and it is better to trade things that are cheap for you, but valued by the other negotiator, for things that are valued to you, but cheap for the other negotiator.

"Let's get one thing clear: is this discussion going to be conducted in vague generalities or specific generalities?"

Venue. Where the negotiations take place is often a matter of indifference, but occasionally it can be important to one or both negotiators.

A home venue might have an advantage to one of the parties: they control the environment, they can manipulate the HOS-PITALITY, they feel more relaxed closer to their coalition members whom they can quickly consult, they have access to records, files and data, and they are visibly 'in charge'.

One party's advantage is not necessarily another party's disadvantage. Negotiators cannot WALK OUT of their own premises. They cannot easily hide behind not having AUTHORITY, if the people with the alleged authority are on the next floor. Any failures in the services to the negotiation (telephones, telexes not working, refreshments not appearing on time, secretarial facilities not available, physical comforts below standard), or any embarrassments at all (strikes, demonstrations, floods, blackouts, fire and emergency alarms, rudeness of staff and such like) are more likely to undermine the composure of the hosts than the guests.

Disadvantages there may be, though some of these are unavoidable if you are negotiating at the client's premises because of circumstance (in a foreign country for instance). One problem is the security of your recess rooms and communications with your head office. Not every opponent is unprincipled enough to bug your recess room and to read copies of your telexes and transcripts of your phone conversations, but if premature disclosure of your views on the situation is likely to undermine your position you have fewer remedies on their home ground than you do on neutral ground. In Communist regime countries there are no neutral venues, and you can take it for granted that this elementary surveillance goes on irrespective of your status (they spy on their own General Secretary of the Communist Party, so what is so special about you?).

Even in the innocent world where there are no cheats, you still lack support facilities at somebody else's venue (those that are offered must at least raise a suspicion as to their neutrality). Whether this improves with recourse to your hotel is open to question. Take your own support staff with you?

What are you looking for in an ideal venue?

• Good size negotiating room with space to walk about and work in comfort.

• Comfortable furniture, lighting and ventilation.

• Recess rooms for each team, with direct dial and secure telephones and access to telex.

• Discrete venue staff, who go about their work quietly and do not interfere in events.

• Everything cleaned and tidied during breaks, and all refreshments replenished regularly.

Vulnerable/vulnerability. Ask yourself where you are vulnerable in a negotiation, or in a business situation. It might help you to protect your flanks from surprises.

For example, a short-term lease leaves you vulnerable to a notice to quit when it is least convenient; a long-term lease might bind you in when you see better opportunities elsewhere. These considerations prompt you to cover your vulnerability in your PROPOSALS.

A management is vulnerable just before an order surge arrives – the employees might take advantage of the pressure to extract concessions; an absent partner is vulnerable to decisions made without him; a supplier is vulnerable to competition offering similar lines; we are all vulnerable to accidents.

Thinking about vulnerabilities is a cure for arrogance and conceit, if it produces constructive measures to avert being ambushed when it would be least expected or welcomed.

W

Waking up the dead. Risky intervention tactic.

Faced with a determined negotiator and not making much progress, it is tempting to try to explore differences of view in his team. You invite a member of the other team who has remained silent throughout the session to comment: 'What do you think, Mr Sujamo?'; 'Have you any suggestions about how to break this impasse, Ms Allbright?' This is risky. The other negotiator might resent your interference and retaliate by stiffening his position. If his team is disciplined, you are unlikely to succeed.

Walk out. It does not always work. They don't come running after you: they leave you to stew.

For what purpose are you walking out? To signal your total disapproval of something they have said, suggested, done or implied? Can you demonstrate disapproval in some other way? Why not just tell them what you feel? In what way does the walk out add to your message?

What do you do when you are faced with a walk out by the other negotiator? Do you change your negotiating position, or do you dig in? As a pressure tactic it lacks a focus because it is not clear what the other negotiator is meant to do when you walk out.

The other team might note that you are obviously serious about your stance; they might regard you as unstable. The walk out is an emotional instrument and as such it is open to various interpretations. If they have to deal with you (a COLLECTIVE BARGAINING dispute, a diplomatic problem, a spouse or child argument), the walk out might bring things to a head, though not necessarily the way you intended (they wanted you to strike, to DEADLOCK, to abandon the matrimonial home etc.).

How do you recommence negotiations after a walk out? The parting shots may preclude an early resumption of face-to-face contact. Why not lower the temperature or signifiance of the walk out by calling for an ADJOURNMENT, even an abrupt one? The impact is immediate, but the damage is less public. You adjourn to 'cool off', to 'think about things', to seek advice etc. It is much easier to resume negotiations after an adjournment than after a walk out.

'**We should have been told**'. Disavowal of responsibility tactic. You have exceeded an agreed budget and are seeking an additional payment for the extra work you have undertaken for a client. They deny responsibility on the grounds that 'they should have been told' before you incurred extra expenses. As you did not tell them, they refuse to pay, no matter that the additional work was necessary, or was 'authorized' by one of their staff without authority to do so. You are stuck with the cost. Perhaps you can persuade them to pay something towards the extra cost on the grounds of your relationship (if you have one), or in recognition that the procedures for approving extra work were not clear but will be from then on (through an official Variation Order system under which all variations in the original contract must be authorized by a named official if payment is to be made, and in return, if an official variation order is made, the client guarantees payment of the extra costs).

'**What do you know?**'. Long shot tactic to elicit information.
The other negotiator opens by asking you how much you know about the issues. You tell him. He finds out more about your knowledge of the details than perhaps you intended to let him know at this stage. Your selection and presentation of details also signals your priorities. (See 'I'M ONLY A SIMPLE GROCER!)
Counter: 'Not a lot. Perhaps you could go over the issues for me?'

What if? Questioning technique to elucidate potential negotiating issues.
Useful technique when faced with DEADLOCK. It helps explore possible avenues down which solutions to the deadlock might be found. For example, 'What if we were to consider delaying the payment deadlines, would that help you with your budgeting?' Or 'What if we re-arranged our two companies into a joint venture, would that meet your concerns about disclosing proprietary information?'
Also useful when faced with a proposition in a field you are not familiar with. The offer may look alright but you have no criteria against which to judge it. Ask 'what if?' questions about everything imaginable in the proposition and note what information comes out of the answers. 'What if you make 200,000

instead of your budgeted 50,000 in the first year? What larger share would I get in those circumstances?' 'What if you decide to sell your business to a third party, how would my interest in the project to protected?

In fields you are familiar with, the 'what if?' technique is also useful. It can highlight deficiencies in the contract terms which experience has taught you to be wary of, or which you have INHIBITIONS about. A good check list of 'what if?' questions drawn up before you negotiate is a useful PREPARATION tool.

Win–win. I win, you win, so we both win. The goal of an EFFECTIVE NEGOTIATOR (see NON-ZERO SUM).

In negotiating we have four possible outcomes defined in terms of winning or losing. These are shown in figure 12.

Figure 12

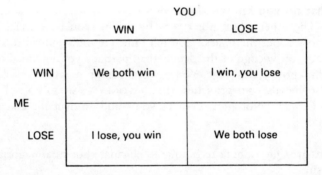

		YOU	
		WIN	LOSE
ME	WIN	We both win	I win, you lose
	LOSE	I lose, you win	We both lose

DEADLOCK, in which we have found it impossible to agree, is a lose–lose outcome (bottom right box). The time we have spent in the negotiation has been wasted (in the sense that we could have been doing something else, perhaps more profitably), and if our relations have been soured we may experience long term disagreeable consequences. We could also end in mutually costly litigation.

Either of us winning with the other losing is likewise an unattractive outcome. If I win at your expense (I sell you a second-hand wreck disguised as a road-worthy car), I risk destroying my reputation, or our relationship, and the expense of litigation. If for any reason you are unhappy with the deal, or how we arrived at it, my winning is a Pyrrhic victory. It could cost me dear later.

The win–win outcome is the most desirable. It gives both of us a stake in the agreement and its implementation. We are both happy with our side of the bargain and on the basis of our experience, both of us are also happy to consider doing more business in future (and to pass on our helpful judgements about each other to third parties).

Y

Yes, but. Bargaining tactic.

'Your offer is acceptable, *but* for one small point.'

You accept the reservation by meeting it in some way, and then expect agreement:

'Fine. We can accept the offer now, *but* there is this issue we must get agreement upon.'

If you go along with this small issue, another one will pop up, and for as many acceptances as you can make, they have another 'yes, but'.

Counter: Identify all the reservations, and address them in one package:

'I see. What other points do you have that require our attention before we can reach agreement?'

Listen to their comments:

'Thank you for raising those points. Now are there any others at all? No? Well, in that case, let me respond in the following way, but be clear, this is in response to all outstanding points you wish to raise. I take it that you have no others? OK?'

The 'yes, but' is exorcised. Any additional attempts at the tactic are repudiated as negotiating in 'bad faith'. Insistence on proceeding with further points invites retaliation with the 'no, but':

'I cannot accept movement on this entirely new point, but if you accept a change in this earlier point, I am prepared to consider a change in what you are now asking.'

For every new change they want, you require a change in a previously offered point.

Yesable proposition. Seller's tactic based on the momentum generated by the buyer saying 'yes' to a series of proposals. If they keep saying 'yes' they will eventually say 'yes' to the closing proposition (in theory).

'You do have a problem with copying costs?'

'Yes.'
'You accept that the Corex Copier copies more times per cent than any other on the market?'
'Yes.'
'You want to start making big savings on copier costs right away.'
'Yes.'
'Will you OK this request for a Corex Copier for delivery in 72 hours?'
'Yes.'

Not always so predictable (shades of the PERRY MASON TACTIC), but likely to be tried on you from time to time.

Counter: YES, BUT.

'You win some and you lose some'. Do not underestimate the need to 'save face'. It motivates almost every negotiator. You have put a lot of effort into an issue, argued long and strong for an outcome, perhaps even thrown in the odd THREAT or two, but in the end you realize you cannot get anything like what you want. What do you do? Press on with the conflict? Keep the teeth clenched like the proverbial Bulldog?

See THE SOMME FALLACY.

Its often better from the negotiator's point of view to admit defeat gracefully. Laugh it off:

• 'Well, George, you win some and you lose some, and this is not my winning day.'

• 'In sum, we will not accept liability for the premium you paid without our authority to clear customs over the weekend.'

'C'est la vie. It was worth trying.'

Z

Zero-sum. Jargon from GAME THEORY. What you gain, they lose. Suppose your wage demand is for an increase of 100 a week. If this is conceded (for whatever reason), the employer's costs rise by 100 (he is 100 a week worse off than before), and your income rises by 100 (you are 100 a week better off). The sum of your (positive) gain plus his (negative) loss is zero (hence, zero-sum).

This is true for all possible settlements of your wage claim: if you gain 50, his losses are –50 and (50 + –50 = 0); if you gain 25, his losses are –25 (25 + –25 = 0). Your interests are diametrically opposed: you are in a state of pure conflict.

Negotiation can be analysed as a zero-sum game (but see NON-ZERO SUM). In pure conflict negotiations you perceive your opponent to be malevolent: he is trying to gain at your direct expense. There can be no cooperation or collusion between you to find a mutually advantageous solution because all solutions are mutually disadvantageous.

Zeuthen's conflict avoidance model. Compares the gains likely to be made by accepting what is on offer with the net gains likely to be made by engaging in conflict (STRIKE or LOCK-OUT) (after F. Zeuthen, *Problems of Monopoly and Economic Warfare*, London, Routledge, 1930).

There is a range of practicable bargains (the settlement range), and any wage rate within this range is more advantageous to either party than a conflict. Outside the settlement range ('the fighting sphere'), compromise is less advantageous than resort to conflict. The limits to fighting are given by the expected result of fighting plus or minus the expected fighting costs. The workers will not accept a wage rate lower than they could receive by a fight, less the losses they take by going on strike; correspondingly for the employers.

Zeuthen's model is a two-stage process. First, the bargainer compares the certain value obtainable from accepting the other party's current offer with the expected value he obtains by holding to his current demand together with the expected value of a breakdown in the negotiations and mutual resort to conflict. This calculation produces the maximum probability of conflict he is willing to accept in preference to accepting the other side's current offer.

Second, the bargainer whose willingness to accept the risk of conflict is smallest (the one who is most anxious to avoid conflict) is the one who makes the next concession. If it is the worker's agent, the union demand for a wage increase is reduced; if it is the employer, the company's offer of a wage rate is increased.

The size of a bargainer's concession is determined by how much a particular concession increases his willingness to risk a strike if it is unacceptable to the other side. Naturally, each party endeavours to persuade the other that any move short of the gap between them induces a preference for a strike (raising their apparent 'eagerness for a fight' in the perception of their opponent).

Mistaken assessments of the other's eagerness for a fight, or miscalculations of one's own net benefits of conflict, lead to a negotiated wage rate above or below what was practicable if the parties had made different assessments. It boils down to an assessment of which of the parties feels strong enough to resort to, or ride out, conflict.

Suggestions for Further Reading

If you wish to consult some additional reading on negotiation, I recommend any of the following titles as being among the best books on negotiation in print. They can be ordered from any good bookshop or direct from the publisher.

General

Fisher, Roger & Ury, William: *Getting To Yes: negotiating agreement without giving in.* 1981, Century-Hutchinson, London; Houghton Mifflin, Boston.

Kennedy, Gavin: *Everything is Negotiable.* Arrow Books, London; Prentice-Hall, Englewood Cliffs, New Jersey.

Kennedy, Gavin, Benson, John & McMillan, John: *Managing Negotiations.* 3rd edn, 1987, Prentice-Hall, London; Englewood Cliffs, New Jersey.

Lax, David A. & Sebenuis, James K: *The Manager as Negotiator: bargaining for co-operation and competitive gain.* 1987, Free Press Inc., New York; Collier Macmillan, London.

Lewiki, Roy J. & Litterer, Joseph A.: *Negotiation: readings, exercises, and cases.* 1985, R.D. Irwin Inc., Homewood, Illinois.

Morrison, William F.: *The Pre-Negotiation Planning Book.* 1985, John Wiley & Sons, New York; Chichester.

Raiffa, Howard: *The Art and Science of Negotiation.* 1982, Harvard University Press, Boston; London.

Business negotiation

Hearn, Patrick: *International Business Agreements: a practical guide to the negotiation and formulation of agency, distribution and intellectual property licensing agreements.* 1987, Gower Publishing Co., Croft Road, Aldershot; Brookfield, Vermont.

Graham, John L. & Sano, Yoshihiro: *Smart Bargaining: doing business with the Japanese.* Ballinger Publishing Co., Cambridge, Massachussets.

Kennedy, Gavin: *Negotiate Anywhere: how to succeed in international markets.* Arrow Books, London.

Marsh, P. D. V : *Contract Negotiation Handbook.* 2nd edn, 1984, Gower Publishing Co, Aldershot; Brookfield, Vermont.

McCall, J. B. & Warrington, M. B.: *Marketing by Agreement: a cross-cultural approach to business negotiations.* 1984, John Wiley and Sons, New York; Chichester.

Winkler, John: *Bargaining for Results.* 1981, Heinemann, London.

For regular material on the whole range of negotiation, you can subscribe to the quarterly:

Negotiation Journal, Plenum Publishing Corp, 233 Spring Street, New York, NY; 88/90 Middlesex Street, London, E1 7EZ.